USS PRINCETON

DAVID R. LEICK

USS PRINCETON

The Life and Loss of "Sweet P"

OSPREY PUBLISHING
Bloomsbury Publishing Plc
Kemp House, Chawley Park, Cumnor Hill, Oxford OX2 9PH, UK
29 Earlsfort Terrace, Dublin 2, Ireland
1385 Broadway, 5th Floor, New York, NY 10018, USA
E-mail: info@ospreypublishing.com
www.ospreypublishing.com

OSPREY is a trademark of Osprey Publishing Ltd

First published in Great Britain in 2024

© David R. Leick, 2024

David R. Leick has asserted his right under the Copyright, Designs and Patents Act, 1988, to be identified as Author of this work.

For legal purposes the Acknowledgments on pp. 14–15 constitute an extension of this copyright page.

All rights reserved. No part of this publication may be reproduced or transmitted in any form or by any means, electronic or mechanical, including photocopying, recording, or any information storage or retrieval system, without prior permission in writing from the publishers.

A catalog record for this book is available from the British Library.

ISBN: HB 9781472868589; eBook 9781472868572; ePDF 9781472868596; XML 9781472868619; Audio 9781472868602

24 25 26 27 28   10 9 8 7 6 5 4 3 2 1

Edited by Tony Holmes
Maps by www.bounford.com
Index by Alan Rutter

Typeset by Deanta Global Publishing Services, Chennai, India
Printed and bound in Great Britain by CPI (Group) UK Ltd, Croydon CR0 4YY

Osprey Publishing supports the Woodland Trust, the UK's leading woodland conservation charity.

To find out more about our authors and books visit www.ospreypublishing.com. Here you will find extracts, author interviews, details of forthcoming events and the option to sign up for our newsletter.

Contents

	List of Illustrations and Maps	6
	Acknowledgments	14
	Prologue	16
1	"Sweet P"	23
2	Joining the Fleet	43
3	A Time for Battle	57
4	Task Force 58	93
5	"Fighting 27"	127
6	*Forager*	141
7	"Uncle Sam's Cyclone"	179
8	Task Group 38.3 East of Luzon	197
9	A New Battle	219
10	*Princeton* Eternally Defiant	235
11	So Long "Sweet P"	247
	Epilogue	261
	Appendix 1: US Navy Ranks	265
	Appendix 2: Specifications	267
	Appendix 3: VF-27 Aces	270
	Appendix 4: Casualties	271
	Bibliography	291
	Index	297

List of Illustrations and Maps

USS *Tallahassee* (CL-61) under construction at the New York Shipbuilding Corporation's yard in Camden, New Jersey, in July 1941. (Naval History and Heritage Command)
Workmen at the Camden shipyard in April 1942. (Naval History and Heritage Command)
Princeton being prepared for launching at the Camden shipyard on October 16, 1942. (Naval History and Heritage Command)
The stern section of *Princeton*, photographed at the Camden shipyard on October 16, 1942. (Naval History and Heritage Command)
Princeton slides down the slipway into the Delaware River on October 18, 1942. (Naval History and Heritage Command)
Margaret Dodds with Lillian Brakeley and Rear Adm Milo F. Draemel at *Princeton*'s launching. (Naval History and Heritage Command)
Adm Frederick C. Sherman and Rear Adms Harold M. Martin and George R. Henderson. (Naval History and Heritage Command)
Princeton anchored in the Delaware River in March 1943. (Naval History and Heritage Command)
Princeton heads down the Delaware River during a test sailing from the Philadelphia Naval Shipyard in late March 1943. (Naval History and Heritage Command)
Princeton heads for the Gulf of Paria in May 1943. (Naval History and Heritage Command)
Stern-to-bow photograph of *Princeton* sailing down the eastern seaboard. (Naval History and Heritage Command)

LIST OF ILLUSTRATIONS AND MAPS

Bow-to-stern photograph of *Princeton*. (Naval History and Heritage Command)
Lt Cdr Henry L. Miller, CAG of CVLG-23 and the CO of VF-23 in 1943–44. (Naval History and Heritage Command)
Adm Ernest J. King, Commander-in-Chief, United States Fleet and Chief of Naval Operations. (Naval History and Heritage Command)
Rear Adm Charles A. Pownall, commander of TF 50. (Naval History and Heritage Command)
CINCPACFLT Adm Chester W. Nimitz and Vice Adm William F. Halsey, then commander of TF 16, on January 20, 1943. (Naval History and Heritage Command)
Vice Adm Halsey with TF 16 staff on USS *Enterprise* (CV-6). (Naval History and Heritage Command)
Vice Adm Raymond A. Spruance. (Naval History and Heritage Command)
A F6F-3 Hellcat from VF-6, attached to *Princeton*'s CVLG-23. (Tony Holmes Collection)
VF-6 pilot Lt(jg) Thaddeus Coleman. (Tony Holmes Collection)
VF-23 raid on Baker Island. (Tony Holmes Collection)
Armorers prepare incendiary bombs during Operation *Galvanic*. (Tony Holmes Collection)
A TBM-1C lands back aboard a light carrier in 1943. (Tony Holmes Collection)
Annotated image of *Princeton* at anchor off the Puget Sound Naval Shipyard in Bremerton, Washington state, in January 1944. (Naval History and Heritage Command)
Princeton steams off Seattle, Washington state, on January 3, 1944. (Naval History and Heritage Command)
Lt Cdr Ernest W. Wood. (US Navy)
Lt Cdr Frederick A. Bardshar. (US Navy)
VF-27's pilot cadre. (Tony Holmes Collection)
Vice Adm Jisaburo Ozawa. (Tony Holmes Collection)
Vice Adm Marc A. Mitscher. (Naval History and Heritage Command)
Fifth Fleet vessels in Majuro Atoll in between operations in 1944. (US Navy)
Armorers load a Mk 13 torpedo into a TBM-1. (Tony Holmes Collection)

An F6F-5 Hellcat of VF-27. (Tony Holmes Collection)
An IJNAF D4Y2 "Judy" dive-bomber of 653rd Kokutai. (Tony Holmes Collection)
F6F-5 *PAPER DOLL* of VF-27. (Tony Holmes Collection)
Princeton's stern filling with smoke after being hit by a single bomb amidships. (Naval History and Heritage Command)
Princeton 20 minutes after being hit. (Naval History and Heritage Command)
Princeton being hosed down by firefighting teams from USS *Reno* (CL-96). (Naval History and Heritage Command)
Hoses on board *Reno* focus on *Princeton*'s stern following the hangar bay explosions. (Naval History and Heritage Command)
USS *Birmingham* (CL-62) approaches *Princeton*. (Naval History and Heritage Command)
Birmingham closes in on *Princeton*. (Naval History and Heritage Command)
Princeton's port forward area, as seen from the bow of *Birmingham*. (Naval History and Heritage Command)
Princeton's bow looms over *Birmingham*. (Naval History and Heritage Command)
Damage control party inspects *Princeton*'s hangar bay. (Naval History and Heritage Command)
Princeton's port side. (Naval History and Heritage Command)
Princeton's forward elevator. (Naval History and Heritage Command)
Damage control parties receive instructions on *Princeton*'s forward port flightdeck. (Naval History and Heritage Command)
Princeton survivors on a whaleboat launched by USS *Cassin Young* (DD-793). (Naval History and Heritage Command)
A sailor prepares to climb up a rope thrown from *Cassin Young*. (Naval History and Heritage Command)
Capt Thomas B. Inglis. (Naval History and Heritage Command)
Smoke plume rises from *Princeton*. (Naval History and Heritage Command)
Cdr Bruce Harwood. (Naval History and Heritage Command)
Princeton's port midships area. (Naval History and Heritage Command)
Birmingham following the explosion at 1523 hrs. (Naval History and Heritage Command)

LIST OF ILLUSTRATIONS AND MAPS

Capt John M. Hoskins. (Naval History and Heritage Command)
Princeton blows up after being torpedoed by *Reno*. (Naval History and Heritage Command)
Birmingham sails through San Francisco Bay in November 1944. (Naval History and Heritage Command)
The damage sustained to *Birmingham*. (Naval History and Heritage Command)
Under Secretary of the Navy Ralph A. Bard presents Capt William H. Buracker with the Legion of Merit. (Tony Holmes Collection)
The Essex-class carrier USS *Princeton* (CV-37) in November 1948. (Tony Holmes Collection)

MAPS

Map 1: Operations of the Pacific Fleet, September 1943– October 1944   10
Map 2: Tactical disposition of Task Force 58, June 19, 1944   12
Map 3: Tactical disposition of Task Force 38, October 24, 1944   13

USS *PRINCETON*

Operations of the Pacific Fleet, September 1943–October 1944

LIST OF ILLUSTRATIONS AND MAPS

1. September 1–14, 1943: Baker Island.
2. September 18–19, 1943: Gilberts raid on Tarawa, Makin and Abemama.
3. November 1–2, 1943: northern Solomons (Buka and Bonis airfields on Bougainville Island).
4. November 5, 1943: first Rabaul raid.
5. November 11, 1943: second Rabaul raid.
6. November 19, 1943: strike on Nauru Island.
7. November 20–24, 1943: assault on the Gilbert Islands as part of Operation *Galvanic*.
8. January 29–31, 1944: strikes on Wotje and Taroa atolls (Marshall Islands) as part of Operation *Flintlock*.
9. February 3, 1944: strikes on Engebi Island (Marshall Islands).
10. February 10–13, 1944: strikes on Eniwetok Atoll (Marshall Islands).
11. February 16–17, 1944: supported landings on Engebi Island (Marshall Islands) as part of Operation *Catchpole*.
12. February 18, 1944: strikes on Eniwetok Atoll as part of Operation *Catchpole*.
13. February 22, 1944: strikes on Parry Island as part of Operation *Catchpole*.
14. March 31–April 1, 1944: strikes on Palau.
15. April 13–24, 1944: strikes on northern New Guinea as part of Operations *Persecution* and *Reckless*.
16. April 29–30, 1944: Truk raid.
17. June 15–July 28, 1944: strikes on Mariana Islands as part of Operation *Forager*.
18. September 6–8, 1944: strikes on Palau.
19. September 9–10, 1944: strikes on northern Mindanao.
20. September 11, 1944: strikes on the Visayas.
21. September 21–22, 1944: strikes on Luzon.
22. September 24, 1944: strike on Masbate Island.
23. October 10, 1944: strike on Okinawa.
24. October 11–14, 1944: strikes on Formosa.
25. October 14, 1944: strikes on northern Luzon.
26. October 22–24, 1944: strikes on Luzon.
27. October 24, 1944: *Princeton* lost.

USS *PRINCETON*

Tactical disposition of Task Force 58, June 19, 1944

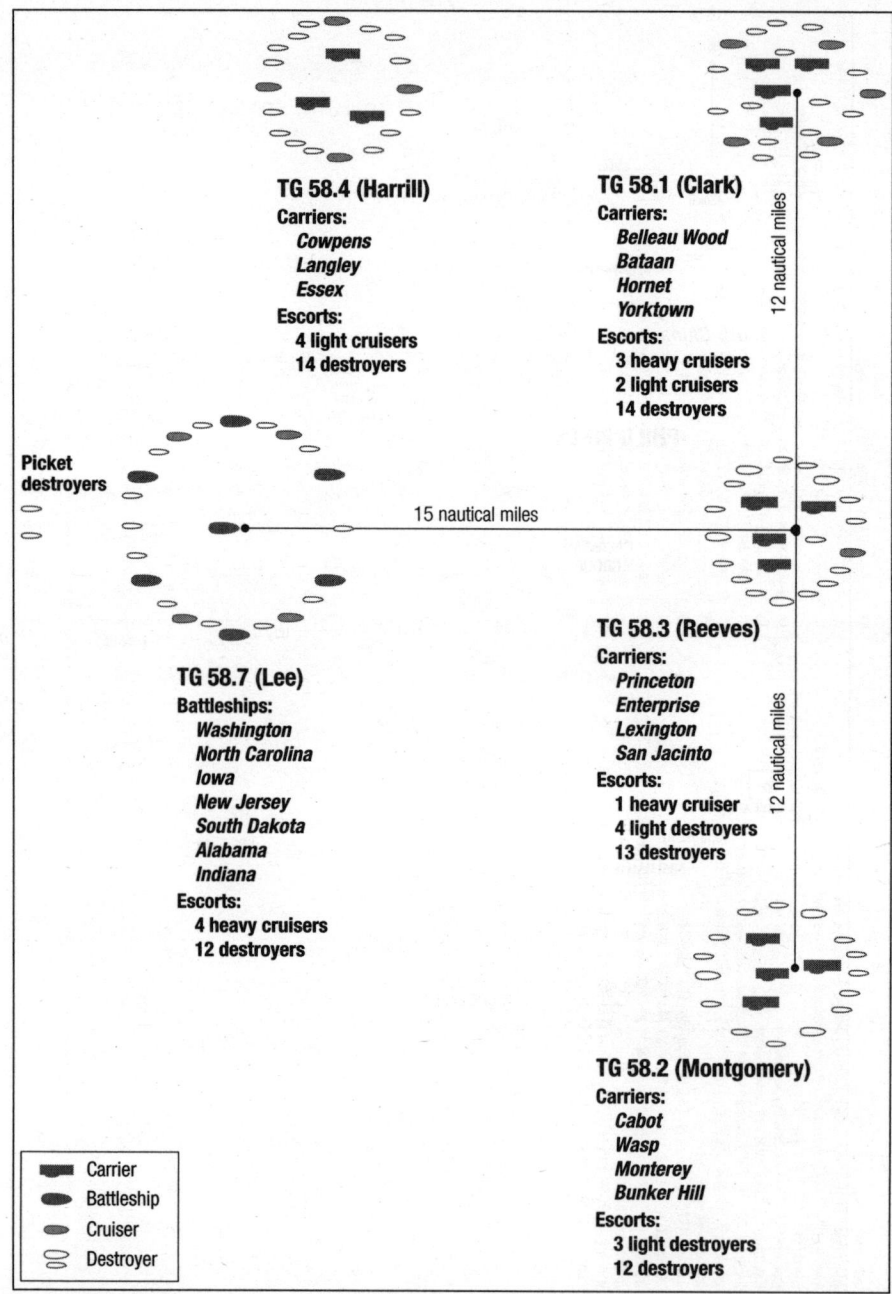

LIST OF ILLUSTRATIONS AND MAPS

Tactical disposition of Task Force 38, October 24, 1944

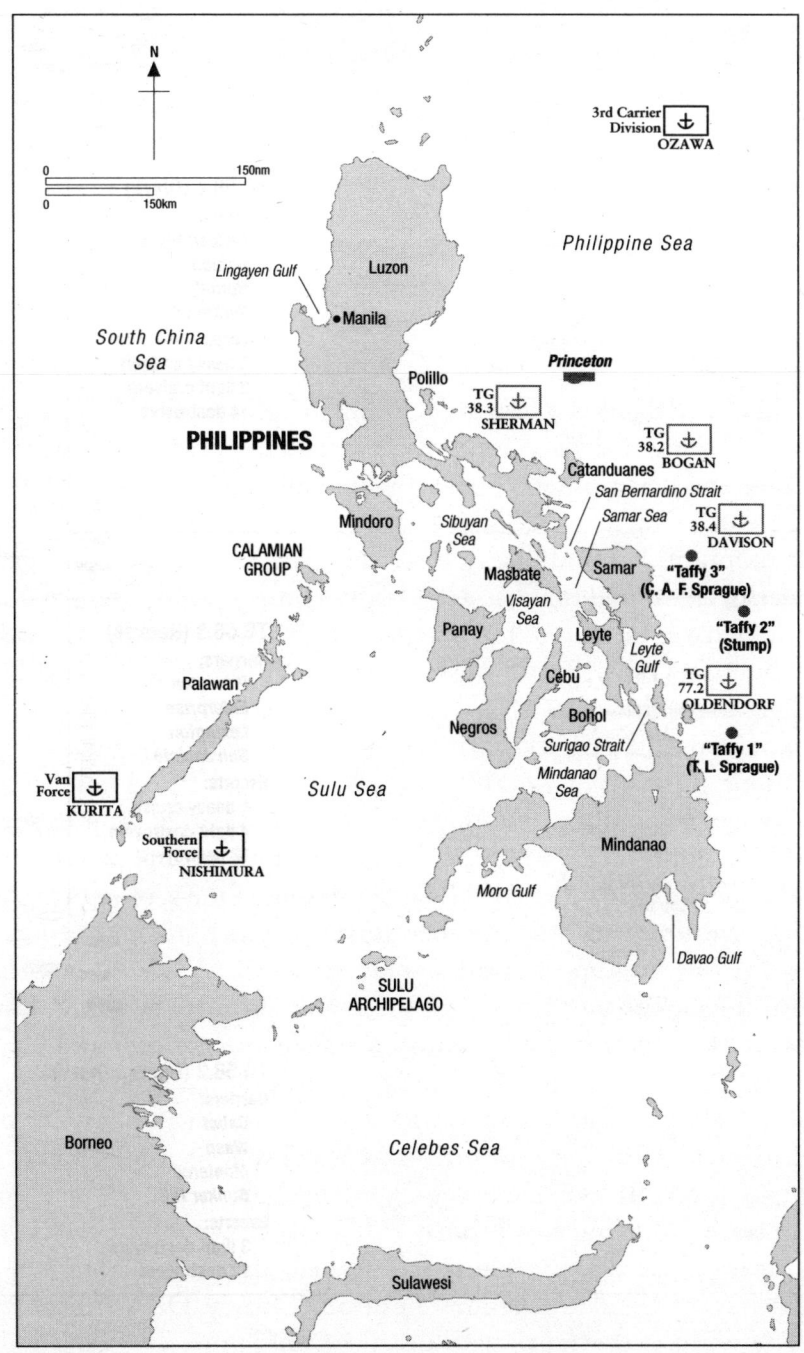

Acknowledgments

I would like to thank my dear wife, Robin, for all that she has done. She has stood by my side since 2003 when we said our vows and has shown true love and devotion ever since. I would also like to give my love to our precious daughter, Meghan, a gift to us 13 years ago that we are so thankful for. I would like to thank my parents and sister for such a wonderful childhood that has left a lasting, positive impression and has contributed a great deal to my life as an adult. Our father, Dale, passed away in 2017 and he is still missed very much to this day – I wish he was here to see this.

I would also like to acknowledge my maternal grandparents, Bruce and Virgie Burk. After working at the Mare Island Naval Shipyard in San Francisco Bay during World War II, my grandfather went to sea in the Pacific as a Merchant Marine, having taken that route due to a rare blood type and being denied enlistment in one of the service branches. During that time, my grandmother drove a laundry truck in Oakland, across the bay, in support of the war effort as well.

Also due acknowledgment are the many authors, Edwin P. Hoyt being at the forefront, who allowed me to pursue my interest in military history. I contacted leading Pacific War author/historian Barrett Tillman after I had finished my manuscript, and he put me in touch with Tony Holmes at Osprey Publishing. Thanks to you two for your assistance and guidance. A special thanks goes out to both Tony and his Publisher, Marcus Cowper, at Osprey, for they opened the door to allow a long-held dream to come true. I would like to thank Alexandra Boulton, Osprey Desk Editor, for her fine work and attention to detail on this project. I would also

ACKNOWLEDGMENTS

like to thank author/historians Mark Stille and Jeffrey Cox for their wonderful endorsements of this book.

A very special acknowledgment goes to Thomas I. Bradshaw and Marsha L. Clark who co-wrote *Carrier Down – The Sinking of the USS Princeton (CVL-23)*, published in 1990. Their collaboration, the result of more than ten years' worth of interviews with survivors from USS *Princeton* (CVL-23) and USS *Birmingham* (CL-62), has become priceless, and it has led to an updated tale that can be found in the pages of this book. *Carrier Down* was published through Eakin Press (Wild Horse Media Group) of Fort Worth, Texas, and I would like to thank them, and specifically Billy Huckaby, for their permission to use several quotes from that book. Permission was required from Barrett Tillman to use quotes from his book *Hellcat Aces of World War 2* as well, and I would like to thank him for that permission and his endorsement of this book. High praise to you, Barrett – you got the ball rolling.

Finally, I would like to express my gratitude to all the officers and enlisted men of the US Marine Corps. I must extend a heartfelt thank you for a friendship and brotherhood that no author, no matter how good, will ever be able to put into words.

Prologue

The United States was brought into World War II by the Imperial Japanese Navy (IJN) carrying out a surprise military strike against American bases and other installations on the island of Oahu, Hawaii, just before 0800 hrs on Sunday, December 7, 1941.

Japan's attack, led by Adm Chuichi Nagumo, was intended to be a preventative action that would severely cripple the US Navy's Pacific Fleet, stopping it from interfering with Japan's very carefully laid plans of immediate and near future military actions in Southeast Asia and surrounding regions. These plans included conquering the territories and military installations of the British Empire, the Netherlands and the United States. In addition to Pearl Harbor, and over the course of seven hours, there were coordinated Japanese combined forces attacks on the Philippines, Guam and Wake Island, all held by the United States. The British Empire was attacked in Malaya, Singapore and Hong Kong, along with Thailand, the Dutch East Indies, the Gilbert Islands and Borneo.

Two waves of 353 attack aircraft launched from six IJN carriers succeeded in sinking four battleships and a number of smaller vessels, damaging many more, and destroying in excess of 180 aircraft. Some 2,403 Americans were killed and a further 1,178 wounded at targeted Hawaiian bases. Japanese losses amounted to 30 aircraft, 55 aircrew and five midget submarines. Vital facilities such as the fuel farm, submarine piers and headquarters building were overlooked, prompting the airmen of the Imperial Japanese Naval Air Force (IJNAF) to plead with Adm Nagumo to launch a third strike wave. Maintaining his precious carriers on station just 230 miles north of Oahu, he elected to refuel and head back to Japan.

PROLOGUE

Japan's key objective during the initial part of the conflict, known as the Southern Operation, was to seize key economic resources in the Dutch East Indies and Malaya, particularly the oil fields, which would then allow the nation to free itself from an Allied embargo that had been implemented in July 1941.

Japan had planned to wage a limited war where its military forces would seize key objectives and then establish a defensive perimeter to thwart Allied counterattacks. The US Navy would have no choice militarily and would be lured into Japanese waters, leading to its destruction and forcing the United States and its allies into a negotiated peace. The attack on Pearl Harbor coupled with the early Pacific offensives was intended to give Japan the six to twelve months that Adm Isoroku Yamamoto, Commander-in-Chief of the Combined Fleet, needed to complete that defensive perimeter in the Pacific Ocean Area.

The early period in the war was divided into two operational phases. The first phase was broken up into three separate parts in which the major objectives of the Philippines, British Malaya, the Dutch East Indies, Burma, Borneo and Rabaul would be occupied. The second phase called for further expansion into the South Pacific by seizing eastern New Guinea, New Britain, Fiji, Samoa and strategic points in Australia. In the Central Pacific, Midway Island was targeted, as well as the Aleutian Islands in the North Pacific, as these key areas would provide the Japanese with a defense in depth and would deny the Allies staging areas from where counterattacks could be mounted.

The Japanese occupation of Southeast Asia could be termed the first global conflict in that it mounted an armed resistance to the control and intervention of Asian economies and prosperity that had been taken from these nations by a Eurocentric world system through the implementation of colonialism. To the people of Southeast Asia who had lived under European rule for generations, along with increasing American intervention, the Japanese had espoused their vision of a greater Co-Prosperity Sphere – ultimately, an Asia for Asians.

From as early as 1935, Japanese military strategists had concluded that the Southeast Asian region was of considerable importance because of its oil reserves, rubber and other resources. Indochina, Malaya and the Philippines were added to that list in 1940.

Western powers that included the United States, Britain, Australia and the exiled government of the Netherlands (due to the Nazi occupation of

Western Europe in the spring and early summer of 1940) stopped selling oil, iron ore and steel to Japan in an effort to discourage it from further expansion. This denied Japan the raw materials it needed to continue its military operations in China and French Indochina, prompting the Japanese government and their nationalist partners to view this as an act of aggression. Imported oil made up approximately 80 percent of domestic consumption, and if its supply was cut off it would grind Japan's economy and military operations present and future to a halt.

By November 1941 Japan's plans for further military aggression were complete, being only slightly adjusted over the next month. Japanese military planners counted on Great Britain and the Soviet Union not being able to respond with any considerable force, if at all, to a Japanese attack because of the current conflict in Europe.

Japanese leadership understood that a total military victory against the United States was impossible in a traditional sense, so they counted on quick military victories early in the conflict, breaking American will and consequently pushing them to the negotiating table to recognize Japanese dominance in Asia. Japanese leadership looked to base the coming war against the United States upon the model of past successful conflicts against China (1894–95) and Imperial Russia (1904–05). In these conflicts, a strong continental power was defeated by the opposing force conquering a limited group of military objectives, not by the total occupation of a nation and the crippling of its industrial base.

On December 2, 1941, the order to "Climb Mount Niitaka" had been sent, setting in motion the start of the offensives after all necessary preparations for the attacks had already been carried out in late November. Units of the IJN and the Imperial Japanese Army (IJA) commenced moving forces into position to launch simultaneous surprise attacks on the United States and the British Empire after prolonged tensions and failed negotiations.

By then Japan was already firmly established in Korea, Manchuria and northeast China, and it was in possession of key ports on Hainan and Formosa, as well as in the Mariana, Caroline and Marshall Island groups. It also had the whole French Indochina region to stage from. Japan's main aim was still the conquest of China, which emphasized the seizure of the oil fields in the Dutch East Indies, with a close second on the list being the closing of the Burma Road over which Allied supplies continued to flow, thus keeping Chinese troops in the fight.

PROLOGUE

Both moves meant war with Britain and the United States, and a vital part of the Japanese strategy was the establishment of a sprawling defensive perimeter stretching from Burma right around to the Aleutian Islands of Alaska. Only in this way could it hope to hold off American military might once the nation's immense manpower and industrial resources were mobilized. On December 7 (December 8 in Asia/Western Pacific time zones), the Japanese vision of a Greater East Asia Co-Prosperity Sphere would be realized by force.

With the bulk of their ground forces tied up in China, the Japanese could only employ 11 infantry divisions for these offensives, so speed was vital before the Allies could reinforce their troops or mount legitimate counterattacks. The IJN had far more aircraft carriers in-theater than its opponents and its surface task forces were very well trained, especially in nightfighting. Furthermore, they had no language barriers to overcome.

The Allied forces at that time were a complete contrast, with scattered naval vessels and no central command. To their detriment, the two main Pacific naval bases, Pearl Harbor and Singapore, were nearly 7,000 miles apart. The IJA fielded just slightly more troops than the Allies, and Japanese soldiers were usually better trained and experienced in amphibious operations, with the added weight of air superiority both overall and locally. Only the US Pacific Fleet posed an immediate danger to Japanese plans, which led to the decision to attack it at Pearl Harbor as opposed to engaging the US Navy while other multiple, simultaneous operations were being conducted.

The Japanese chose the time and place for their amphibious operations, and all were well escorted by cruiser and destroyer forces, while air cover was maintained by land-based aircraft or from carriers, and battleships and heavy cruisers supplied additional firepower.

What followed was a professional deployment of ground, naval and air forces carrying out a very well planned and executed combined arms campaign that focused on a concentration of force at the point of attack. The first wave of simultaneous Japanese attacks included Pearl Harbor, the Philippines, Guam, Wake Island, and the British territories of Malaya, Singapore and Hong Kong. Opposing them were Allied forces that were both poorly trained and equipped.

The same day Pearl Harbor was attacked, Hong Kong was invaded from mainland China, with fighting taking place until Christmas Day when the British and Dominion forces surrendered. Simultaneously, Japanese troops landed on the east coast of the Kra Isthmus of Thailand and northeast Malaya and started a drive south toward Singapore. Landings also took place in the Philippines between December 10–22, catching Gen Douglas MacArthur, commander of US Army Forces in the Far East, completely off balance – he and his forces would never recover from these initial, surprise attacks.

Also on December 10, the Royal Navy lost the capital ships HMS *Repulse* and HMS *Prince of Wales* to an overpowering, well-coordinated air attack that sent both vessels to the bottom of the South China Sea in a little over an hour. Guam, in the Marianas, was captured and Makin and Tarawa atolls in the Gilberts chain were occupied.

A glimmer of good news surfaced as Wake Island was attacked on December 11, with the landings being repulsed by a small group of stubborn Marines. A force was dispatched from Pearl Harbor to reinforce them, but it was called back and the small garrison was eventually overwhelmed on December 23. The first landings took place in northern Borneo in mid-December, and they continued into late January 1942.

Earlier that same month British Army Gen Archibald Wavell had been made commander of the American-British-Dutch-Australian Command (ABDACOM), but it was a cumbersome, ineffective organization burdened by language barriers and other logistical hang-ups. The dominoes continued to fall for the Allies in January, with Kuala Lumpur being captured on the 11th, advances being made in the Dutch East Indies with landings in Borneo and in the Celebes, and Burma being invaded toward the end of the month. January also saw the Japanese expand into the southeast Pacific with landings at Kavieng on New Ireland and Rabaul on New Britain.

Seeming to be everywhere at once, Japanese forces commenced their occupation of Singapore on February 8. Seven days later, an exhausted IJA force one-third the size of the Allied force attempting to defend Singapore accepted its surrender, seizing the "key" to Southeast Asia and the Southwest Pacific in the process. On February 18, the IJNAF attacked the Australian port of Darwin – the main staging area for the supply of Allied forces in Java – and sank eight ships, including a US Navy destroyer and several valuable transports. The port was effectively put out of action at the cost of just two aircraft.

In a series of surface battles spanning February 27–March 1, ABDACOM naval forces attempting to disrupt the Japanese invasion of the Dutch East Indies were nearly annihilated. The sharp surface actions led to only three elderly US Navy destroyers managing to escape the IJN's dominance in the region. On March 8, the Burmese capital Rangoon, entry point for the Burma Road, fell to the Japanese – the British Army had barely escaped the lightning advance of the IJA. That same day in New Guinea, north of Port Moresby on the northeastern coast of Papua, Japanese troops entered Lae and Salamaua on the Huon Gulf unopposed.

Gen MacArthur and members of his family, along with hand-picked staff officers, left the Philippines on March 11. MacArthur, having turned his command over to Lt Gen Jonathan M. Wainwright, proceeded to board one of several US Navy PT boats that had sneaked through Manila Bay to the island of Corregidor. He reached Mindanao two days later, and from there MacArthur and his party flew to Australia in two B-17 Flying Fortresses. They eventually arrived in Melbourne by train on March 21.

Nine days earlier, northern Sumatra had been occupied, and the rest of March was spent consolidating the Japanese hold throughout the many islands. Its southern perimeter had been secured in less than four months, with naval forces patrolling the Indian Ocean south of Java to stop the escape of Allied shipping. Japan's first operational phase was duly completed when carrier-based IJNAF aircraft conducted a series of raids into the Indian Ocean that effectively drove the Royal Navy westward beyond its bases in Ceylon. Further expansion in this theater was only halted because of the IJN's operational requirements in the Pacific.

The IJA made its final push on Bataan and, on April 9, American and Filipino forces surrendered. The island fortress of Corregidor held out until May 6. Some resistance continued on other Philippine islands, and the Americans, along with their fellow Filipino prisoners of war (PoW), were subjected to the infamous Bataan Death March, beatings, starvation, disease, executions and imprisonment by their Japanese captors through to September 1945.

By the time Corregidor fell, five months had passed since the start of the Pacific War. Of all the initial objectives of the Japanese Empire, only one remained unachieved. The invaders had up until now conquered the Dutch East Indies, advanced down the Malayan Peninsula to capture

Singapore, seized Hong Kong and accepted the surrender of Allied forces in the Philippines. Their unprecedented military campaigns had expanded through a series of islands in the Pacific Ocean, and achieved important air and naval victories that left the Allied fleet in ruins.

With the fall of Rangoon, the Burma operation was on track, so the Imperial General Headquarters in Japan now planned to shift to Phase Two of operations – looking east out into the Pacific toward Midway and the United States, south toward Australia and New Guinea and west toward Ceylon and India.

In the midst of the military disasters befalling the Allies in Southeast Asia and the Pacific, President Franklin D. Roosevelt appointed newly promoted Adm Chester W. Nimitz as Commander-in-Chief, US Pacific Fleet (CINCPACFLT), effective as of December 31, 1941. Nimitz and his staff immediately turned to the Rainbow 5 War Plan, a number of war plans devised by the Joint Planning Committee during the inter-war years that outlined potential US strategies for hypothetical war scenarios. They started formulating raids against the occupied Marshall and Gilbert Islands in an attempt to give the Japanese war machine pause as the vital shipping lanes from the United States to Australia were now threatened.

I

"Sweet P"

The Cleveland-class light cruiser USS *Tallahassee* (CL-61) was laid down on June 2, 1941 at Camden, New Jersey, by the New York Shipbuilding Corporation in anticipation of American involvement in World War II. Although the attack on Pearl Harbor was still six months away, the situation in the Pacific had intensified with Japan signing the Tripartite Pact with Germany and Italy on September 27, 1940, and Gen Hideki Tojo of the IJA becoming Prime Minister on October 18, 1941.

During continued negotiations between Japan and the United States, the Roosevelt Administration made a counter proposal in November to end the conflict in China by demanding the removal of all Japanese troops from the country and the signing of non-aggression pacts with all Pacific western powers. These demands, coupled with a strangling oil embargo on Japan's war machine, were met with firm resistance and looked upon as an unspoken declaration of war.

Eleven months prior to the November 1941 proposal, President Roosevelt had delivered his Arsenal of Democracy speech on December 29, 1940. Proving that this was not simply political rhetoric, the President (who was a former Assistant Secretary of the Navy) instigated studies into whether the nine hulls of the planned Cleveland-class cruisers then under construction could be converted into small aircraft carriers. This proposal was made to the General Board of the US Navy, specifically the Bureau of Ships (BuShips). Its studies of proposed cruiser-size aircraft carrier designs had shown that the type had serious limitations, and in October 1941 BuShips reported that such a conversion suffered from too many compromises for it to be a legitimate undertaking, and that the vessel produced would not be effective.

BuShips' Preliminary Design section opposed the project because "it would upset the orderly construction of this series of cruisers, and would produce small, costly aircraft carriers of limited effectiveness [not much, if at all] earlier than the large Essex-class now building." Additionally, the Bureau of Air (BuAer) chimed in, stating the design "has a number of undesirable aeronautical features which combine to jeopardize seriously the probable usefulness of these vessels ... flight operations would be both hazardous and difficult."

President Roosevelt immediately ordered another study that got the General Board's attention, for it had left a loophole in its assessment – if a smaller flightdeck, fewer aircraft, or less effectiveness were acceptable, the conversion could, of course, be completed sooner. This was precisely the point, for the President wanted these vessels available for service as quickly as possible. Making use of resources already in the pipeline in the form of the partially completed cruiser hulls would allow aircraft carriers to be completed expeditiously and put sea-based air power into the war, specifically the Pacific Theater, far in advance of dedicated fleet carriers then also under construction.

The Cleveland-class light cruisers, of which 36 were ordered, were originally authorized as a follow-on to the Brooklyn-class light cruisers. The largest single class of cruisers in US Navy history, the nine Cleveland-class light cruiser hulls were the logical choice for conversion because of the numbers available and the fact that they were considered to be the smallest vessels that could be adapted as carriers with the speed required for fleet operations and adequate flightdeck space to provide a useful aircraft capacity.

Adm Harold R. Stark, at that time Chief of Naval Operations (CNO), wrote to BuShips less than a month after the attack on Pearl Harbor to confirm that one of the Cleveland-class light cruisers would be converted into an aircraft carrier. BuShips got to work the next day using its earlier plans, but soon shifted to a design based on the Sangamon-class escort carrier, four examples of which were built on fleet-oiler hulls and were larger and more capable than the C3 merchant-ship conversions that had preceded them. Additionally, the Sangamon-class conversions were comparable in dimensions and displacement to light cruisers, which meant the two designs had flightdecks that were identical in size.

Overcoming initial structural issues, BuShips designers were able to build a flat hangar bay – essential for the safe handling of aircraft – that ran between the forward and after deck elevators 4ft above the cruiser main deck. With the hangar bay being critical to effective daily operations in respect to the maintenance, fueling and arming of aircraft, a hangar clearance height of 17ft 4in. (comparable to the US Navy's purpose-built fleet carriers) was accomplished by using flightdeck girders that were only 3ft deep. The smaller girders at the base of the flightdeck were included in the design by waiving the requirement for suspending spare aircraft from the overhead of the hangar bay, as was common practice in fleet carrier hangars.

Another innovative design to keep the hangar bay spaces well ventilated, and thus prevent gasoline vapor build-up, was the installation of large openings like warehouse doors along the edges of the hangar bay at the aft end that could be individually closed off if necessary. This feature paid off many times over as it allowed live ordnance and fueled-up aircraft to be pushed through the openings and over the side when the ship came under attack, or to rid the space of objects that could prove hazardous to the vessel.

The Independence-class light carriers, as the converted Cleveland-class light cruisers were known to the US Navy, had a relatively short and narrow flightdeck and hangar, with a small island superstructure. The addition of the latter, along with the flightdeck and hangar, added a significant increase in the ship's topside weight and balance. To prevent the altered vessels from being top-heavy, naval architects considered using 400 tons of ballast to make the light carriers ride lower in the water, thus increasing stability. Eventually, this problem was solved by adding blisters with a total weight of 315 tons to the hull, increasing the beam by 5ft. This in turn added space for an additional 635 tons of fuel storage to the original cruiser design, allowing 225 tons (122,000 gallons) of aviation gasoline to be taken aboard.

The vessels would have a cruising radius of 10,000 miles at 15 knots, which was better than the Cleveland-class cruisers they were based on, but only two-thirds that of the 27,000-ton Essex-class fleet carriers. The blisters, while necessary, hindered the top speed by 1.5 knots to 31.6 knots, which was good enough to allow the Independence-class light carriers to operate with the Essex-class vessels. Overall, the standard displacement of an Independence-class light carrier was 11,000 tons, compared to 11,744 tons for a Cleveland-class cruiser, while the carrier's draft was 26ft, a foot deeper than the cruiser's.

The light carriers were slated to have a belt of armor installed, and the blisters caused problems since Class A armor could not be used as it was found to be too difficult to cut and weld when it came to attaching it to the blisters. Class B armor was needed, which, unfortunately, added an additional 360 tons to the displacement and 3in. to the draft, thus reducing the top speed by a quarter knot. Furthermore, unexpected delays were encountered in the delivery of Class B armor, so the first two ships of the class, USS *Independence* (CV-22) and USS *Princeton* (CV-23), were completed without an armored belt to allow them to be commissioned on schedule and get the carriers to the fleet in a timely manner.

Modifications continued as the cruiser's ammunition magazines were converted to bomb storage, allowing a total of 331 tons of aviation ordnance to be carried. A space to the rear of the hangar was also created to house 24 torpedoes, which would ride the aft aircraft elevator to the flightdeck. Fifteen-pound Special Treatment Steel (STS) 0.38in. thick was applied to the side of the hangar around the torpedo storage area and exposed control spaces to protect these vulnerable spots. Bomb elevators and ammunition hoists were likewise protected with 25lb and 30lb STS.

The original main powerplant of a Cleveland-class cruiser, consisting of four Babcock & Wilcox boilers feeding four Parsons geared turbines that provided 100,000 shaft horsepower, was retained, but the disposal of exhaust stack gas became a problem. After different modifications were considered, four simple smoke pipes were arranged in pairs and retrunked to the starboard side.

The Independence-class carriers all received the same island structure, which was little more than a small open bridge some 6ft wide positioned 4ft from the starboard edge of the flightdeck near the forward elevator. The island was equipped with the captain's and navigator's sea cabins, a chart room, an open bridge and sky lookout platforms extending 4ft to either side. These compact workspaces took economy of movement into consideration, allowing the ship's captain to get to these vital compartments in roughly 20 steps. The addition of the island had to be counterbalanced by the addition of 82 tons of concrete in four blister compartments below the second platform deck level on the port side of the carrier.

As construction neared completion, it was found that the aviation handling facilities were better than predicted in the earlier design studies, although the hangar bay was smaller than even the Sangamon-class escort carriers (designated CVEs) at 215ft in length and a width of just 58ft. Fortunately, the ships were equipped with two aircraft elevators that had faster cycles than the CVEs.

As *Independence* was fitting out, extensions were added to the flightdeck between the stacks to allow aircraft that were not running properly to be quickly moved out of the way. Another extension on the port side next to the forward elevator allowed aircraft to bypass the elevator when it was in the lowered position, while also serving as a jettison ramp. A Type H Mk 2 Mod 1 hydraulic catapult was installed on the port side of the flightdeck, with a second later added to the starboard side. A 14,000lb-capacity aircraft crane positioned forward of the island assisted with the loading/unloading of aircraft and other large pieces of equipment. With these and other necessary additions, the ship's growing weight was always a constant concern, and no detail was left overlooked. That included replacing all the doors to the officers' quarters with much lighter curtains.

On January 10, 1942, USS *Amsterdam* (CL-59), laid down on May 1, 1941 as a light cruiser, was reordered for conversion to an aircraft carrier as *Independence*, lead carrier of the Independence-class. The following month, on February 14, the new CNO, Adm Ernest J. King, reviewed the conversion plans and added two more vessels. Maintaining naval custom, the nine small flattops were named after battles or former US Navy vessels, and *Tallahassee*, laid down on June 2, 1941, was reordered as *Princeton*, while USS *New Haven* (CL-76), laid down on August 11, 1941, became USS *Belleau Wood* (CV-24). The remaining six, USS *Cowpens* (CV-25), USS *Monterey* (CV-26), USS *Langley* (CV-27), USS *Cabot* (CV-28), USS *Bataan* (CV-29), and USS *San Jacinto* (CV-30), followed in succession, with all nine commissioned before the end of 1943.

The ships of the Independence class displaced 11,000 tons, or 15,800 tons fully loaded, with an overall length at just under 623ft, a basic beam of 71ft 6in., a flightdeck length of 552ft and a width of 109.2ft.

The light carriers could operate with a total of 45 aircraft, although 30–35 was more typical once delivered to the fleet. Defense of these vessels consisted of 26 Bofors 40mm guns split between two quad mounts, eight dual mounts and 16 single mounts. They were originally designed to carry a complement of 140 officers and 1,321 enlisted men, but as wartime requirements led to demands for more sailors to operate added weaponry and equipment, this later increased to a total of 1,569 enlisted men, with those numbers being slightly more than half the crew of a larger Essex-class fleet carrier. Accommodation was always tight.

FIGHTBACK IN THE PACIFIC

While the construction of this new class of carrier was underway, the war in the Pacific carried on without pause as Adm Nimitz and his staff moved forward with a series of daring raids into the Central and South Pacific. The Imperial General Headquarters had counted on the devastating Pearl Harbor raid having a psychological effect on the US Navy, but things did not quite work out as it had planned. It believed that the Americans would enter the war as a defeated military force that undertook every upcoming campaign against their opponents with the expectation of further loss. The Japanese were convinced that the Americans would conduct themselves as the Chinese and Russians had after handing them defeats in 1894 and 1904, respectively. The exact opposite took place, however, as the US Navy reacted with fury and revenge, exhibiting no sense of inferiority whatsoever.

With the minimal forces they had at their disposal, Adm Nimitz and Vice Adm William F. "Bull" Halsey were able to finalize a plan that entailed Halsey's Task Force (TF) 8 linking up with the carrier USS *Yorktown* (CV-5) (part of TF 17) as it arrived in American Samoa to deliver troops for garrison duty and jungle training. The two task forces would then split up and hit their objectives simultaneously. USS *Enterprise* (CV-6) would attack the Marshall Islands of Kwajalein, Maloelap and Wotje, and *Yorktown* would hit Makin and Jaluit atolls in the Gilberts. The strikes were duly carried out on February 1, 1942 and they were chalked up as a success due to the fact that the Japanese defenders were caught completely by surprise as the task forces "hit-and-run" without receiving any damage in return.

Adm Yamamoto had estimated that the IJN would dominate the Pacific Theater for six months before the US Navy would mount any effective counterattack. It actually came in less than eight weeks, shocking the Imperial General Headquarters in Tokyo which was left alarmed by the effectiveness of the US Navy's audacious raids.

Such strikes, at that time anchored by Halsey's audacity and fighting spirit, did not stop with the Marshalls–Gilberts raids. In fact, they had only just started. An extremely bold raid was planned for February 20 that called for USS *Lexington* (CV-2), with an escort of four cruisers and ten destroyers, to steam deep into enemy-held waters around Rabaul and strike the newly established IJN base there.

While making their run-in to the target, TF 11, under the command of Rear Adm Wilson Brown, was spotted by an IJNAF reconnaissance aircraft and an enemy bomber attack soon materialized. The Naval Aviators from *Lexington* put up a fierce fight in defense of their ships and downed 18 IJNAF Mitsubishi G4M medium bombers in an engagement that would earn Lt Edward "Butch" O'Hare of VF-3 the Congressional Medal of Honor after he brought down five aircraft in succession while at the controls of his Grumman F4F-3 Wildcat. Rear Adm Brown then withdrew, not wanting to keep his task force in hostile waters any longer than necessary.

Three weeks after hitting the Marshalls, Halsey, this time at the helm of TF 16, would attack Wake Island on February 24 and Marcus Island on March 4. Both raids were again successful, with the strike on Wake sending several thousands gallons of fuel up in flames, destroying a number of IJNAF aircraft and leaving the island's airfield inoperable for several months. The Marcus raid was significant in that the island was only 1,000 miles from Tokyo and 600 miles from major military installations in the Bonin Island chain and waters under complete Japanese control.

IJA troops landed unopposed on the north coast of New Guinea at Lae and Salamaua on March 8 and had become an immediate threat to both Port Moresby and Australia. In the first ever US Navy operation involving a two-carrier task force, Rear Adm Frank J. Fletcher took *Yorktown* and *Lexington* into the Coral Sea, northwest of Port Moresby, and launched his aircraft on March 10. Their target was Japanese shipping, and three vessels of differing sizes were sunk after pilots had navigated their way over the imposing Owen Stanley Range into (and back out of) the target area.

Although this raid was a success, both it and the previous attacks would pale in comparison to what came next from Halsey and TF 16. He took the combined force of two carriers, *Enterprise* and USS *Hornet* (CV-8), plus support ships, on a daring mission to launch US Army Air Force (USAAF) North American B-25 Mitchell medium bombers off the deck of the latter carrier in a raid to attack targets in Tokyo and other selected cities.

On April 18, while the task force was still 750 miles from Japan, it was sighted by a Japanese picket boat that signaled Tokyo. Col James Doolittle, the mission leader, and *Hornet*'s skipper, Capt Marc Mitscher, decided to launch the B-25s immediately – ten hours early and 200 miles farther from Japan than originally planned. Doolittle and his raiders had 467ft (155.7 yards) of takeoff distance. All 16 medium bombers launched safely between 0820 and 0919 hrs and then flew toward Japan at wave-top height. The aircraft arrived over their targets at about midday Tokyo time, six hours after launch, climbed to 1,500ft and bombed ten military and industrial targets in Tokyo, two in Yokohama and one each in Yokosuka, Nagoya, Kobe and Osaka, and then egressed to secret landing strips in China.

Although damage inflicted by the raid was minimal, it would offer a stern warning to the Imperial General Headquarters that the capital of the Japanese Empire was within reach of medium bombers flying from US Navy carriers. This raid, along with the Pacific Fleet's pin prick attacks on the Japanese Pacific perimeter over the previous three months, had put the IJN's plans to invade Midway, in the Central Pacific, in motion.

Overcome by "victory disease," the IJN made the fatal mistake of splitting its forces and underestimating the US Navy, resulting in a strategic defeat at the Battle of the Coral Sea on May 4–8. The Americans then pulled off an intelligence coup that saw them break the Japanese naval code detailing Yamamoto's next move in the Pacific War. The US Navy was duly able to position itself in an ideal position to ambush the IJN's Combined Fleet, which had no idea that three American carriers were waiting for it at Midway. Dive-bombers from *Enterprise* and *Yorktown* pummeled the 1st Carrier Striking Force on June 4–5, sinking four of its fleet carriers in an epic confrontation that would then pivot the initiative in the Pacific in favor of the Americans.

"SWEET P"

The US Marine Corps' 1st Marine Division would literally walk ashore at Guadalcanal, in the Solomon Islands, on August 7, 1942, catching the island's Japanese defenders by surprise. The fighting that ensued on land, at sea and in the air over control of the newly completed runway at Henderson Field would see some of the bloodiest clashes of the campaign as both sides struggled to maintain a toehold in the South Pacific. The war of attrition that developed in-theater would eventually drain the IJNAF of men and materiel, putting Japan on the defensive and opening up the vast Pacific Ocean for an American counteroffensive against the nation's eastern flank that would eventually take the war to Tokyo's doorstep.

LIGHT CARRIERS LAUNCHED

The ships that would soon participate in that action were now close to ready as *Independence* slid into the Delaware River on August 22, 1942 and *Princeton* followed it on October 18. A newspaper account said the latter vessel was launched "with informality," and the accompanying $25 affair was in keeping with the cost limit imposed by the US Navy for such an event in wartime. Margaret Dodds, wife of the president of Princeton University, christened the new carrier by cracking a bottle of champagne against its hull. Although there were no formal speeches during the launch, hundreds of shipyard workers within eyesight of the carrier paused just long enough to watch *Princeton* slide into the water.

With the first and second milestones of the construction of a naval vessel complete, the third was about to begin as the carrier was prepared for its commissioning. Once eased into the fitting dock at the New York Shipbuilding Corporation yards, members of the outfitting detail – roughly 300 enlisted crewmen who had survived the October 27, 1942 sinking of *Hornet* during the Battle of the Santa Cruz Islands – began reporting in. Added to that group were a number of officers from *Hornet*, USS *Wasp* (CV-7), USS *Saratoga* (CV-3) and *Enterprise*. Capt George R. Henderson was among the ex-*Hornet* officers, and he was assigned to *Princeton* as its first commanding officer, accompanied by a nucleus of other officers who had seen combat in the Pacific on board not just carriers but battleships and cruisers as well.

Not all the "old salts" were enthusiastic about the new light carriers, with some preferring the formidable new Essex-class vessels that would be joining the fleet alongside the smaller carriers. Some of the Independence-class warships sailed with 70 percent of their enlisted personnel and half of their officer cadre having no prior sea experience. Indeed, many of these men had never been on board an ocean-going vessel of any kind, let alone a large warship. The US Navy was doing all it could to wrangle the experienced sailors down and assign them to the new ships, much to the chagrin of Lou Mitnich, an experienced fireman 1st class.

Expecting leave after his transfer from a heavy cruiser, he was instead ordered to report to the *Belleau Wood* as it neared completion in Camden, right behind *Princeton*. Mitnich recalled:

> I had rushed in a chit for leave, but the officer, after looking through some papers, said, "You're the man we are looking for. B division has been waiting weeks for a fireman like you." I retired wearily and prepared to hit the sack. After breakfast the next morning, I met the chiefs and some boys and was ready to get my first glimpse of the *Belleau Wood*. Suddenly someone yelled, "That's her!" You could have knocked me over with a feather. All the time I had thought the *Belleau Wood* was one of the big Essex-class carriers, but there she was, a little ugly flattop with a starboard list to boot. For a moment I wished I'd joined the Army.

All of the Independence-class ships were built by the New York Shipbuilding Corporation at Camden, with a company representative making a point to attend the initial meeting in January 1942, for much of the conversion design work changing the vessel from a light cruiser to light carrier would be done by the builder. The company, established at the turn of the century by Henry G. Morse with financial backing from Andrew Mellon and Henry Frick, was originally to have been located on Staten Island, as the name implies. Morse then decided that Camden, which offered better land, rail facilities and access to a great number of experienced shipyard workers, was a superior location and the new shipyard was built there, but the name remained unchanged.

The shipyard opened in 1900, and by World War I it had become the largest of its kind in the world and a major builder of US Navy warships. "New York Ship," as it was also known, had an impeccable shipbuilding record, with 70 vessels built by the company seeing service in World War II. Implementing American ingenuity and common sense, the shipyard installed overhead cranes that connected all parts of the site and built a roof over the shipbuilding ways to avoid delays caused by bad weather – these were just two of the innovations it implemented.

Among the many warships they built, the shipyard workers were especially proud of the nine light carriers of the Independence class, and the vessels were referred to collectively in wartime company advertisements as the "sunsetters" for their role in the defeat of Japan, the "land of the rising sun."

The presence of combat experience among the carrier's crew would paid dividends during the outfitting, especially when it came to gun placement. Capt Henderson and *Princeton*'s gunnery officer, Lt Cdr Walt Phaler, stepped in to correct issues on more than one occasion. Initially, single 5in./38 guns were to be mounted on the carrier's forecastle and fantail, prompting Henderson and Phaler to step in and insist upon mounting 40mm quad Bofors mounts – a much better antiaircraft weapon with a high rate of fire. There was initial resistance to this change, with those objecting citing the additional time needed to source the new weapons and the increased staffing required to man them, but the two officers won out, and their decision would pay dividends considering the nature of the warfare that they would soon be facing in the Pacific.

Following the attack on Pearl Harbor, the existing 1.1in. quad mount and 0.50-cal. machine guns were determined to be inadequate when it came to defending a ship from an attack by enemy aircraft, and these were rapidly replaced by 20mm Oerlikon and 40mm Bofors cannon that would prove their worth many times over in the coming engagements.

Princeton was towed across the Delaware River to the Philadelphia Naval Shipyard from the Camden yards on the morning of February 25, 1943, and as soon as the ship was secure, the 450 men who had been quartered at nearby facilities boarded their new home. Formal commissioning took place that afternoon as the festivities commenced, with the Philadelphia Naval Shipyard Band playing the National Anthem, followed by a brief speech by Capt Henderson. Chief Boatswain R. C. Hawk then piped his boatswain's mates and set the watch, signifying that the ship was under the control of its crew.

To celebrate its new status, George A. Brakeley, vice-president of Princeton University, was on hand to present Capt Henderson with a silver ladle, tray and punch bowl – replicas of the items made by Paul Revere – on behalf of alumni and friends. A representative of the New York Princeton University Club was also present, and he gave Capt Henderson a Currier and Ives print of the composite gunboat USS *Princeton* (PG-13) of 1898, the new ship's namesake.

Meanwhile, a few miles north of Philadelphia at Willow Grove airfield, Light Carrier Air Group (CVLG) 23, led by Lt Cdr George M. Chafee, was established on November 16, 1942 with orders to begin training as *Princeton*'s first air group, with initial training conducted in North American SNJ Texans and F4F-4 Wildcats. The Naval Aviators and other carrier air group personnel had no complaints concerning the off-time venues and night life in nearby Philadelphia, but the foul weather in Pennsylvania during the winter months cut into flying time and CVLG-23 transferred to US Marine Corps Recruit Depot Parris Island, South Carolina, on January 6, 1943. Shortly thereafter, Lt Cdr Chafee was detached to become air officer for the new light carrier USS *Cabot* (CV-28) and he was replaced by Lt Cdr Henry L. Miller. A notable highlight of their training period while at Parris Island was a visit by President Roosevelt in April 1943.

As training proceeded, the men received a first-hand account of the Doolittle Raid from Lt Cdr Miller. In March 1942, USAAF personnel, with their B-25s, had arrived at Eglin Auxiliary Field No. 1 in Florida to start their training for the mission against mainland Japan. Then Lt Miller, stationed nearby at Naval Air Station (NAS) Pensacola, Florida, was assigned to the operation as a training officer, and he assisted the pilots in a multitude of tasks that included taking off from the flightdeck of an aircraft carrier.

Once the training was completed, crews flew their aircraft to McClellan Field in Sacramento, California, for final modifications and inspection. They then transferred to NAS Alameda at Oakland, on San Francisco Bay, and embarked their 16 B-25s on board *Hornet* for the journey across the Pacific. Lt Miller accompanied them throughout the process, being on board the carrier for the launch. He was also named an honorary Doolittle Raider for his contribution to the success of this extremely dangerous mission.

The carrier air group was training hard to prepare for the shakedown cruise, and that included ground school, aircraft and fighter direction procedures and enemy aircraft and ship identification. Lt W. L. Curtis, *Princeton*'s landing signal officer (LSO), arrived at Parris Island to conduct field-carrier landing practice that consisted, as much as possible, of landings on the airfield with procedures and conditions resembling those on a carrier.

Princeton was scheduled to depart on its shakedown cruise six weeks after commissioning, but leaks in the carrier's gasoline tanks required alterations and complete retesting of the fuel systems, which set the departure date to the Caribbean back several days. At the naval shipyard in Philadelphia, this additional time was put to good use, with the crew continuing to train in a variety of subjects and undertaking trials that included a test sailing down the Delaware River and back and the firing of dead weight shots while alongside the dock to test the carrier's two catapults. There were a wide range of drills that included man overboard, fire suppression and abandon ship, as well as the tremendous labor involved in the loading of provisions, stores, ammunition and fuel into a previously empty ship.

Tens of thousands of young men, if not drafted first, flocked to the nearest recruiting stations following the attack on Pearl Harbor, signing up for the branch of service that most interested them. A large number hailed from small midwestern towns, and having never seen the ocean before, many of them joined the US Navy as non-swimmers. Catering for such individuals among *Princeton*'s crew, the Camden YMCA made its facilities available so non-swimmers could receive instruction and all sailors could exercise.

The men enjoyed their time off to the fullest, with all hands granted a three-section liberty schedule. This meant that both officers and men could go ashore in Philadelphia three nights out of four. "This was a strenuous period for the personnel officer, chaplain and division officers," recalled Lt Cdr Edward L. Clifford, aide to the ship's executive officer. "The men found plenty of trouble, although most of it was relatively harmless."

More than 500 sailors were cut loose for liberty on their nights off in Philadelphia, and those officers mentioned by Clifford must have been like worrisome mothers as they were fully aware that many of the men had never seen neon lights before, let alone a large east coast city.

Most of them had only known the Great Depression, having been born in the early to mid 1920s and lived hard lives from the start. They came from a generation that was raised in homes with a scarcity of food, being forced to wear hand-me-downs that were probably not to their liking. There is a good chance that some of them grew up in homes with dirt floors. These young men were now getting three square meals a day of US Navy chow, and they probably felt pretty dapper in their sharp new uniforms as they stepped out into town with a few dollars in their pockets – things were good.

Princeton's crew also took time to organize ship's parties and on March 17 an event was thrown in one of the base buildings. Ilona Massey, Arthur Treacher and other cast members of the Ziegfeld Follies, which were in a pre-New York opening run in Philadelphia, were invited. The Follies girls performed, danced with the men, and generally provided entertainment during what proved to be a very nice evening for the crew. In April, the ship's officers held a party at the Warwick Hotel in Philadelphia, with wives and sweethearts accompanying the men, along with other guests. It was the first time the officers had gathered socially as a group since reporting in, and the event was also a great success.

The parties were soon over, however, for it was time to get back to business as the embarkation date for *Princeton*'s carrier air group was fast approaching. From early to mid-May, CVLG-23 flew from Pungo Field, an auxiliary air station near NAS Norfolk, Virginia. While there, pilots accomplished carrier qualification on board *Princeton* as it sailed in Chesapeake Bay. Led by Lt Cdr Miller, who "double hatted" as both the carrier air group (CAG) commander and commanding officer (CO) of fighter squadron VF-23, the pilots and aircraft landed aboard the vessel prior to commencing carrier qualifications. "Fighting 23" embarked 12 F4F-4 Wildcats, and two F6F-3 Hellcats were also made available to the squadron so that its pilots could complete their required landings in the new Grumman fighter.

Composite Squadron (VC) 23, with Lt Cdr Martin T. Hatcher commanding, comprised the group's other unit. It came aboard with nine Grumman TBF-1 Avenger torpedo-bombers and nine Douglas SBD-5 Dauntless dive-bombers.

Princeton wrapped up its dockside work-ups, training and drills and reported for duty on May 18, 1943. The following day, it left Philadelphia and headed down the Delaware River. At the mouth of

Delaware Bay, off Cape May, it was joined by the Gleaves-class destroyers USS *Stockton* (DD-646) and USS *Stevenson* (DD-645). They escorted the new carrier and crew into the Chesapeake Bay, a run that took just one day in the open ocean. Nevertheless, *Princeton* was plagued by a rash of seasickness among its officers and men who were experiencing their first taste of the open ocean. Welcome to the US Navy.

While *Princeton* cruised up and down Chesapeake Bay, the pilots made repeated landings and takeoffs, accompanied by the expected number of barrier crashes and other accidents. Luckily no serious injuries occurred.

Accidents, crashes and death are a constant companion in this dangerous business, and CVLG-23 lost two pilots, Ens Albert Robbins and Ens Richard Selman, while at Parris Island when their SNJ trainer crashed at Hilton Head Island, not far from the airfield. Just a week after that incident, Ens Robert Young was killed when his Wildcat turned over and trapped him inside the cockpit after he had ditched. Although there were other accidents which saw pilots crash in swamps and onto beaches, the Naval Aviators involved all survived unscathed.

On May 27, CVLG-23 flew from Pungo to NAS Norfolk, where its aircraft were loaded aboard *Princeton*. The following morning, as the carrier sailed out of Hampton Roads, it was joined by the Fletcher-class destroyers USS *Fullam* (DD-474), USS *Ringgold* (DD-500) and USS *Wadsworth* (DD-516) on their journey south. The four vessels headed down Chesapeake Bay on their way to Trinidad, just off the northeast coast of Venezuela, for their shakedown cruise – the final step in the training process. The small group reached the Gulf of Paria and dropped anchor at Port of Spain on June 2.

The Caribbean island of Trinidad had been selected because of its location bordering the eastern side of the Gulf of Paria, a body of water 60 miles long and 30 miles wide. What made this location so unique was that the gulf had only two entrances – the Dragon's Mouth at the northern end and the Serpent's Mouth at the southern end – which could be protected against enemy submarines by patrolling destroyers. The gulf was an ideal spot for US flattops and their carrier air groups to discover, or "shakedown," any discrepancies that might need correction.

Over the following four weeks CVLG-23 was put through a grueling schedule, working six days a week, sunup to sundown. When night carrier landing qualifications were underway, sailors worked well past dusk, and an all-out effort was made by *Princeton*'s officers and petty officers to emphasize the need for caution during hazardous flightdeck operations.

The captain held absolute responsibility for the combat readiness of his ship and for the safety, well-being and efficiency of the crew. His ability, experience and leadership often determined what kind of "personality" the ship would develop. The commanding officers of these new light carriers had varied backgrounds, and while some would not measure up to the leadership demands of carrier combat, there were a good many that would persevere and see success at the highest levels.

The CO of *Belleau Wood*, Capt A. M. "Mel" Pride, was a former enlisted man, a "mustang," who had worked his way up the ranks from machinist mate 3rd class to captain. Having earned his Wings of Gold in World War I, Pride was a rear admiral by the end of World War II. Capt Robert P. McConnell, CO of *Cowpens*, had been the captain of USS *Langley* (AV-3) when it was sunk south of Java on February 27, 1942.

Taking his responsibility and the position of leadership that he held very seriously, Capt Henderson, mincing no words, penned the following notice in the first edition of the ship's newspaper:

> This is a fast-moving war. Everyone must keep his eyes and ears alert. It has been said before but cannot be repeated too often: one or more among you, because of carelessness, will not return from this cruise. The experience of other carriers on their shakedown indicates this. Dangers aboard a carrier are more numerous than aboard most naval vessels. Planes continually landing and taking off render a careless person unsafe on the flightdeck. Elevators without guards are a constant hazard. Plans-of-the-day have emphasized the dangers of propellers in motion. Handling ammunition, ascending and descending numerous ladders, and working at our various jobs with potentially dangerous equipment, calls for eternal vigilance. While we keep our conscious mind on the immediate task at hand, let's keep our subconscious on the goal for which we fight. It is our obligation to do our work safely.

Aircraft carrier flightdeck operations are an awe-inspiring working environment that prompts one to ask how so many actions taking place on board a moving ship can happen like clockwork without one disaster after another taking place. While in the Gulf of Paria, takeoffs were divided between down the deck runs and catapult launches, and, in both cases, the carrier was turned into the wind so that sufficient speed was attained to create a 32-knot airflow over the deck from bow to stern, giving aircraft being launched enough lift to become airborne. Additionally, it also provided aircraft coming in for landing the proper conditions to approach the bobbing and rolling carrier at a minimum speed so the pilot could "trap" his machine on a flightdeck that was 307ft shorter and 35ft narrower than the flattop on an Essex-class carrier.

Often, takeoffs immediately preceded the landing sequence, with one group of aircraft headed skywards moments before a landing took place. The emphasis was always on swift execution, since the carrier and escorting vessels were more vulnerable to enemy submarine attack when cruising on a predictable course while undertaking air operations.

A key figure in the landing cycle of carrier operations was the LSO. A pilot himself, he fully understood the problems faced by fellow Naval Aviators and the demands placed on them. Whenever possible, the LSO would spend pre-cruise time with the pilots he would be working with while the carrier was at sea. During their tour of duty together, the LSO and the pilots would exchange thoughts and suggestions to make a highly risky and extremely dangerous undertaking as safe as possible. If a Naval Aviator made a landing the LSO considered poor enough to have endangered the carrier and flightdeck crew, as well as putting himself and the aircraft in jeopardy, the LSO would make a point of tracking the pilot down and talking him through the event.

On carriers like *Princeton*, the LSO's duty station consisted of a platform jutting out from the aft end of the flightdeck on the port side. Standing there with his eyes trained on the inbound aircraft, his job was to guide each incoming pilot by means of a pair of paddles, one in each hand. During night operations, the paddles were replaced by a pair of lighted wands, the LSO following the course of the aircraft with the help of its wingtip and other fuselage lights.

He communicated with the pilot via a set of hand and arm signals. When one of several arrestor cables strung across the width of the flightdeck was successfully caught by the recovering aircraft's lowered tailhook, members of the flightdeck crew scrambled to the rear of the machine as fast as possible to disengage the hook, allowing the pilot to taxi out of the way of the next incoming aircraft. An efficient and experienced flightdeck crew could bring aircraft aboard at 30-second intervals.

On the second day in the gulf, the Wildcats flown by Ens Jack M. Abell, Ens William G. Buckalew and Ens Robert S. Tyner ran into heavy weather while flying an intercept mission and lost radio contact with the ship. Heading for the nearest land, the trio eventually made an emergency landing at an airfield at Carúpano, in Venezuela. The three overcame severe linguistic handicaps that surely involved hand and arm signals mixed with drawn-out pronunciations and managed to wire details of their predicament to Port of Spain, Trinidad. The following day *Princeton* launched Avengers loaded with fuel tanks in their bombbays, these aircraft flying to Carúpano to allow the Wildcats to refuel and return to the ship.

As Capt Henderson had pointed out in his letter to the crew at the beginning of their training evolution, the flightdeck of an aircraft carrier is a dangerous place. Inevitably, as *Princeton* and CVLG-23 went about their business, mishaps and accidents took place, with deadly consequences.

Ens Buckalew continued to experience his fair share of bad luck when his Wildcat, while on approach for a night landing, angled slightly to the right of *Princeton*'s flightdeck. The LSO gave him a "cut" signal, instructing the pilot to throttle back immediately and land, but the Wildcat still missed the center of the flightdeck. The tailhook struck "something solid" (it could not be determined precisely what in the darkness) on the side of the flightdeck and the impact tore it loose, along with the last 4ft of the Wildcat's fuselage. Buckalew was able to maintain control of the fighter as it rolled into one of the crash barriers erected across the width of the flightdeck. He climbed out of the cockpit and walked away from a 7,000lb aircraft that had just been torn in half.

Two days later, on June 6, 1943, the Wildcat flown by Ens Oscar Cantrell failed to return to the carrier after a routine training flight. His division had flown into a light cloud while climbing, and upon emerging from it, Cantrell's fellow pilots noticed that he was missing. A subsequent search failed to locate the Wildcat or its pilot.

The carriers of the Independence class often did not receive their final drafts of men until just before commissioning. The difficulties of learning to operate and maintain a large and complex ship, with flight operations also having to be factored in, were compounded by the need to transform a body of officers and men into a cohesive team that could fight and win. Many of the skills needed were taught ashore at various schools and training centers, but experienced sailors were a precious commodity. *Princeton* seemed to have been fortunate for it attracted a quality group of men, as the shakedown numbers reveal.

The grueling pace set during the month-long stay in the gulf was indicated by a total of 1,242 landings, with that number long standing as a record for any comparable carrier during a shakedown cruise. Each of VF-23's pilots made a minimum of 30 landings in both Wildcats and Hellcats, including two night deck landings in the latter type. This meant that VF-23 and VC-23 became the first units to qualify in night landings on light carriers.

Princeton's crew did get time off from their hectic schedule, as Mondays were designated a day of rest, with personnel from both the carrier and CVLG-23 granted shore liberty between 1100 hrs and 1800 hrs. A key venue for a run ashore was Maqueripe Beach Club, which was almost an hour by vehicle from Port of Spain. It provided sailors with the opportunity to swim, play basketball and baseball, or just relax. Others headed to Port of Spain itself and the Queens Park Hotel Bar, famous for a beverage called the "Planter's Punch." Both venues were a wonderful respite from a blazing hot flightdeck or a crowded, muggy working space below decks.

Princeton's crew and CVLG-23 developed an excellent working relationship as the ship's company came to realize that they would be going into combat with a very well-trained and highly competent carrier air group. Enthusiasm is contagious, and it spread to the sailors on board *Princeton*'s escort destroyers. Not being ones to break from a naval tradition that states whenever you pack sailors into a bar fists start flying, enlisted personnel from *Ringgold* and sailors from the carrier *Belleau Wood*, which was also in the gulf on its shakedown, realized they had a difference of opinion when it came to the merits of the two flattops, so it was time to brawl. No major injuries were reported.

As a final exercise before *Princeton* departed Trinidad, a realistic abandon-ship drill was held during which a third of the men went over the side into the water. As the motor launches raced to recover them, battling a six-knot running tide, it provided for some added excitement while they scooped the life-jacketed sailors out of the sea. A few newer members of the crew were non-swimmers, and they were found clinging to fantail lines behind the carrier.

As its shakedown cruise came to a close, *Princeton* steamed out of the Gulf of Paria and headed for Philadelphia escorted by the Fletcher-class destroyers USS *McKee* (DD-575) and USS *Dashiell* (DD-659). While off the coast of Trinidad, the carrier made a high-speed run – its powerplant allowed the vessel to reach a top speed of 33 knots in choppy seas. This was a performance deemed more than acceptable, and it would prove to be absolutely necessary when these vessels were ordered to operate side-by-side with the new, fast, Essex-class carriers.

In early July 1943, 150 miles from landfall, *Princeton* launched all of its aircraft, with their destination being NAS Willow Grove (it had been commissioned as a naval air station in January 1943), as the carrier continued to the Philadelphia Naval Shipyard. The shakedown cruise had indicated that *Princeton* needed certain gear and equipment, and while it was tied up dockside in Philadelphia, half of the crew and maintenance personnel from CVLG-23 were given well-deserved five-day leave. The remaining sailors went ashore when their shipmates returned from leave.

2

Joining the Fleet

While work was being done to get *Princeton* and the rest of the Pacific Fleet ready for war, Allied and naval planners were finalizing their doctrine on how the war was to be waged. During the Casablanca Conference held in French Morocco in January 1943, Allied leaders had decided that a Central Pacific offensive should go forward. This decision resolved the dispute continually brought up by Gen MacArthur that the US Army, rather than the US Navy, should have operational control across the board in the Pacific. The question of whether or not to capture or bypass the Philippines was deferred for the moment, and this issue would not be resolved until the following year, when the newly constructed Pacific Fleet had proven that it could conduct a swift offensive against the Japanese Empire's eastern flank.

The Central Pacific was the logical choice for the offensive, as it was in this region that naval strategists had fought mock battles and established carrier doctrine in the interwar years through their fleet problem training operations. Adm King assured the Joint Chiefs of Staff that they could put aside all apprehension concerning the validity of the new carrier task forces, and that their performance would provide proof that the fast carriers could hit hard and sustain a legitimate counteroffensive.

In the summer of 1943, the high-level Joint Strategic Survey Committee recommended that Allied strategy in the Pacific be reoriented from Gen MacArthur's Southwest Area to Adm Nimitz's Central Pacific. This brought immediate blowback as MacArthur protested strongly for the obvious reason that the Southwest Pacific and the US Army would take a backseat to Nimitz and the US Navy. He and his supporters wanted Nimitz's carriers to guard the flank of MacArthur's drive up the New Guinea coast, engaging in hit-and-run raids while Lt Gen George Kenney's land-based Fifth Air Force would handle the main supporting role.

On June 15, 1943 the Joint Chiefs of Staff informed MacArthur that the significantly bolstered Central Pacific naval forces would not be allowed to stagnate, or be forced into constricted waters in support of US Army operations ashore. They would be tasked with attacking the Marshalls and possibly the Gilberts in mid-November of that year. The operation was to be US Navy planned and led, oriented around two new concepts of warfare, namely the Fast Carrier Task Force and the US Navy–US Marine Corps amphibious assault force.

By mid-1943, Nimitz's reversal of fortune in the Pacific had become obvious. Guadalcanal had been declared secure in February of that year, and Operation *Cartwheel* – the advance on the Japanese stronghold at Rabaul – had commenced in the South Pacific with the capture of New Georgia in July. In New Guinea, MacArthur's forces had secured the Kokoda Trail, Milne Bay and Buna, and a pincer movement by the two forces was now underway and would soon be in position to eventually capture or isolate Rabaul.

On March 15, 1943, Adm King had established a new system for identifying US naval forces. In anticipation of ships and aircraft arriving in quantity in-theater, Pacific Fleet forces would eventually be reorganized into three separate, numbered, fleets. Halsey's South Pacific Force was redesignated Third Fleet, while Allied Naval Forces, Southwest Pacific Area, operating under MacArthur and, from November 1943, directly commanded by Vice Adm Thomas C. Kinkaid, became Seventh Fleet. The Central Pacific Force, under Nimitz's control, would remain unnumbered until April 1944, when it became Fifth Fleet.

The Central Pacific Force would be led by Vice Adm Raymond A. Spruance from August 1943. Having commanded at the Battle of Midway, he had served as Nimitz's chief of staff from mid-1942 and deputy commander to CINCPACFLT from September of that same year. Spruance was a cool, calculating professional who was known for meticulous planning and the careful weighing of risks. The improved American position in the Central Pacific had reduced the need to take risks, as had been the case in 1942, and Spruance could now afford to be more methodical and cautious when it came to engaging the enemy.

The Central Pacific Force would also include an amphibious element, designated Fifth Amphibious Force, under Rear Adm Richmond K. "Terrible" Turner who was a hard task master, and as the war progressed, American skill in amphibious operations continuously improved. The US Marine Corps troops assigned to Fifth Amphibious Force's V Amphibious Corps had Maj Gen Holland M. "Howlin' Mad" Smith as their commander, and he would work closely with Turner in the planning and execution of the upcoming landings.

Nimitz's staff, after several months of heated debate on the proper deployment of Central Pacific Force's powerful new fleet of warships, issued a formal statement on fast carrier policy, dated August 21, 1943. The fast carriers were (1) to attack the enemy on land and sea, the carriers being the principal offensive element of the fleet; (2) to provide direct air support for amphibious operations; and (3) to provide air support to task forces in which carriers were not the principal element. Carrier-based aircraft would gain command of the air and destroy the enemy air force, conduct air searches, provide fighter cover in landings and maintain combat air patrols (CAPs) over the fleet. Their effectiveness depended upon tactical concentration, as splitting up the carriers would dissipate their strength.

The Fast Carrier Task Force, once committed to combat, would be debuting new equipment in battle in the form of the Essex-class carrier, the Independence-class light carrier, the F6F Hellcat fighter, and new radios and radar systems for aircraft and ships. Defending these vessels would be the proximity-fuzed 5in./38 shell, an arsenal of 20mm and 40mm antiaircraft guns and a host of new ships manned in the main by crews who had never previously engaged the enemy.

READY FOR ACTION

With orders to proceed to Pearl Harbor, CVLG-23 personnel and the ship's company were ordered to return aboard *Princeton* by mid-afternoon on July 20, 1943, as the vessel would sail the following day. The ship's officers soon discovered that 22 crew had either missed the sailing time accidentally or jumped ship intentionally. All of them were eventually rounded up and disciplined to varying degrees, depending upon their intent. Undoubtedly, *Princeton*'s officers heard some very interesting explanations as to where these men had been and what they had been up to.

Five days prior, on July 15, 1943, the vessel had been reclassified as a light aircraft carrier and redesignated CVL-23. The carrier air group's designation remained as CVLG-23, however. "Fighting 23" in the meantime had enthusiastically replaced its F4F-4 Wildcats with 12 F6F-3 Hellcats.

At dawn on July 21, *Princeton* sailed down the Delaware River and across the Delaware Bay before heading out to sea in company with *Belleau Wood*, which had CVLG-24 embarked. *Princeton* launched Hellcats for CAPs as the two carriers and their escorts sailed down the east coast and crossed the Caribbean Sea. The carriers reached the Panama Canal on July 26, where they linked up with brand new Essex-class carrier USS *Lexington* (CV-16), with CVG-16 embarked, and the three ships passed through the canal. Two days later, following a short shore leave, the three carriers left the Canal Zone on July 28 under the directive to proceed to Pearl Harbor, with six destroyers providing escort.

The war suddenly drew closer as the ships moved into the Pacific, and the past grumblings of the rigorous training grind took on a whole new meaning as the 3,000-mile voyage from the western side of the Panama Canal to Hawaii was conducted under wartime conditions. The seas around them were a hunting ground for enemy submarines, and the three carriers with no combat experience, along with their escorting destroyers, operated as a task unit in enemy territory.

The epic carrier battles of 1942 had put the US Navy in the driver's seat, but not without the loss of four carriers and one left severely damaged during a five-month stretch. *Saratoga* had been torpedoed while patrolling west of Hawaii in January 1942 and laid up for nearly six months undergoing repairs. At the Battle of the Coral Sea, *Lexington* was hit by two armor-piercing bombs and two torpedoes, and after the crew had spent several hours fighting fires and the vessel was wracked by severe internal explosions, it was scuttled on May 8. *Yorktown* was hit by two bombs and two aerial torpedoes at the Battle of Midway, leaving it dead in the water with a severe list. The carrier was lost after being torpedoed by a Japanese submarine on June 7. *Wasp* was struck by three torpedoes on September 15 while operating some 150 miles southeast of San Cristobal Island in the South Pacific, and it was soon rocked by several catastrophic explosions that caused the carrier to sink. *Hornet* was hit by multiple bombs, torpedoes and a damaged Aichi D3A "Val" dive-bomber flown by a suicidal pilot during the Battle of the Santa Cruz Islands on October 26, 1942 after repeated attacks by Japanese aircraft. Following several attempts to tow the carrier to safety, further air raids led to its abandonment and scuttling.

During the long trip west, exercises were conducted to familiarize fighter pilots with the process of being directed into battle by the carrier's radar team in the Combat Direction Center (CDC). Pilots from *Princeton* took turns flying CAP with Naval Aviators from squadrons on board *Lexington* and *Belleau Wood*, and the competitive nature of the men involved soon had the two light carriers timing their launches, making sure they were not the ones who were lagging. As pilots and flightdeck personnel battled it out over bragging rights on launch times, the newer members of the ship's crew had an opportunity for the first time to practice keeping station in a cruising formation – the very important task of maintaining the proper distances from the other ships in formation, and following the proper speed set by the lead vessel in the group.

On August 7, 1943, when the carriers were two days from reaching Pearl Harbor, the Pacific Fleet directed the three ships to stage a simulated attack against various targets on Oahu to determine the defenders' alertness. The aircrew were quite enthused about carrying out this training mission because it meant they would be allowed to land ashore immediately following the simulated attack. Staff personnel from the different squadrons carefully planned their raid and, on the 9th, an hour before dawn, *Lexington*, *Princeton* and *Belleau Wood* launched their aircraft from a position about 100 miles east of Oahu.

"The simulated attacks were carried out successfully," said CVLG-23 CAG, Lt Cdr Miller, "with no interceptions by Army fighters, and our planes landed at [NAS] Barbers Point at 0900 that morning. Transportation was readily available, the beds had Simmons mattresses, and the officers' club was quickly given a favorable rating, except that other air groups were already on the base, and it was sometimes a bit hard to get by them to the bar."

NAS Barbers Point had only been completed in April 1943 by the US Navy's Seabees of the 5th Naval Construction Battalion, and the sprawling new facility which encompassed nearly 4,000 acres boasted three runways thousands of feet in length. The newly arrived fighter squadrons were placed under the jurisdiction of the USAAF's VII Interceptor Command, and at least one division from VF-23 was on alert call every morning and generally scrambled. Between the alerts, both of CVLG-23's squadrons trained in group exercises, gunnery and navigation hops.

The ships put in to Pearl Harbor that same day and immediately turned to refueling and provisioning. One did not have to look very far to see that the Arsenal of Democracy was in full effect. In addition to *Lexington*, *Princeton* and *Belleau Wood*, other carriers in port were the new USS *Yorktown* (CV-10), USS *Essex* (CV-9), *Independence* and the Royal Navy's HMS *Victorious*. Seven carriers had never previously been seen in port at Pearl Harbor at the same time.

Nimitz had begun to receive a steady flow of new ships from mid-1943, despite the fact that these vessels were not slated to arrive in the Pacific until 1944. However, the shipyards in the United States had gone into high gear, allowing the US Navy to start commissioning some of the first Essex-class carriers earlier than planned. In just two months, Nimitz would have ten of these fast carriers and seven Independence-class light carriers at his disposal. He would also have two new fast battleships, eight heavy and four light cruisers and 66 destroyers. The US Navy, after suffering tremendous losses in both men and materiel over the first 18 months of the campaign in the South Pacific, was now in the process of effectively receiving a brand new fleet.

RAPID EXPANSION

Adm King, wearing two hats as Commander-in-Chief, United States Fleet and CNO, also apparently deemed himself "monarch" of the American shipbuilding industry. Showing no restraint whatsoever, he seized the opportunity to build an armada that almost defies belief. Congress granted the US Navy the most generous "open cheque" in history following the July 1940 Two-Ocean Navy Act, and that greenlighted King to set about fulfilling his grandiose vision of a wartime fleet, with the defeat of Japan as the end game and absolutely no logic justified for anything else. King simply decided, with no regard whatsoever concerning the US Army's needs, that since the war cost his country $200 million a day, building more ships would defeat America's enemies quicker and, in the long run, would save the taxpayers' money.

The US Navy's total war expenditure was $100 billion, with more than one-third of this figure being spent on ship construction which saw fleet tonnage balloon from three million to almost 30 million between 1941–45. In these years, US shipyards built seven battleships, 28 aircraft carriers and 1,194 other essential ships. These new additions joined the 713 ships already in service with the fleet by December 1943. By late 1944, the US Navy was larger than the combined strengths of all the navies in the world, while the Pacific Fleet outnumbered the IJN four-to-one in terms of ships and significantly more in combat firepower.

Prior to the attack on Pearl Harbor, the US Navy mustered 8,000 officers, and each year thereafter during the war an additional 95,000 were granted reserve commissions, becoming "90-day wonders" at the end of their three months' training. The US Navy grabbed the best and the brightest, with the Independence-class carrier *Langley*, for example, having an advertising executive, a lawyer, a college teacher and an Atlanta architect who specialized in designing Methodist churches on their fighter direction staff.

America's shipbuilding industry answered the call with staggering growth. Mare Island Naval Shipyard in San Francisco Bay, California, for example, expanded from 6,000 employees in 1939 to 40,000 in 1944, while the Boston Naval Shipyard went from 8,700 employees in June 1941 to 50,000 three years later. A private shipbuilder in New Jersey accepted a monstrous order for 42 cruisers. More than a million workers were building and repairing ships by 1944, with 82 percent of them clustered on both coasts, while two million more workers served in supporting industries. Toward the end of the war, the United States was having trouble finding enough men to actually man these ships.

To maximize production and make use of America's superior rail infrastructure, the industry started "thinking outside of the box" and implemented extraordinary ingenuity. Smaller vessels (submarines and destroyer escorts, for example) were built in sections at plants located in cities far inland such as Denver, Colorado, and then transported them by rail to one of the coasts for completion. Troop landing ships (LSTs) were constructed in the thousands on the Great Lakes and sailed to coastal ports. One LST came within 100ft of going over the Niagara Falls before grounding, its crew having suffered a navigation error while heading for the eastern seaboard.

Aircraft at that time simply did not have the heavy lift capabilities of today's modern types, so large movements of troops and materiel depended upon ships. Sitting on California's Pacific coastline made the Bay Area a logical ship production site, with direct rail links between there and the industrial centers in the Midwest and East Coast enabling a steady flow of steel and other essential materials. Mare Island, established in 1854, began with a single floating drydock and progressed over the decades to become the San Francisco Bay Area's major contributor of naval vessels during World War II.

The Bay Area was fortunate in that it had two major local shipyards, Bethlehem Shipbuilding Corporation and Moore Drydock Company, that had gained invaluable experience in large-scale rapid production during World War I. At the outbreak of World War II, it still had core management and labor groups on hand as a result of both companies being able to keep their workforces employed during the difficult depression years of the 1930s. Men like Joseph Moore, Warren Bechtel and Henry Kaiser epitomized the "can do" spirit that was prevalent in the early 1900s, and they applied their skills in organization, management and innovation to oversee successful shipbuilding programs in the 1940s.

While Joe Moore had been a shipbuilder for decades, Kaiser and Bechtel were new to the business. They were not, however, new to building large things, and they fully understood that a crucial component for success was reliable engineers and foremen.

The key to accelerated shipbuilding was welding, for the riveting of steel plates not only took time but required two workers to carry it out. The advantages of welding were not only speed but strength – properly welded joints and seams were as strong, or stronger, than the surrounding steel. Automatic seam-welding machines and new alloys and welding methods added even greater speed to the process.

A skilled welder could make a quality seam by positioning his body at any angle to achieve that weld. Novice welders, on the other hand, as many of the new shipyard workers were, had neither the skill nor the experience to match the efficiency of their veteran counterparts. Applying careful thought through all the processes in order to rectify this problem, one solution was to position seams so that the welder could work in a "down-hand" position at all times. The electrodes could be held at waist level or below to avoid fatigue, and that often meant bringing the piece undergoing work to the welder. Large vertical parts to be welded were turned horizontal, while sections that were eventually going to be ceilings and overhead structures were welded inverted then reversed when completed. Additionally, scaffolding was widely employed to place the welders in an optimum position.

It was these types of skilled workers, coupled with excellent management teams, that enabled the much-needed carriers to be completed during the course of 1943. Coming into service at much the same time as the first eight Essex-class carriers, the nine Independence-class ships made up a vital component of the Fast Carrier Task Force. While they could only carry roughly 30–35 aircraft, as opposed to the large 90-aircraft deck load of the Essex-class vessels, the light carriers nevertheless contributed significantly to the campaigns in the central and western Pacific from mid-1943 through to war's end in September 1945, providing 40 percent of the Fast Carrier Task Force's fighters and 36 percent of its torpedo-bombers.

Compromises had to be made, however, when converting the light cruisers into light carriers, and the armored protection built into these vessels was modest. With their ships lacking the purpose-built magazines seen in the Essex-class carriers, munitions handlers were forced to store pallets of bombs in the hangar bay – a factor that would rear its ugly head in late 1944.

RADAR

American scientists and engineers immediately went to work on improving the radar technology that was turned over to them by the British as a part of the Lend-Lease deal. These improvements, and the implementation of this technology in the fleet, would allow radar to play a key role in the fighting in the Central Pacific from late 1943. The quality of the equipment fitted to the Essex- and Independence-class carriers, as well as other vessels in the Central Pacific Force, was markedly different to the basic radar used by the prewar carriers at the outbreak of hostilities.

A Plan Position Indicator radar display in the CDC allowed a multicarrier task force to maintain a high-speed formation in heavy weather or at night. A dead reckoning tracer was used for navigation and tracking surface ships, while identification-friend-foe (IFF) radar transponders in both ships and aircraft allowed fast identification of hostile ships and aircraft; pilots could potentially get a rude wakening when they forgot to turn on the IFF transponders in their aircraft if they ventured too close to the fleet. Radio communication was vastly improved by use of a four-channel very high frequency (VHF) radio, which used channel variation to prevent enemy interception of transmissions while at the same time allowing simultaneous radio contact with other ships and aircraft in the task force.

VHF was a vast improvement over the earlier single-channel high-frequency radio, which had been easily swamped with transmissions in the 1942 battles because the system lacked the necessary capabilities. With electronic support, fighter direction officers (FDOs) could transform carrier air defense from its lowly state during the battles of 1942 and take it to another level.

Princeton featured SK air-search and SC and SG surface-search radars when built, while SM fighter-direction radar was added later. As the primary air-search radar, the SK had a large 17ft x 17ft "mattress" antenna, with IFF antennas attached to the top edge. The SK had a range of 100 miles under normal conditions, and it was mounted atop a stub mast located just forward of the after pair of smoke pipes. The secondary air-search radar was the smaller SC-2, which had a range of about 80 miles. Along with the SC-2, the island carried an SG surface-search radar and the YE aircraft homing beacon. Because of the physical separation of the antennas for the two air-search radars, the Independence-class light carriers suffered fewer of the mutual interference problems experienced by the larger Essex-class ships.

The 5in./38 gun batteries were originally controlled by two Mk 37 fire control directors and a Mk 4 fire control radar. This gear proved inadequate in distinguishing low-level aircraft from surface clutter, so the systems were replaced with the Mk 12 and Mk 22 combination. Mk 51 gyro-stabilizing optical directors with integrated lead-angle calculators were used to control the 40mm Bofors batteries.

For their antiaircraft defense, both the Independence- and Essex-class carriers were bristling with the 40mm quad mount Bofors and 20mm Oerlikon cannon, with the Essex class additionally being armed with 5in./38 guns as their main battery. The 40mm quadruple mount had been developed by mounting two twin mounts side by side, with the additional improvement of power operation to both twin and quad mounts. The 40mm Bofors fired a two-pound projectile at a muzzle velocity of 2,900ft per second, with a rate of fire at 160 rounds per minute depending upon the elevation of the gun barrels. Its maximum range was just over six miles, which made it extremely effective. US Navy ships accommodated as many 40mm mounts as possible.

The 0.50-cal. machine gun seen in great numbers on board US Navy warships in the early stages of the war in the Pacific was rapidly replaced by the Oerlikon 20mm cannon – a single barrel, advanced primer ignition blowback antiaircraft weapon that was manually operated for short-range interception. Newer models of the gun had a muzzle velocity of 3,400ft per second, and it could fire 450 rounds per minute. With a cylindrical and, later, belt-fed feed system, it had a maximum firing range of 7,400 yards, effective out to 4,800 yards. The combination of 20mm and 40mm weapons allowed US Navy warships to throw up a truly devastating amount of lead at medium to close range when targeted by enemy aircraft.

The protection of ships from aerial attack was paramount, and carrier air defense received a decided boost after American scientists labored for two-and-a-half years to produce the proximity fuze – a radio transmitter and receiver built into the head of a 5in. shell that would gauge its own distance from the target before detonating. When the shell was 70ft from an enemy aircraft, a strong ripple pattern of radio waves set off a chain reaction of triggers, culminating in detonation. A near-miss by an exploding shell usually generated sufficient shrapnel to bring an aircraft down.

The effectiveness of the 5in. gun, which was the major defensive firepower of an Essex-class carrier, was therefore increased three to four times. The 5in./38 gun, dual-mounted in six turrets flanking the island of an Essex-class carrier, had a long-distance range of ten miles and a ceiling of six miles, and it could fire 12 to 15 rounds per minute. The proximity or variable time (VT) fuze, as it was deceptively named, had entered fleet service at the beginning of 1943. Until then, all American antiaircraft shells had only detonated upon impact with their target, resulting in the 5in./38 gun being a highly unreliable defensive weapon against a swift, small aircraft.

A few VT-fuzed shells had been used at the end of the Guadalcanal campaign, but the new device would be first put to the test on a large scale on board the fast carriers. The combat success of the Brooklyn-class light cruiser USS *Helena* (CL-50) on January 5, 1943 off Guadalcanal, when the ship's gunners fired a 5in. projectile that brought down a fleeing "Val" dive-bomber, was the desired outcome following several years of technological, industrial and military endeavor involving scores of researchers and more than 100 factories nationwide. By war's end, an army of workers had assembled and installed more than 22 million innovative VT fuzes (each one containing around 130 miniaturized electronic parts) into 5in. shells at a cost then of more than $1 billion (roughly $15 billion in today's money).

SUPERIOR AIRCRAFT

By mid-1943 the US Navy possessed a fleet of aircraft that were superior to the IJNAF's land- and carrier-based aircraft. Similarly, the best fighter and bomber types flown by the Imperial Japanese Army Air Force (IJAAF) were also inferior to American carrier-based aircraft. This was a result of Naval Aviators and aeronautical engineers paying close attention to the revolutionary developments in aircraft development in Europe. Aircraft designs were also influenced by the US Navy's detailed analysis of aerial combat in the skies over Europe and Asia prior to the United States entering the war.

New fighters, scout/dive-bombers and torpedo-bombers were either rolling out of the factories and finding their way to carrier decks or undergoing trials by the summer of 1943. *Princeton*, and all other light carriers, would embark 24 F6F-3 Hellcat fighters and nine TBF-1 Avenger torpedo-bombers. Each Essex-class carrier would sail with three squadrons embarked, equipped with 36 Hellcats, 36 scout/dive-bombers (most were still flying the SBD Dauntless at this time while problems with the troublesome Curtiss SB2C Helldiver were sorted out) and 18 Avengers.

The aging, heroic Dauntless scout/dive-bomber did not have the range or speed to keep up with the newer aircraft now entering fleet service. Its bombload was also under requirements. By the summer of 1943, the SBD was well on the way to being replaced by the SB2C, although the fleet's transition to the Helldiver was anything but smooth. The new dive-bomber was plagued by both a slow rate of production and poor build quality that led to disastrous carrier trials. Wing fold mechanisms and arresting gear malfunctioned, fuselage and wing skins wrinkled, tailwheels collapsed and the hydraulic system leaked, forcing the US Navy to send aircraft back to the factory for rectification work.

Although these problems were eventually sorted out, allowing the Helldiver to play an important role in the Central Pacific, its place on the flightdeck of Essex-class carriers (SB2Cs never embarked operationally on Independence-class vessels) was progressively taken by bomb-equipped Hellcats and, from late 1944, Vought F4U Corsairs, as the US Navy created fighter-bomber (VBF) squadrons. These units effectively undertook the same missions as dedicated fighter units, with the addition of ground attack after the Hellcat and Corsair were cleared to carry bombs.

Although the flightdecks of Independence-class carriers were dominated by F6F Hellcats, examples of the rugged and versatile Avenger torpedo-bomber (both TBF and General Motors-built TBM variants) were also embarked. Capable of dropping a single 2,000lb Mk 13 torpedo, Mk 24 mine or up to 2,000lbs of bombs, it was armed with a single fixed M2 Browning 0.50-cal. machine gun in each wing, a 0.50-cal. weapon in a rotating dorsal turret and a flexible M1919 Browning 0.30-cal. "stinger" machine gun located in the underside of the fuselage, aft of the bomb-bay.

While the F4F Wildcat had held its own during the first 18 months of the Pacific War, the US Navy needed an appreciably better fighter to beat the impressive Mitsubishi A6M Zero-sen, which had caught the Allies on the back foot in 1941–42. Grumman duly delivered with the F6F-3 Hellcat, which featured the powerful 2,000hp Pratt & Whitney R-2800 Double Wasp radial engine with a two-speed, two-stage supercharger and water injection driving a three-bladed Hamilton Standard propeller. The Hellcat had a top speed of 385mph, some 30mph faster than the A6M5 variant of the Zero-sen, and a better rate of climb, although its service ceiling of 38,800ft was only some 300ft higher than that achievable in the IJNAF fighter.

The F6F-3 could sustain tremendous punishment and, at the same time, dish it out. The fighter was armed with six M2 Browning 0.50-cal. air-cooled machine guns, three in each wing, with 400 rounds per gun. To protect the pilot, the fighter was fitted with a bullet-resistant windscreen and 212lbs of cockpit armor. The oil tank and oil cooler were also shielded by armor. A 60-gallon self-sealing fuel tank made of rubber and encased in a canvas hammock to nullify the effect of bullet punctures was installed under the cockpit floor, with single 87-gallon tanks of identical construction being fitted in either wing root. Additionally, the aircraft could carry a single 150-gallon drop tank under the fuselage attached to a center-section hardpoint to give it a combat radius of 945 miles.

The Hellcat was built with a high-mounted cockpit and a downward slope of the fuselage forward of the pilot that enhanced his view, aiding the pilot not only in combat, but with carrier approaches. This made the F6F an ideal carrier-based fighter.

The territory that spanned the vast Pacific Theater could not be taken unless air supremacy was secured, thus the airmen had to gain combat experience by actually engaging the enemy – the time for training had ended. During August 1943, Rear Adm Spruance ordered several operations, having decided that the time had come to put the fleet and new tactical doctrine to the test in battle. Adm Nimitz then released several of Central Pacific Force's new carriers for hit-and-run raids against enemy outposts, anticipating that the fast carriers would also soon be called upon to beef up Vice Adm Halsey's Third Fleet as it went on the offensive in the South Pacific.

3
A Time for Battle

Princeton and *Independence* immediately went into action on August 18, 1943, carrying out a quick run into the South Pacific to transport US Navy Seabees and personnel of the Seventh Air Force tasked with occupying Nakufetau and Nanumea in the Ellice Islands. The sailors and soldiers began building airfields on the islands to support further battles, while *Princeton* turned right around and returned to Hawaii.

The subsequent days and nights at Pearl Harbor were rife with rumors as the scuttlebutt was now in high gear concerning *Princeton*'s future deployments in the war zone. For the time being, there was the work routine and duty that takes place while military units are tied down and waiting in rear areas – training flights, fuel consumption tests, gunnery hops and pre-dawn CAPs.

Whenever possible, liberty was granted in Honolulu, but at the time the immediate Waikiki area was ruled out-of-bounds because of a local outbreak of dengue fever – a highly infectious viral disease that causes severe joint pain, headaches and a rash. Making sure the deployment checklists were completed, CVLG-23 was then informed that they would be heading into the combat zone very soon and all personnel needed their tetanus shots.

Medical issues now taken care of, all hands were ordered aboard the carrier and aircraft were loaded minus the Dauntless dive-bomber. The SBDs were removed from all light carrier rosters and 12 pilots were attached to *Princeton* from VF-6, along with their Hellcats, bringing the ship's fighter strength to 33 pilots and 24 F6F-3s, along with the original nine Avenger torpedo-bombers. *Independence* and *Belleau Wood* would also receive veteran fliers from VF-6, with the unit's commanding officer and the US Navy's first ace of World War II, Lt Cdr Edward "Butch" O'Hare, embarking in *Independence*.

Princeton's first proper combat mission began on August 25, 1943 when TF 11 sortied from Pearl Harbor. Two task forces, TFs 11 and 15, would conduct simultaneous raids on Baker and Marcus Islands, and as the ranking Naval Aviator afloat, Rear Adm Charles A. "Baldy" Pownall commanded the Marcus operation with TF 15 while Rear Adm Willis A. "Ching" Lee, Commander, Battleships Pacific, conducted the occupation of Baker. Ironically, Lee led a force *without* battleships while on board his flagship, USS *Hercules* (AK-41), a transport converted for the purpose of command and control during landing operations. Rear Adm Arthur W. Radford hoisted his flag in *Princeton*, with Capt George R. Henderson at the helm, in command of Task Group (TG) 11.2. The latter also included *Belleau Wood*, with CVLG-24 embarked.

The task force intended to land the US Army's 804th Aviation Battalion on tiny Baker Island (which covers just 0.81 square miles) so that it could construct an airfield there for land-based bombers to carry out raids on Japanese installations. Six transports carrying troops and supplies, and four escorting Fletcher-class destroyers – USS *Spence* (DD-512), USS *Trathen* (DD-530), USS *Boyd* (DD-544) and USS *Bradford* (DD-545) – would accompany the carriers, with a fighter-direction team on board *Trathen*. A US possession since 1936, the deserted atoll, located more than 1,200 miles southwest of Pearl Harbor and a short distance above the equator, had been abandoned in 1942 following attacks by enemy ships and aircraft.

While Marcus was a live target for the new carriers, despite it being of little value to the Allies, other islands fitted into the overall scheme of the Central Pacific offensive. One of them was Baker, a strategically located islet due east of the Gilberts. With new airfields on Baker, the recently occupied Phoenix Islands southeast of it, and on Ellice Islands to the southwest, the USAAF would have a triangle of bases from which to fly strikes against the Gilberts. The occupation of Baker completed the triangle.

While the ship's officers and crew were being briefed separately, air personnel were called together and told they were to operate with

Belleau Wood in supplying air cover for the occupation of Baker Island. For the aircrew of CVLG-23, who had been in training so long for this moment, the word that IJNAF aircraft might make an appearance was exciting news.

While underway, a full schedule of CAPs was flown from the two light carriers during daylight hours, while land-based Lockheed PV-1 Venturas flying from Canton Island undertook night patrols over the ships. For those not in the air, briefings were the order of the day, with CVLG-23's intelligence officers providing aircrew with as much information as possible about Baker Island, its surrounding waters, the planned occupation and enemy aircraft that might be encountered.

While the six-day voyage was generally uneventful, there was one mishap on board *Princeton*. VF-6's Lt(jg) Robert "Dixie" Loesch, while attempting to land, careened over the carrier's port side and crashed into the sea. He escaped without serious injuries, but his F6F, which had been CAG Miller's favorite aircraft, nicknamed *The Imp*, was lost.

On August 31 the two carriers departed the convoy to provide air cover while the transports continued to the landing areas, with USS *Ashland* (LSD-1) pioneering the use of the landing ship, dock amphibious warfare vessel. At dawn the following day (September 1), the first troops moved ashore and started unloading supplies and equipment, with *Princeton* aircraft overhead.

A VF-6 division under Lt(jg) Loesch had launched at noon and was assigned a CAP station over the landing force. Loesch had first entered combat a year before when "Fighting Six" was engaged in the Battle of the Eastern Solomons, and he had scored his first victory in that engagement while flying a Wildcat. Now his division received a vector from the fighter director on *Trathen*, ordering the four Hellcats at 10,000ft toward a "bogey" 32 miles away heading east toward the task group at 7,000ft.

The intruder was a Kawanishi H8K "Emily" flying boat, and apparently it never saw the four fighters coming. Loesch and his wingman, Ens Albert W. Nyquist, made a high nose-to-nose gunnery run, opening fire at 500 yards and pressing the attack down to 100 yards. They both fired about 300 rounds, getting a good concentration of hits on the cockpit and inboard engines. The "Emily" fell away in an easy right-hand dive, completing a 180-degree turn as it exploded upon striking the water. The VF-6 pilots had dispatched the Japanese flying boat so quickly that its crew had not had time to send a radio report of the landings.

History was made three times over that day, for the downed "Emily" represented the first victory to be credited to the F6F, Lt(jg) Loesch had become the first pilot to score in both a Wildcat and a Hellcat and, finally, the kill was the first claimed by an aircraft flying from *Princeton*.

During the early hours of August 31, Rear Adm "Baldy" Pownall had TF 15 on station off Marcus Island, some 2,700 miles west of Pearl Harbor and only 1,000 miles from Japan. The sea was calm, with a clear sky and the planet Mars glowing in the direction of the target while the fleet carriers *Yorktown* and *Essex* and the light carrier *Independence* commenced launching into the pre-dawn darkness. The carriers maneuvered to give their aircraft suitable airspeed by churning up to 30 knots and heading for any breeze. Destroyers swung in front to mark a launching horizon with their lights and the "big-gun" ships gave the carriers sea room. At 0422 hrs the first Hellcat rolled down *Yorktown*'s deck and into the sky.

The carrier-based aircraft had caught the enemy by surprise. Strafing fighters hit picket boats on the way in and then destroyed seven parked G4M "Betty" torpedo-bombers, while the Avengers and Dauntlesses targeted the airstrip and buildings. The TBFs carried single 2,000lb "blockbusters," the heaviest bombs dropped by the aircraft to date, while the SBDs expended 1,000lb "daisy cutter" fragmentation bombs. Five "deck loads" of strikes were flown against Marcus, two each from *Essex* and *Yorktown* and one from *Independence*. Since *Yorktown*'s CVG-5 led the operation, its fighter unit, VF-5, could claim to be the first to fly the Hellcat into combat, while the pilots of VF-9 (assigned to CVG-9 embarked in *Essex*) had strafed IJN picket boats on the way in, allowing them to claim that they had fired the first shots in anger from the F6F.

While *Princeton* was being refueled on September 2, *Belleau Wood* took over CAP duties and the day quietly passed by. However, on the 3rd, with *Princeton* back as "duty" carrier, things were rather different. At 1200 hrs Lt H. W. Crews took off from the carrier as part of a six-Hellcat flight, and after receiving a vector from *Trathen*, the "Fighting Six" aircraft flown by future ace Lt(jg) Thaddeus T. Coleman and Ens Edward Phillipe split off from the group and raced 20 miles to intercept another "Emily." They eventually "splashed" it after a running gunfight.

"It looked as though the Japs were very regular and prompt about arriving over the same area on odd days at about 1300 hrs," noted CAG Miller. "Consequently, everyone wanted the noon flight, and the *Belleau Wood* fighter squadron indicated that they thought the *Princeton* squadron was being favored. The admiral allowed the *Belleau Wood* pilots to take the Baker Island patrols. As luck would have it, on September 8 – an even day – two *Princeton* pilots, [future ace] Lt Harold Funk and Lt(jg) Leslie Kerr [from VF-23], were patrolling the offshore area miles from Baker when, lo and behold, a Jap plane approached from a different direction than the earlier two. Number three hit the water in short order."

As Miller explained, the two fighters were vectored onto the "Emily" and attacked, bracketing the flying boat from a range of 400–500 yards. The crew of the aircraft returned fire, but the F6F-3s made another run on the "Emily," hitting it forward of the cockpit and starting a fire in the nose. The gunners fell silent as the flames engulfed the flying boat, and it plummeted 8,000ft until it hit the water, disintegrating on impact. VF-23 had claimed its first aerial victories.

During these interceptions the Hellcat pilots had photographed the large, four-engined flying boats so that intelligence analysts could examine them – the H8K had only recently been encountered by US Navy pilots. The Baker Island operation lasted until September 14 for *Princeton*, and it would be a far different experience for the crews involved in comparison with the amphibious landings scheduled in the near future.

Although the operation was deemed a success, the neophytes on board *Princeton* unfortunately had to skip the age-old initiation ceremony for sailors crossing the equator for the first time – the carrier had crossed from the northern to the southern hemisphere several times while operating in the Baker Island area, as the atoll was situated just north of the equator.

The takeaways from the simultaneous raids were successful deployment of both the command vessel and the landing ship, dock at Baker. Additionally, Rear Adm Pownall had personally contacted Rear Adm Charles A. Lockwood, Commander, Submarines, Pacific Fleet, before the operation and requested that one of his vessels maintain a presence in the waters off Marcus to rescue downed fliers – Lockwood gave him USS *Snook* (SS-279). Adm Nimitz endorsed the idea, and it soon evolved into the Submarine Lifeguard League, a standard practice during every subsequent fast carrier operation.

Before departing Baker Island, an aircraft was flown to Canton Island to pick up mail. In short order, VF-23's executive officer, Lt Funk, discovered that he had received orders to report to San Diego to assume command of FM-2 Wildcat-equipped VF-26. There were "hot" rumors circulating at the time that *Princeton* would be involved in the upcoming attacks on the Japanese stronghold of Tarawa. Funk, who had also learned from his new orders that he had been promoted to lieutenant commander, did not want to miss out on the action at Tarawa, so his orders were "forgotten" for the moment.

Very quickly, scuttlebutt became fact. Tarawa, Makin and Abemama in the Gilbert Islands were to be the next targets to stop Japanese pressure on the occupation of the Ellice Islands and to provide the fleet with further operational experience. As soon as Rear Adm Radford's TF 11 and Rear Adm Pownall's TF 15 returned to Pearl Harbor, *Princeton* would sail for the Gilbert Islands as strikes were planned for September 18–19.

The Tarawa operation would follow the pattern of Marcus, with the important exception being that photographs were to be taken of the landing beaches for the upcoming late November assault. Rear Adm Pownall would hoist his flag on board fleet carrier *Lexington*, with Capt Felix B. Stump at the helm. "Lady Lex" would be joined again by *Belleau Wood*, commanded by Capt Pride, and, of course, *Princeton*. Together, they would again be designated TF 15, with this operation aimed at testing the advantages of the multicarrier task force when the latter was comprised mainly of light carriers. Further enhancing the task force's firepower were the Cleveland-class light cruisers USS *Santa Fe* (CL-60), USS *Birmingham* (CL-62) and USS *Mobile* (CL-63) along with ten destroyers, including *Princeton*'s shakedown companion, *Ringgold*.

The squadron air intelligence officers broke out maps, charts, and slides for briefing sessions, and informed the Naval Aviators that they would be getting a little help from the Seventh Air Force in the form of 25 bombers preceding the US Navy attack with a strike on the night of November 17–18. Furthermore, USS *Steelhead* (SS-280) would arrive on station just prior to the operation to provide submarine rescue services.

As the task group approached Tarawa, personnel rose early to prepare for the long days ahead. For the Makin strike, *Princeton* fighter pilots Lt H. W. Crews and his wingman, Ens P. H. "Junior" Gordon, volunteered to accompany the torpedo-bombers. Launching at 0338 hrs, the aircraft successfully bombed and strafed enemy installations, setting four IJNAF floatplanes alight that were subsequently listed as destroyed. This morning sortie set the pace for September 18, with *Princeton* carrying out a long day of flight operations that saw 170 pilot hours logged by CVLG-23 on that day alone.

The larger strike against Tarawa, some 92 miles away from TF 15, launched an hour after the Makin aircraft had taken off. It consisted of VF-23 Hellcats and five VC-23 Avengers from *Princeton*, joined by seven TBF-1s from Torpedo Squadron (VT) 16 and SBD-5s of VC-24 from *Lexington*'s CVG-16 and *Belleau Wood*'s CVLG-24, respectively. After a 35-minute flight, they were "welcomed" by heavy antiaircraft fire as they bombed and strafed vessels, gun batteries, parked aircraft and barracks buildings. They also sank two motor torpedo boats in the lagoon and left eight G4M "Betty" bombers burning. The effectiveness of the attack was, overall, questionable, as superb enemy camouflage had done an excellent job of deceiving the pilots. During these attacks, the Hellcat pilots had spotted four "Bettys" off in the distance fleeing the action, but they did not intercept them.

Princeton's Hellcats provided the CAP umbrella over the task force, and that afternoon at 1413 hrs a division of four fighters flown by Lt(jg)s J. P. Altemus (of VF-6), L. W. Haynes, J. D. Madison and J. W. Syme were vectored toward a "Betty." Tearing into it, they made no fewer than seven runs against the bomber. After the third pass a fire broke out around the "Betty's" starboard engine and flames enveloped the cockpit, causing the bomber to drop to just 50ft above the water and then explode. It was "Fighting 23's" fourth kill, and ultimately Madison and Syme were each given a half-credit. "Fighting 23" thus far had destroyed every one of the four aircraft they had encountered, prompting Rear Adm Pownall to signal the squadron that night, "Congratulations to all hands. Your alertness to meet the enemy in any way he chooses to fight was one of the many highlights of the day. It was a job well done."

CVLG-23 sustained its first combat loss during the Tarawa mission. One of *Princeton*'s Avengers, flown by Lt(jg) Charles Bransfield, was hit by antiaircraft fire and made a forced landing in the sea five miles off the island's shoreline. Bransfield and his men were observed getting out of the ditched aircraft and clambering into a rubber life raft before the aircraft sank. Unfortunately, *Steelhead* could not rescue them, and following the occupation of Makin in 1944, it was learned from a Catholic priest on the island that the downed aircrew had come ashore and been quickly captured, after which they were sent to Japan as PoWs.

TF 15 flew a total of seven strikes that day, losing four aircraft in the process. Several aircraft from *Lexington* took a series of low oblique photographs of the lagoon-side of Betio Island, in the Tarawa Atoll, which helped planners prepare for the landings. They did not, however, show the reefs clearly – vital information required for the success of the mission, as landing craft would be coming in through the lagoon and putting Marines ashore on Betio's beaches in just two months' time.

The vertical photographs required for the landing went down with the Avenger tasked with taking these images, for it was one of the four aircraft lost that day. Pownall's staff recognized the importance of acquiring the vertical photographs and recommended sending another aircraft in to complete the task, but Pownall refused, showing signs of irritation and nervousness that had also surfaced during the Marcus raid.

The next order of business for *Princeton* was to return to Pearl Harbor so that repairs could be carried out on its catapult, which had recently broken down. Upon crossing the equator on September 22, King Neptune and his Royal Court at last made an appearance. This gave crew members with previous equator-crossing credentials a chance to initiate those who had not yet done so. In the lore of the sea, those who have been duly inducted by King Neptune and his Royal Court are designated shellbacks, but before their initiation they are lowly pollywogs.

The pollywogs vastly outnumbered the shellbacks and subsequently, as VF-23's historian wryly noted, "considerable punishment was meted out on both sides." The evening prior to the ship crossing the equator:

> [The] Pollywogs were duly served subpoenas, listing individual offenses which had been committed during our sojourn aboard, and notification was given of costumes which would be worn the following day. After an adequate performance had been given on the flightdeck, culminated by all pollywogs running the gauntlet through a long double line of eagerly awaiting Shellbacks, Neptunus Rex accepted all new hands into the Royal Domain.

"Events leading up to Neptune's appearance were hectic," said Lt Cdr Miller. He continued:

> For days before the actual ritual, a wide variety of haircuts could be observed about the carrier. It seems shellbacks would catch an unwary pollywog and treat him to a less than artistic hair trim. However, the worm turned. The evening before the scheduled convening of Neptune's court, Lt Chuck Kenyon from the fighter squadron was called on the ship's loudspeaker to report to the flightdeck. Kenyon and some fellow pollywogs realized that this was actually a summons to a shellback-administered haircut. Kenyon and his companions holed up in the pilot's ready room and sent out word that they were ready to receive any and all shellbacks.
>
> A band of shellbacks accepted the invitation, and the result was a real melee with chairs, coffee mugs, backpacks, chart boards and even bodies flying everywhere. Fortunately, the captain happened by the ready room, and quiet was restored for the time being.

The initiation finished the next morning, when the shellbacks formed two lines on deck, paddles in hand, and all pollywogs were made to run the gauntlet before receiving cards confirming their shellback status.

TF 15 returned to Pearl Harbor in the fall of 1943, and at that time CVLG-23 flew ashore to NAS Ford Island. The 12 pilots from VF-6 who had performed well while attached to the carrier air group returned to their parent squadron as VF-23 was doubled in size, taking its strength up to 24 F6F-3 Hellcats.

With its catapult repaired and fresh supplies loaded, *Princeton* was made ready for sea. Ashore, CVLG-23 engaged in field carrier landings and gunnery drills, and its personnel certainly did not miss out on visits to Honolulu and its many attractions.

MORE ACTION

CAG Miller had been enjoying a quiet Sunday morning ashore at Pearl Harbor on October 10, 1943 when he received a phone call from *Princeton*'s air officer and was summoned to the ship to be briefed on operations unfolding in the South Pacific.

The Japanese had abandoned Guadalcanal in February 1943, concluding a grueling six-month campaign that brought the first American offensive operation of World War II to a victorious conclusion. This hard-won victory also marked the beginning of an equally grueling advance up the Solomon Islands chain directed at the notorious enemy stronghold of Rabaul at the northeastern end of New Britain.

Princeton had been ordered back into action, and its sailors and personnel from CVLG-23 started moving at a rapid pace to get the vessel and its embarked carrier air group ready to sail. VF-23 and VC-23 were recalled to NAS Ford Island from the outlying airfield at NAS Kaneohe Bay and their aircraft were craned aboard the light carrier. Seven new pilots, all "nuggets" without combat experience, were put ashore and attached to VF-1. In exchange, VF-23 received 12 of VF-1's more experienced pilots – two lieutenants, one lieutenant(junior grade) and nine ensigns.

By midnight on October 10, the same day that Lt Cdr Miller had been called back to the ship, all personnel and equipment were on board the carrier. Miraculously, aircraft repairs that had been slated to take days had been wrapped up in mere hours. The following morning, *Princeton* left Pearl Harbor with a lone destroyer, the Gleaves-class vessel USS *Edwards* (DD-619). As the two ships moved out into open water, the task group that had just completed an attack on Wake Island was entering Pearl Harbor. *Princeton* would have been a part of that operation had it not been for an inoperative catapult. The Wake Island raid on October 5 had seen the first combat between the Hellcat and Zero-sen, during which future ace Ens Robert W. Duncan of *Yorktown*'s VF-5 became the first F6F pilot to down an A6M.

Edwards served both as an antisubmarine escort and as a rescue vessel during flight operations. While the latter were underway, the destroyer cruised astern the carrier, and in the event an aircraft ditched on takeoff or landing, the fast and highly maneuverable *Edwards* was there to pick up any surviving pilots and aircrew.

Off Hawaii, all new pilots who had not been flightdeck-qualified were checked out during a series of launches and landings from *Princeton*. With that accomplished, the carrier and *Edwards* turned to the southwest and headed for Espiritu Santo, the largest island in the New Hebrides archipelago. It was home to Naval Advance Base Espiritu Santo, a major facility built by US Navy Seabees. Aside from being used by the Pacific Fleet, the base also supported operations by the US Army, USAAF, US Coast Guard and US Marine Corps.

Immediately after the attack on Pearl Harbor, the US Navy had recognized the demand for bases that could repair and resupply Pacific Fleet vessels at advanced locations, rather than ships having to sail hundreds of miles back to Pearl Harbor or, even further, to bases on the West Coast of the mainland United States. Located far enough away from the immediate Japanese threat, Espiritu Santo was quickly identified as the ideal location for the first facility of its kind in the Pacific. It duly became capable of servicing all elements of fleet operations from logistics in fuel, food and ammunition, to transport and embarkation for combat operations or returning to the United States. The ship repair facilities and drydocks were capable of handling most damage and routine maintenance, and Naval Advance Base Espiritu Santo also served as a major rest and recreation destination for the Pacific Fleet. By war's end it had become the second-largest base in-theater.

During the nine-day voyage from Hawaii, *Princeton* crossed the equator for the 35th time and, once again, all pollywogs on board were given a necessarily shortened welcome into King Neptune's realm. On October 17 the two ships crossed the International Date Line, and upon their arrival at Espiritu Santo three days later, Capt Henderson received orders teaming *Princeton* and the recently repaired *Saratoga*, with CVG-12 embarked, along with other warships already at Espiritu Santo. They would be joining TF 38, under the command of Vice Adm William Halsey, which would support the impending invasion of Bougainville, in the Solomon Islands. In preparation for upcoming operations, both carriers and their escorts were fortunate enough to have some time to work together. Over the next two days *Princeton* and *Saratoga* cruised offshore to give pilots, aircrew and ships' personnel some important training time.

Now in the South Pacific war zone, CVLG-23 personnel were given orders by *Princeton*'s first lieutenant to send home any gear not absolutely essential to the upcoming operation. Members of the ship's crew had gone through a similar "house-cleaning" earlier, which was a precaution often employed to protect personal belongings in the event of a sinking or major damage to the ship.

After five frenzied days of loading supplies and provisions, *Princeton* and *Saratoga* sailed from Espiritu Santo on October 29 as part of the Relief Carrier Group. Assigned to TF 38, it was commanded by Rear Adm Frederick C. Sherman, who was flying his flag in *Saratoga*. The carriers were accompanied by the Atlanta-class light antiaircraft cruisers USS *San Diego* (CL-53) and USS *San Juan* (CL-54) and six destroyers. TF 38 would take part in Operation *Cartwheel*, which was the Allied plan to advance in the direction of Rabaul, which had been turned into a fortress by the Japanese – among its many defenses was a massive IJNAF complex that was home to seven airfields. *Cartwheel* consisted of a number of phases that included Operation *Cherryblossom* on November 1, 1943, which saw the 3rd Marine Division landing at Cape Torokina near Empress Augusta Bay on Bougainville Island.

Saratoga and *Princeton* would not strike at Rabaul alone. They would in fact be supported by a combined services force provided by Aircraft, Solomons consisting of the USAAF's Thirteenth Air Force and US Navy, US Marine Corps and Royal New Zealand Air Force (RNZAF) squadrons. Additionally, Fifth Air Force aircraft would be flying from bases in Australia, having been tasked with hitting targets around Rabaul.

TF 38's CVG-12 and CVLG-23 were directed to neutralize Buka and Bonis airfields at the northwestern tip of Bougainville during the crucial first hours of the amphibious landing on November 1, and they would be joined by a mixed group of land-based squadrons for subsequent close air support (CAS) operations. Participating units from the US Navy and US Marine Corps included VC-38 (TBFs) and VF-17 (F4Us), Marine Scout Bombing Squadron (VMSB) 144

(SBDs), Marine Torpedo Bomber Squadrons (VMTBs) 143 and 233 (TBFs) and Marine Fighting Squadrons (VMFs) 215 and 221 (F4Us).

The voyage to the Solomons was uneventful, except for a forced water landing by VF-23's Lt(jg) J. W. Syme, who experienced engine trouble while chasing after an unidentified aircraft. A destroyer was dispatched to look for the downed Naval Aviator, and it found him in his rubber raft sampling some of the emergency rations from his backpack.

Operating well to the west in open waters, this was the first time that the fast carriers had seen action in the South Pacific since the dark days of the Guadalcanal campaign in late 1942, as Rear Adm Sherman directed the vessels to launch their aircraft in attacks on Japanese airfields and installations in the North Solomon Islands. The admiral and his staff hoped that these raids would diminish Japanese aerial resistance against the landings, the strike groups launching before dawn on November 1. There was some confusion as the attack formations joined up, and two more Hellcats from VF-23 suffered mechanical failures that led to their pilots having to ditch in the sea. The destroyer crews were on the spot, though, and both pilots were rescued. Tragically, however, two Avengers from VC-23 collided in mid-air and then crashed, killing four of the six men in the aircraft involved. The two lucky survivors were pulled from the sea.

Throughout the first days of November, bombing and strafing attacks were carried out against the two airfields at Buka and Bonis, which straddled either side of the Buka Passage. A CAP averaging 38 fighters rotated over the beaches and disrupted major Japanese aerial counterattacks while troops from the 3rd Marine Division moved ashore at Cape Torokina, approximately midway up Bougainville's southwestern coast. Additional support was provided by the cruisers of TF 39 under Rear Adm Aaron S. "Tip" Merrill as they shelled selected targets in the area.

Aircraft from *Princeton* bombed and strafed the airfield, antiaircraft guns and ground installations at Bonis, with some of the Hellcats descending to tree-top level to attack an enemy merchantman southeast of Sohano Island. Lt Cdr Miller and his wingman, Lt(jg) Joe Webb, joined the party, conducting two strafing runs on a second cargo ship and forcing the Japanese to beach it. Other aircraft contributed to the destruction, leaving the runway at Bonis cratered, antiaircraft batteries destroyed and serious damage inflicted on several parked "Betty" bombers.

On the night of November 1–2, an IJN force of two heavy cruisers, two light cruisers, and six destroyers attempted to counterattack the troop transports off Bougainville. Rear Adm Merrill engaged the vessels with four light cruisers and eight destroyers, turning back the Japanese assault and sinking an enemy light cruiser and a destroyer in what would become known as the Battle of Empress Augusta Bay.

The following morning, *Saratoga* and *Princeton* sent two coordinated strikes against enemy airfields at Bonis. Basically a repeat of the day before, but no less dangerous, the aircraft involved strafed enemy positions, struck another cargo ship and set fire to an aviation gasoline storage area near the airfield. The Japanese defenders fought back fiercely, and while conducting a low-level strafing run, Ens Leonard Keener was shot down and killed, marking VF-23's first combat loss. CVLG-23's pilots reported heavy antiaircraft fire throughout the day from 13.2mm and 20mm guns as several of the Hellcats returned to the ship with multiple holes.

As Sherman's task force withdrew from the area to refuel, they were the recipients of a well-deserved pat on the back from the US Navy's high command. Very pleased with the results of the two-day operation, the ships involved received the following message: "Admiral Halsey has congratulated the task force on the strikes at Buka and says well done. As a result, Buka is not now contributing to the Jap war effort."

On the afternoon of November 2, while mostly US Navy and US Marine Corps aviation units carried out successful air strikes and CAP duties for the Bougainville landings, a different scenario unfolded for the USAAF as it conducted a strike against Rabaul.

Finally getting a break in the weather, B-25 Mitchells from three bombardment groups, escorted by Lockheed P-38 Lightnings from three fighter squadrons, became part of what could only be explained as a scene taken directly from a sensationalized Hollywood movie as they descended upon Rabaul. The intensity of the aerial combat in the South Pacific had not waned despite recent Allied successes, and the 78 USAAF aircraft were intercepted by no fewer than 112 Zero-sens flown in the main by seasoned IJNAF pilots. Nine B-25s and an equal number of P-38s were lost that day, resulting in the November 2 raid being referred to as "Bloody Tuesday" in Fifth Air Force annals.

Halsey's bold landings at Bougainville triggered an immediate IJN response from Adm Mineichi Koga, Commander-in-Chief of the Combined Fleet, who released carrier aircraft from 1st Carrier Division for an urgent transfer to Rabaul from their base at Truk. On November 1, 173 aircraft from two fleet carriers and one light carrier landed at Rabaul, taking its strength up to 375 machines. That same day, Koga dispatched Vice Adm Takeo Kurita with seven heavy cruisers, one light cruiser and four destroyers to Rabaul, with their mission being to destroy Halsey's warships in and around the US Marine Corps beachhead at Torokina – it was protected only by light cruisers and destroyers.

Halsey had no intelligence of these movements while Sherman's TF 38 headed south on November 2, away from Rabaul and the strengthening IJN force. His greater concern that day was the fact that Rear Adm Merrill's covering force was now both outgunned and exhausted following its recent heroic action at Empress Augusta Bay, which had seen TF 39 engaged in combat for nearly 36 hours straight.

IJN intentions were confirmed on November 4 when a USAAF Consolidated B-24 Liberator spotted Kurita's fleet, minus a heavy cruiser and destroyer that were absent due to orders received to tow two smaller craft back to Truk. The crew of the bomber immediately reported 19 ships heading toward the western entrance of Saint George's Channel at Rabaul. At about the same time that Halsey had received the news of Merrill's victory, he was handed a message with the details of Kurita's force. The news sent a chill down his spine, causing him to comment, "Presumably they would refuel, then run down to Torokina the following night and sink our transports and bombard our precarious positions."

With most of the Pacific Fleet preparing to support the invasion of the Gilbert Islands and Rear Adm Merrill's TF 39 retiring to Purvis Bay after fending off attacks by more than 100 aircraft following a hair-raising night battle in which they claimed 30 of their attackers destroyed, Halsey simply did not have adequate surface forces nearby to stop Kurita's powerful armada. There was, however, a small carrier detachment in the form of Rear Adm Sherman's TF 38 that had just left the area after the bombardment of Buka and Bonis.

The landings on the west coast of Bougainville were now seriously threatened, and Halsey had to make the excruciating decision to commit his tiny carrier force that had only just withdrawn. The best chance of success was to attack the enemy cruisers by surprise while anchored and refueling in Rabaul's Simpson Harbor, but this would be extremely risky for the aircraft involved. The strike force at Halsey's disposal, if he sortied every aircraft embarked in *Saratoga* and *Princeton*, totaled just under 100 aircraft, and it would be outnumbered by the massive force that had recently been flown into Rabaul. Furthermore, the target would be defended by dozens of antiaircraft batteries both ashore and on board the IJN vessels in Simpson Harbor.

If all of TF 38's aircraft attacked Rabaul, the carriers would be stripped of their air defense, leaving them vulnerable. The vessels' protection would have to be allocated to local land-based fighters from airfields in the Solomons that were within range of Rabaul. Even with the availability of land-based fighter cover, the two carriers would still be in a position of vulnerability if the mission went ahead due to both vessels being within range of IJNAF dive- and torpedo-bombers at Rabaul. Halsey was reluctant to place any of his ships in harm's way, stating that he "sincerely expected both air groups to be cut to pieces and both carriers stricken, if not lost."

As he fretted over the dilemma facing him, the situation for Allied forces ashore at Bougainville and TF 39 did not improve with time. *Saratoga* was an older carrier, being only the third such vessel commissioned (in November 1927) by the US Navy. By November 1943, it had gained a reputation for being where the action was not. Seemingly always in the wrong place, the vessel had been torpedoed twice earlier in the war and subsequently spent more than its fair share of time in port. Considered a "second-stringer" and a "bench warmer," the carrier had earned for itself some brutal nicknames from Pacific Fleet sailors, including "Pond Lily," "Reluctant Dragon" and "Sara Maru" (Maru is Japanese for a civilian ship). But *Saratoga*, like a steely-eyed poker player, had an ace up its sleeve in the form of CVG-12, led by veteran Naval Aviator Cdr Henry H. Caldwell.

Although the carrier air group had been in the Pacific for a year, its trio of squadrons had yet to see any action. Nevertheless, CVG-12 had used the time out of the frontline wisely, training hard as a team to become a "top-notch outfit" due primarily to the fighter tactics that had been developed by VF-12 CO, Cdr "Jumpin" Joe Clifton. He had stressed to his men the importance of maintaining top cover for the dive- and torpedo-bombers while they were in their attack runs, thus providing them with protection when they were at their most vulnerable.

Princeton and its escorts had pulled back to refuel and were awaiting further instructions when they received a dispatch from Halsey ordering "Task Force 38 proceed maximum formation speed [to] launch all-out strike on shipping in Rabaul and north thereof (order of targets: cruisers, destroyers). Retire thereafter."

On the evening of November 4, 500 miles southeast of Rabaul and clear of any land-based threat, things were sufficiently calm on board the carrier to permit the showing of a film in *Princeton*'s hangar bay. While it was still running, the air officers were called to the captain's quarters. A short time later other officers, including the squadron intelligence officers, were summoned. The word they received, which was quickly passed along to the rest of their carrier air groups, was to attack Rabaul in the morning. With only 14 hours' notice, and having been joined by *San Diego* and *San Juan* and nine destroyers, *Saratoga* and *Princeton* headed north at 27 knots to "kick over a hornet's nest."

This was the "big time" Lt Cdr Miller had referred to on more than one occasion when addressing CVLG-23. He told his pilots and aircrew that Rabaul – one of the enemy's principal western Pacific bases – was then serving as an anchorage and supply point for a task force of Japanese heavy cruisers and destroyers. This armada had been sent down from Truk to attack the invasion site at Empress Augusta Bay, and Allied intelligence sources also had indications the IJN was in the process of dispatching additional warships to Rabaul for the planned onslaught.

Good fortune was with TF 38, since the two carriers and their escorts masking themselves in overcast weather while running in toward their target – cloud cover kept the vessels hidden from the IJNAF's long-range flying boats. Their passage to the designated launch point 57 miles southwest of Cape Torokina and 220 miles southeast of Rabaul on the morning of November 5 had been assisted by smooth seas, allowing the destroyers to keep station.

CVG-12, led by CAG Caldwell, sortied every aircraft embarked in *Saratoga* – 33 Hellcats, 16 Avengers and 22 Dauntlesses – and *Princeton* added 19 Hellcats and seven Avengers. As the strike group cleared the carriers, Allied land-based fighters from airstrips at different locations on New Georgia arrived overhead to protect the carriers. Lt Cdr Tommy Blackburn's VF-17, for example, committed three eight-aircraft flights of Corsairs, with each one being on station over the US Navy ships for several hours at a time.

Reassured by the knowledge that their carriers would be well protected by the New Georgia-based fighters in their absence, the aircraft from CVG-12 and CVLG-23 pressed on in the direction of Rabaul. Cdr Joseph Clifton, leading VF-12, later stated, "The main idea of our orders was to cripple as many ships as we could, rather than concentrate on sinking a few." Two hours after launching, the US Navy aircraft reached their target, which was bathed in clear blue skies and visibility out to 50 miles. The plan of attack had had to be patiently worked out by the CAGs and their squadron commanders over the radio on their way to Rabaul due to the mission's compressed time schedule.

Lt Cdr Miller described the scene as *Princeton*'s fighters approached Simpson Harbor. "The target was protected by an umbrella of terrific antiaircraft fire, the likes of which our boys had never experienced before and hope never to see again. Japanese fighter planes swarmed the skies – Zekes, Tonys, Hamps – everything the enemy could make airborne. Hell had broken loose, literally, and planes seemed to fill every inch of the sky."

The IJNAF, in fact, had a total of 59 aircraft in the air to oppose the attack, and the Japanese fighter pilots had expected their US Navy counterparts to break into small groups as they approached the targets. Caldwell "threw them a curveball" by simply directing one large formation through the gauntlet of antiaircraft fire and then letting pilots split up into smaller groups at the last moment before they made their attack runs.

Although they were tempted to engage the IJNAF aircraft spotted overhead Rabaul, the disciplined Hellcat pilots stuck to the plan as one fighter division remained with each bomber flight all the way to the target. Refusing to follow the attacking aircraft through their own antiaircraft fire, the Zero-sen pilots left the US Navy formations alone. Instead, they spent their time "stunting" and engaging in tail chases with each other as they vainly tried to lure the Hellcats away from their assigned groups, thus leaving the Avengers and Dauntlesses unescorted.

Ignoring the intense antiaircraft fire, Caldwell guided CVG-12 across Crater Peninsula and then led his charges upwind of the enemy ships. His SBDs then attacked, while the TBFs descended to masttop level to start their torpedo runs. By that time, the IJN ships were either steaming for the harbor entrance or taking evasive action. As the Avengers and Dauntlesses pulled up from their attacks, the pilots found themselves flying over or around enemy ships for four to five miles. All bar five fighters and five bombers emerged from the attack without casualties, seven pilots and eight aircrew having been killed or posted as missing in action.

Hellcats from VF-12 and VF-23 also flew through withering antiaircraft fire to engage enemy fighters, with pilots from the latter unit claiming ten Japanese aircraft destroyed. One of the Naval Aviators to enjoy success was VF-23's Lt(jg) Stanley Crockett, who along with his wingman, Ens Carlton Roberts, escorted Cdr Henry Caldwell's Avenger as its pilot led the CVG-12 attack. Among the TBF's three-man crew was photographer PH1c Paul Barnett, with his equipment.

Crockett's Hellcat had almost failed to participate in this mission because of mechanical difficulties that made it impossible to lock the aircraft's wings in the extended position. However, he implored his mechanics to make every effort to get the F6F ready as the other aircraft launched. While fighters, dive-bombers and torpedo-bombers from both carriers launched, rendezvoused and then turned onto their attack heading as planned, Crockett was finally able to get airborne as soon as his wings were locked. Having raced to catch up to the strike group, he reached them about 20 miles from the carriers and then maneuvered into position slightly above Caldwell's Avenger as he acknowledged Ens Roberts.

When the trio of aircraft reached a point about five miles from Rabaul, the Hellcats took a corresponding position on either side of the group leader and roared in over the mouth of Simpson Harbor at an altitude of between 13,000–14,000ft. PH1c Barnett soon began taking photographs, despite the antiaircraft fire being thrown up by ships and shore emplacements around the harbor being horrendous. At the same time, enemy fighters began to reach intercept altitude. Unperturbed, Caldwell assigned individual ships to the group and ordered them to attack, then he and his fighter escorts turned north and skirted the northern shore of Crater Peninsula. When the Avenger and the pair of Hellcats reached Talili Bay they turned east to make a daring photographic run across the harbor at an altitude of just 3,500ft, flying directly into the withering antiaircraft artillery barrage being generated by many of the warships and shore batteries.

The aircraft emerged from the hail of bullets and shells over Rapopo airfield, where they were intercepted by a Zero-sen that damaged Ens Roberts' Hellcat. With his main battery cable cut, severing the aircraft's electrical power to the cockpit, Roberts was forced to divert to incomplete Barakoma airfield on Vella Lavella Island – he was out of the fight.

The Avenger was a slow aircraft, and not nearly as maneuverable as a Zero-sen. Nevertheless, Caldwell and Crockett quickly adopted a defensive maneuver that offered both pilots mutual cover to each other's tails as they sought to flee Rabaul. Although a further eight IJNAF fighters then joined in the pursuit, Crockett kept up the weaving back and forth to protect CAG's TBF. The hostile fire hit his engine and sprung the cowl flaps open. The Avenger's rear turret was also disabled and PH1c Barnett had been killed, but Caldwell managed to fend off a series of head-on passes with his single fixed machine gun mounted in the nose.

The IJNAF aircraft then briefly climbed, before again diving down to make one final pass at the Hellcat and Avenger. Crockett met the challenge, shooting down a "Zeke" (the Allied reporting name for the A6M) and damaging another. Nevertheless, rounds tore into his Hellcat's instrument panel, destroying almost everything except the magnetic compass and shooting the throttle handle out of his hand. Perspex shards from the hood littered the cockpit floor. Forced to fly "blind" due to the shattered instrument panel, Crockett also had to fly the fighter with both hands firmly on the stick because of severe damage to the port wing. Blood flowed freely from a gash in his head, rendering his goggles useless, while hits in his arm covered his hands in blood and wounds in his shoulder, knee and leg caused blood to pool on the cockpit floor.

Crockett could have ducked into some nearby clouds for cover, but he instead stayed on Caldwell's wing until they returned to the carriers. CAG brought his Avenger back to *Saratoga* with only one operable wheel, no flaps, no aileron and no radio, landing it on the first attempt. Crockett, in his weakened condition, did not remember landing on *Princeton*'s small flightdeck, and he collapsed upon exiting the aircraft. Sailors immediately carried him to the sick bay. Crockett's Hellcat had been riddled by enemy fire, with 268 holes being discovered in the airframe – 54 of them in the cockpit and 180 in the port fuselage and wing.

Caldwell messaged Crockett, "Group Commander sends fighter pilot Number Three X – your courage, determination and loyalty will be a lasting inspiration to me."

As the aircraft returned to *Princeton* from Rabaul shortly after noon, sailors on board the carrier anxiously scan the sky and count them back in. Rumors began to spread that an entire division had gone down, and as they made the final count CVLG-23 learned that the raid had cost it three Hellcats and three Avengers. The VF-23 pilots lost in the aerial battle were Lts R. E. O'Connell and J. A. Smith and Lt(jg) J. D. Madison, with VC-23 losing Avenger pilots Lt(jg)s G. F. Scott, C. C. Dyer and W. W. Fratus and their aircrew.

Hellcat pilots had claimed 21 victories in the fighting over Rabaul, with VF-23 accounting for ten of those kills, as well as two probables and eight listed as damaged. Avenger and Dauntless pilots and aircrew claimed an additional seven victories, one of which was credited to gunner AMM2c J. S. Warakomski from VC-23.

When the surviving Hellcats and TBFs left Rabaul, CAG Miller recalled that "the place was an inferno. Cruisers and destroyers were hit, some sunk, while Japanese planes were scattered all over the place, total wrecks." The ordeal had exhausted both CVG-12 and CVLG-23, and at 1300 hrs Sherman ordered *Saratoga*, *Princeton* and their escorts to come about and make speed to the south to be within range of Allied shore-based fighter cover. The raid all but eliminated any major threat to the landings at Empress Augusta Bay, badly damaging four heavy cruisers and two light cruisers.

Rear Adm Sherman was as jubilant as Vice Adm Halsey, and he hailed the accomplishment as "a glorious victory, a second Pearl Harbor in reverse." Sherman was not far off, for now the IJN's battleships had lost their cruiser protection. This strike, along with the other aerial attacks and surface actions in the waters surrounding the Solomon Islands, had reduced Japan's cruiser force to four ships after this attack. It had numbered 11 vessels just two months earlier. Bougainville was now safe for Halsey's advance, and the IJN's heavy warships would never visit Rabaul again.

IJNAF reconnaissance aircraft found the retiring vessels of TF 38 at 1445 hrs, and 18 Nakajima B5N "Kate" torpedo-bombers were dispatched to sink the carriers. At 1915 hrs the Japanese aviators spotted a target, but it was the wrong one. The following day Radio Tokyo reported the results of what it called the "First Air Battle of Bougainville." The report listed the American casualties as "One large carrier blown up and sunk, one medium carrier set ablaze and later sunk, and two heavy cruisers and one cruiser and destroyer sunk." That absurd report was chalked up as one of the most inaccurate of the entire Pacific War, the "Kates" having actually attacked two landing craft and a PT boat. They failed to sink the three craft after a sustained 14-minute attack. Rear Adm Theodore Wilkinson, commander of I Marine Amphibious Force, gave PT-167's skipper, Ens Ted Berlin, a pat on the back for his courageous defense of the landing craft, concluding his praise with the line "Fireplug Sprinkles Dog."

Upon learning of the success of his gamble to attack Simpson Harbor, a relieved Halsey radioed Sherman, "report of attack is real music to me. When *Saratoga* is given a chance, she is deadly. *Princeton* too takes a deep initial bow in the South Pacific. May the Jap cripples permanently be buried in Davy Jones' locker. A funeral dirge has been sounded for Tojo's strongest South Pacific base."

Halsey then ordered land-based long-range bombers to find the Japanese ships retiring out of Simpson Harbor on their way to Truk and "sink the cripples." They failed in their attempt to prevent the vessels from reaching their destination though, and Halsey was rumored to have wanted to attack that bastion as well.

He had been pleading for additional carriers in the South Pacific, and Nimitz finally delivered when three more vessels were assigned to Third Fleet on the day Rabaul was attacked. Rear Adm Alfred E. Montgomery, commanding TG 50.3, brought combat-veteran *Essex*, the brand new USS *Bunker Hill* (CV-17) (with untried SB2C Helldiver dive-bombers embarked) and *Independence*, the first of the light carriers to be commissioned. Due to the demands of the upcoming Gilbert Islands operation, getting underway in late November, these three ships remained at Espiritu Santo for three days while the admirals desperately sought more destroyers to add to the task group's screen.

Halsey instructed *Princeton* and *Saratoga*, now operating as TG 50.4, to hit Rabaul from the north while TG 50.3 struck from the south, with the attack date set for November 11. The battle plan called for Montgomery's TG 50.3 to send full deck load strikes, while the CAPs would be manned by land-based US Navy Corsair and Hellcat squadrons. It was a complex operation, as Montgomery's task group would strike from the Solomon Sea while TG 50.3 attacked from due east of the objective. The combined force of five carriers was the largest thus far assembled by the US Navy for a single mission, and it would demonstrate a classic example of the successful projection of naval air power carried out by carrier air groups on a fixed target that USAAF horizontal bombing had thus far failed to destroy.

As noted, the land-based squadrons would provide fighter protection for the task groups while embarked fighter units escorted the carrier-based bombers to Rabaul. The CAP was handed to two New Georgia-based squadrons, Lt John Kelley's VF-33 (equipped with 12 F6F-3s) flying from Segi Point and Lt Cdr Tommy Blackburn's VF-17 (equipped with 24 F4U-1As) flying from Ondonga. Twelve of these fighters were to land aboard each of Montgomery's three carriers, while 32 Corsairs from VMF-212 and VMF-221, flying from the newly opened Barakoma airfield, and a squadron of RNZAF P-40Ns provided overhead protection. The US Navy fighters would refuel on board the carriers after their initial hop from New Georgia and then immediately launch again to provide another layer of protection over the task groups.

By November 8 Halsey's operations officer was finally able to gather enough destroyers to provide Montgomery with an adequate screening force. With the attack still 72 hours away, the Rabaul "hornet's nest" received ample warning of the impending strike.

Having rendezvoused with their escorting destroyers, *Saratoga* and *Princeton* again turned their bows north for Rabaul and launched their morning attack, despite unfavorable weather conditions, from a point near the Green Islands, 225 miles southeast of Rabaul. *Saratoga* and

Princeton, as per the operational plan, would put their aircraft over the target 30 minutes prior to Montgomery's TG 50.3 main strike. The combined force from CVG-12 and CVLG-23, totaling 55 Hellcats, 25 Avengers and 21 Dauntlesses, attacked a light cruiser and four destroyers in Simpson Harbor through rain squalls and cloud cover.

The initial strike also tangled with nearly 70 "Zekes" that had been scrambled well in advance of the US Navy aircraft reaching Rabaul, the pilots and aircrew from TG 50.4 being tasked with keeping the IJNAF fighters busy while the larger TG 50.3 formation closed on Simpson Harbor. Montgomery had launched his aircraft 160 miles southeast of Rabaul, and CVG-9 ran headlong into dozens of "Zekes" at 0900 hrs over Cape St George. After the twisting, turning dogfights and strikes on shipping through clouds and rain had concluded, the US Navy aircraft returned to their carriers.

Both task groups had planned to launch a second strike, but increasingly bad weather prompted Rear Adm Sherman to abort a return to fortress Rabaul. Post-mission reports noted that the target had been hit well enough, with a Japanese destroyer sunk and four other warships damaged, indicating that the mission was not a total bust. "Antiaircraft fire was just as heavy as on our earlier strikes at Rabaul," said Lt Cdr Miller. "The Japanese had planes in the air everywhere, but we had learned from our previous experience."

Adm Halsey expressed his satisfaction with the results: "You have dealt severe blows to the enemy. Your first attack on Rabaul was another shot heard around the world. Your second was equally effective, although hampered by insufficient targets. I know you will carry out successfully future Central Pacific operations. Good hunting and good luck."

At 1313 hrs, little more than an hour after Montgomery's aircraft had returned to their carriers, SK air-search radar fitted to vessels in the task groups picked up an enemy formation at a distance of 119 miles and closing. A lone Zero-sen had spotted TG 50.3 and monitored it while a Japanese counterattack was launched from Rabaul at noon consisting of 69 "Zekes," "Vals" and "Kates," followed by a flight of "Bettys." It was one of the largest anti-carrier strikes mounted by the IJNAF to date.

At 1351 hrs four Hellcats from VF-33 reported enemy aircraft 40 miles away, and when the fighter directors asked how many, a Corsair pilot jumped on the radio and replied, "Jesus Christ, boys, there's a million of them! Let's go to work!" The four F6F-3s from VF-33 made the initial interception, and they were soon joined by the Corsairs of Blackburn's VF-17. The skies above the task group quickly turned into a "furball" of wildly maneuvering aircraft, with some on fire – impacts on the surface of the water marked where they subsequently crashed.

The carriers then adopted a triangular formation within a 2,000-yard radius, with the destroyers ringing them in a 4,000-yard circle. A "circling of the wagons," if you will, effectively pooled their antiaircraft guns for mutual support, rather than the carriers separating as they had done in the past. The IJNAF aircraft attacked in three waves and initially ran into *Essex*'s VF-9 just as the unit's Hellcats were taking off. A dive-bombing attack was followed by two waves of torpedo-bombers, then more dive-bombers. Although the intense action lasted 46 minutes, only ten sailors were wounded, and none mortally.

The IJNAF suffered terrible losses that day, however, with eight "Zekes," 14 "Kates," 17 "Vals" and several "Bettys" being shot down. The defending fighters, supported by antiaircraft batteries on the carriers and their escorts, had successfully fought off a large-scale land-based air attack, and the losses inflicted on the IJNAF more than made up for the modest results of the Simpson Harbor raid earlier in the day. In roughly 30 minutes, US Navy pilots had claimed 50 enemy aircraft destroyed for the loss of six TBFs and eight Hellcats. No ships from either task group were hit. Details pertaining to the losses inflicted on the IJNAF and the damage incurred by vessels in Simpson Harbor were relayed up the Pacific Fleet's chain of command via after action reports, and the forces involved received hearty congratulations from Vice Adm Halsey, Gen Douglas MacArthur and the USAAF's commanding general, Gen Henry H. "Hap" Arnold.

Following the hard-won successes in the fall of 1943, Adm Nimtz had now fully realized the effectiveness of his personnel and their skillful use of the weapons of war that they had recently been provided with. The landing on Bougainville and the strikes on Rabaul had brought a carrier task force that much closer to Truk, which was now the prime target for aerial attack in the western Pacific.

Just 52 of the 173 aircraft sent to defend Rabaul on November 1 made the return flight to Truk shortly after the disastrous attack on the Third Fleet carriers. On November 13, fresh units were transferred from the Marshall Islands to Rabaul to relieve them – a move that would benefit US forces when the landings at Tarawa and Makin commenced exactly one week later.

OPERATION *GALVANIC*

Following the raids on Rabaul, *Princeton*, still attached to TG 50.4, refueled at Espiritu Santo on November 14. Its crew hurriedly took on stores and CVLG-23 welcomed replacement pilots to fill out the squadron rosters, after which the carrier set a course for the Gilbert Islands to support Operation *Galvanic* – the first trial-by-fire for the newly minted Central Pacific Force and its fledgling amphibious assault doctrine against heavily fortified objectives. The latter took the form of Makin, Abemama and Betio islands within Tarawa Atoll. Betio was home to an airstrip and a well dug-in force whose commanding officer claimed that it would take one million men 100 years to take it. The 2nd Marine Division captured it in three days. Described as a time of utmost savagery, the opposing forces locked horns on Betio, whose acreage is nearly equal to that of the Pentagon and its parking lots, in brutal close quarters combat.

Due to unpredictable tides during the morning hours of November 20, the Marine landing craft bottomed out on an exposed reef on the way in through the lagoon to the assault beaches on Betio, forcing the men to disembark and wade 600–800 yards through chest-deep water before finally coming ashore. With the chaotic landing opposed by withering machine-gun fire from pill boxes manned by naval infantry units of the IJN, the assault looked like faltering after casualties started to mount. It had now turned into a squad leader's fight, as small groups of Marines rallied, gained a toehold ashore and proceeded to nearly annihilate the IJN garrison of almost 5,000, while losing more than 1,000 of their own.

The savagery of the operation to seize Tarawa Atoll had actually started four days before the amphibious landings, when Gato-class submarine USS *Corvina* (SS-226), commanded by Lt Cdr Roderick S. Rooney, was sunk by an IJN submarine. The US Navy had deployed ten submarines in support of Operation *Galvanic*, with several being on station in the Marshalls and near Truk, where they were to report and oppose any attempt by the IJN's Combined Fleet to counterattack in reaction to the landings in the Gilberts.

Corvina, on its very first war patrol, was sighted on the surface 85 miles southwest of Truk on November 16 by IJN submarine *I-176*. Having the drop on their opponents, the crew of the Japanese submarine immediately snap-fired a spread of three torpedoes at *Corvina*, two of which struck their target and exploded. The American submarine quickly sunk, taking with it the entire crew of 82. *Corvina* was the only US Navy submarine known to have been sunk by an IJN submarine.

Two days later, on the night of November 18–19, Sargo-class submarine *USS Sculpin* (SS-191), with new CO Lt Cdr Fred Connaway at the helm, was on its ninth war patrol when a large high-speed convoy was detected by radar north of Truk. The crew duly made a fast surface run to get ahead of the convoy and set up an attack in the early morning hours just before dawn. However, *Sculpin* was forced to dive when it was sighted, and the convoy sailed directly toward the submarine. It surfaced after the vessels had passed, but the convoy commander had anticipated this move and left the destroyer *Yamagumo* behind – *Sculpin* surfaced just 600 yards from the destroyer and was immediately spotted. It quickly dove, while *Yamagumo* conducted two depth-charge attacks that inflicted damage and, crucially, knocked out *Sculpin*'s depth gauge.

Running low on battery power, the submarine attempted to surface at 1200 hrs under the cover of a rain squall, but due to the broken depth gauge the vessel broached and was immediately detected by *Yamagumo*. *Sculpin* dived again, but the destroyer laid a damaging pattern of 18 depth charges, which knocked out *Sculpin*'s sonar and caused it to lose depth control. The submarine sank below safe depth, springing so many leaks and taking on so much water that it had to run at high speed to maintain depth, making it easy for *Yamagumo* to track.

When it became apparent the submarine would sink, Connaway opted to fight it out on the surface. As *Sculpin*'s crew manned the deck guns, *Yamagumo*'s very first salvo hit the conning tower, killing Connaway, the executive officer, the gunnery officer and the rest of the bridge watch, while shrapnel cut down the gun crew. At this point, the senior surviving *Sculpin* officer, Lt George Brown, informed Capt John P. Cromwell, who commanded Submarine Divisions 203, 44 and 43, that he intended to scuttle *Sculpin*. Cromwell concurred, but chose to remain on board the vessel. He and 11 others went down with the submarine, while nine were killed topside. Cromwell had been on board *Sculpin* to coordinate a subsequent submarine wolfpack attack, and he chose to go down with the vessel rather than risk revealing to the Japanese under torture information about the impending Gilberts operation and his knowledge of Ultra codebreaking intelligence. Cromwell was posthumously awarded the Medal of Honor, being the most senior submarine officer to receive the US military's highest decoration.

Yamagumo picked up 42 survivors, although one badly wounded sailor was thrown back into the water. The captured men were taken to Truk and interrogated for ten days. By VJ Day only 20 survivors from the crew of 62 remained alive, having ended the war as forced labor in a copper mine.

For *Galvanic*, Rear Adm Spruance, commanding officer of the growing Central Pacific Force, embarked in the Portland-class heavy cruiser USS *Indianapolis* (CA-35). Rear Adm Turner commanded the Fifth Amphibious Force, and he would fly his flag on board the Pearl Harbor-veteran Pennsylvania-class battleship USS *Pennsylvania* (BB-38), while Maj Gen Smith would again command V Amphibious Corps, in charge of the 2nd Marine Division and the US Army's 165th Regimental Combat Team.

Although Turner divided the Fifth Amphibious Force in two, he retained overall control, along with command of the Northern Attack Force (TF 52) which would be charged with taking Makin Island. The latter was closer geographically to the major Japanese base at Truk, and it was presumed to be the axis of greater threat. For this reason Spruance sailed with the Northern Attack Force. Rear Adm Harry W. Hill was given command of the Southern Attack Force (TF 53), with his assignment being the seizure of Betio.

The armada that was bound for the Gilbert Islands included 191 warships in four task forces that consisted of four Essex-class carriers and *Saratoga*, four Independence-class light carriers, seven smaller escort carriers, 13 battleships, eight heavy cruisers, more than a dozen light cruisers and 70 destroyers and destroyer escorts. The transports and cargo ships were carrying 27,600 assault troops, 7,600 garrison troops, 6,000 vehicles (including the US Marine Corps' new Amphibious Vehicle, Tracked, better known as the LVT or amtrac) and 117,000 tons of cargo. These vessels were sustained by 13 fleet oilers and nine merchant oilers, along with the newly innovated mobile logistics base ships.

Providing air coverage for *Galvanic* was the Fast Carrier Task Force Pacific Fleet (TF 50), commanded by Rear Adm Pownall and broken down into four task groups. TG 50.1 was the carrier interceptor group under Pownall's direct command, and he was embarked in the carrier *Yorktown*. This task group also included *Lexington* and the light carrier *Cowpens*, and aircraft from all three vessels would pound Japanese airfields in the Marshalls from November 23.

Meanwhile, TG 50.4, the relief carrier group under the command of Rear Adm Sherman embarked in *Saratoga* and which again included *Princeton*, attacked Nauru Island 380 miles west of the Gilberts on November 19, thus ensuring no IJNAF aircraft on Nauru could intervene in the invasion of the Gilberts. TGs 50.2 and 50.3 provided direct cover to the northern and southern attack groups. Simultaneously, Pownall's TG 50.1 and Radford's TG 50.2 rendezvoused with their battleships and oilers north of the Phoenix Islands and separated in the final approach to the target. Nine fast carriers descended upon their targets in the Gilberts, which were now undefended by surface or air forces. Indeed, the only threats remaining were land-based aircraft few in number and submarines operating out of the Marshall Islands.

Gilberts Task Force Organization, November 15–26, 1943
Commander, TF 50 – Rear Adm C. A. Pownall
Commander, TG 50.1 – Rear Adm C. A. Pownall
    Yorktown – Capt J. J. Clark (CVG-5 embarked)
    Lexington – Capt F. B. Stump (CVG-16 embarked)
    Cowpens – Capt R. P. McConnell (CVLG-25 embarked)
Commander, TG 50.2 – Rear Adm A. W. Radford
    Enterprise – Capt M. B. Gardner (CVG-6 embarked)
    Belleau Wood – Capt A. M. Pride (CVLG-24 embarked)
    Monterey – Capt L. T. Hundt (CVLG-30 embarked)
Commander, TG 50.3 – Rear Adm A. E. Montgomery
    Essex – Capt R. A. Ofstie (CVG-9 embarked)
    Bunker Hill – Capt J. J. Ballentine (CVG-17 embarked)
    Independence – Capt R. L. Johnson (CVLG-22 embarked)

Commander, TG 50.4 – Rear Adm F. C. Sherman
   Saratoga – Capt J. H. Cassady (CVG-12 embarked)
   Princeton – Capt G. R. Henderson (CVLG-23 embarked)
Commander, Support Aircraft – Col W. O. Eareckson, USAAF

Softening up the target beaches at Makin and Tarawa began several days before the Central Pacific Force arrived, with attacks by Vice Adm John H. Hoover's long-range land-based bombers flying from airfields in the South Pacific. Montgomery's TG 50.3 subsequently struck first, bombing Tarawa on November 18, with the other task groups joining in the next day. Pownall's aircraft struck airfields at Mili and Jaluit in the southern Marshalls, Radford's bombed Makin and Sherman's successfully eliminated enemy air strength at Nauru.

Nauru, an island just south of the equator that had been occupied by Japanese forces on August 25, 1942, boasted two airfields that had been built shortly after its capture. These were attacked on November 19 by a joint *Princeton–Saratoga* strike force that saw the carriers launch three strikes during the course of the day that destroyed airfield infrastructure and cratered the runways, rendering them unserviceable. VF-23 also claimed two "Zekes" destroyed and two damaged in aerial combat over the target. All the carrier aircraft involved returned safely.

Princeton and its consorts refueled at a position not far from Nanumea Atoll, then steamed northeast and covered the amphibious force while it headed for Makin and Tarawa. V Amphibious Corps had formed in New Zealand and conducted rehearsals at Efate, part of the Vanuatu island group in the South Pacific. That night (November 19), IJNAF aerial "snoopers" trailed the US Navy vessels until they were driven off by heavy antiaircraft fire from *San Juan* and *San Diego*, along with nine destroyers.

At 0430 hrs on November 20, the US transports completed lowering their landing boats. At 0441 hrs, a red star flare went up over Betio, suggesting that the Japanese were aware the invasion was about to occur. Aircraft had been tracking the slow-moving LSTs of the assault force and they had attempted to attack them under the cover of darkness, only to be repulsed by antiaircraft fire from *Princeton* and the rest of TG 50.4.

The biggest factor that caused so many of the Marine casualties on the 20th was the lack of accurate tide tables for Tarawa. The atoll was prone to unpredictable "dodging tides" – an irregular neap tide that ebbs and flows several times per day at unpredictable intervals, and can maintain constant lower levels for many hours. Rear Adm Turner was aware of the risk of a low dodging tide that would prevent landing craft from getting over the reef. There was also a significant risk that conditions would be even worse if he chose to delay the landing. Turner rolled the dice and the tides won. Amtracs crawled over the reef that day with no problem, but the landing craft got hung up and had to lower their ramps well short of the beach. They were sitting ducks to enemy machine-gun, mortar and artillery fire, and the Marines had no choice but to exit them quickly.

On the night of November 20, long-range "Betty" torpedo-bombers from Kwajalein and Maloelap atolls attacked Montgomery's task group off Tarawa. CAPs and antiaircraft fire from *Essex*, *Bunker Hill* and *Independence* brought down nine of the aircraft, but one managed to get through and torpedo *Independence*, putting it out of the war for six months.

Resistance ended on Betio on November 23, at about the same time that Makin and Abemama fell. Nevertheless, the IJNAF attacks continued, with aircraft from the Marshalls being destroyed by fighters from TG 50.1's VF-16 on November 23 and 24. These actions proved to be the largest aerial clashes of *Galvanic*.

Operating with Pownall's TG 50.1, Capt Stump had positioned *Lexington* between Makin Island in the Gilberts and Mili Island in the Marshalls. This proved to be the ideal location for intercepting any hostile aircraft that might venture into the fray in response to the landings at Tarawa. The carrier's fighter pilots, noting that they had experienced little in the way of aerial combat of late, would see the drought come to an end on November 23. Lt Cdr Paul Buie, CO of VF-16 and a future ace, had maneuvered three divisions of Hellcats (12 fighters in total) into the right place at the right time at mid-morning.

Put into what Buie called "a fighter pilot's dream position," *Lexington*'s FDO called with a contact and directed the fliers 4,000ft above 21 approaching "Zekes." With the Hellcats attacking from out of the sun, the IJNAF pilots were completely oblivious to the descending fighters as Buie led his charges in a coordinated overhead and side attack at

23,000ft. He quickly splashed two "Zekes," and by the time the first two passes had been made, all that remained were a few stragglers at lower levels. All 12 Hellcat pilots returned to *Lexington*, where they claimed a total of 17 destroyed and four probables. Ens Ralph Hanks was the high scorer of the engagement, knocking down five and thus becoming the first Hellcat "ace-in-a-day."

Shortly after noon the following day, Buie was again leading 12 Hellcats in a CAP in roughly the same location when the FDO directed them onto 20 "Zekes" and two "Bettys" at 23,000ft. On this occasion the IJNAF pilots had the altitude advantage, and as the US Navy fighters turned to meet the enemy, a Hellcat was shot down. The enemy quickly lost the advantage, however, with the engagement developing into a vertical combat that ranged from around 20,000ft down to 5,000ft. At the end of the clash, VF-16 claimed a further 13 victories and six probables. During two days of combat, the unit had been credited with a total of 30 enemy aircraft destroyed and 11 probables for the loss of just one Hellcat.

IJN submarines then struck again. In the pre-dawn darkness off Makin on November 24, Casablanca-class escort carrier USS *Liscome Bay* (CVE-56) was hit by a torpedo fired from *I-175* that set off a catastrophic explosion and sent the vessel to the bottom within 23 minutes. Some 645 men were killed, including Rear Adm Henry M. Mullinix, a star Naval Academy football player and the top graduate of his 1916 class. A promising officer whose star was on the rise, Mullinix would almost certainly have been promoted to a fast carrier command. Navy Cross recipient Cook PO Doris Miller, the first black man to receive the honor after his actions during the attack on Pearl Harbor, also perished. Other ships in the area managed to pluck 272 survivors from the water.

Despite *I-175*'s spectacular success, nocturnal aerial torpedo attacks proved to be the preferred method of retaliation for the Japanese – a single IJNAF aircraft appeared over the vessels several evenings in a row. Dubbed "washing machine Charlie" when such aircraft targeted Henderson Field, on Guadalcanal, in 1942–43, the night intruder's alias was now "Tojo the lamplighter" to sailors of the Pacific Fleet. Typically, a lone aircraft would drop flares over Radford's carriers while they were on station off Makin.

However, on the night of November 26, the number of aircraft in the skies over the fleet multiplied to roughly 30 "Bettys" when the torpedo-bombers flew in from the Marshalls to hit TG 50.2. Radford was waiting for them, having launched *Enterprise*'s CAG, Lt Cdr Edward "Butch" O'Hare, and his night team. The latter consisted of two Hellcats from VF-6, whose pilots had been trained in "cooperative nightfighting," and Lt Cdr John Phillips, skipper of VT-6, in his radar-equipped Avenger. Before Phillips could rendezvous with the Hellcats, he engaged two "Bettys" and shot them both down. Shortly thereafter, as O'Hare and his wingman, future ace Ens W. A. Skon, carefully jockeyed into position on either side of Phillips, O'Hare's F6F-3 was struck by rounds from an undetected "Betty" lurking nearby in the dark. The fighter fell away and crashed into the sea. No trace of O'Hare or his Hellcat were ever found.

Several more isolated aerial actions occurred during *Galvanic*, but by the end of organized resistance on the target islands on November 28, Japanese air attacks had also ceased. A total of 71 Marshalls-based aircraft had been shot down during the month, along with several more that had staged from Truk. Additional enemy aircraft were based north of the Gilberts, and if American shipping and garrison forces in the newly captured islands were to remain free from attack, they would have to be eliminated. In contrast to Japanese losses, US carrier aircraft losses for all of November, including Rabaul (but excluding the 23 Avengers and Wildcats that went down with *Liscome Bay*), totaled 47. Porpoise-class submarine USS *Plunger* (SS-179) contributed to the rescue of a number of downed pilots and aircrew from these aircraft, plucking several of them from the sea around the Gilberts.

In support of V Amphibious Corps' struggles against bitter resistance on Betio, and the landings on Abemama and Makin atolls, *Princeton* had launched nine strikes in 19 days and its aircraft had flown 2,278 close air support, CAP and antisubmarine sorties through to November 24. By then the carrier had developed an intense shaft vibration while cruising on station off the Gilberts, and it was sent back to Pearl Harbor with *Saratoga* and a number of battleships, destroyers and other vessels that also needed repairs or equipment upgrades. Prior to departing on November 29, *Princeton* exchanged operational Hellcats and Avengers for damaged aircraft from other carrier air groups and charted a course for Hawaii.

Meanwhile, Spruance ordered Pownall to leave two carriers (*Bunker Hill* and *Monterey*) under the command of Sherman north of the

Gilberts for insurance, while he proceeded to take the rest of the Central Pacific Force to the Marshalls for a large-scale attack on Kwajalein.

Princeton reached Hawaii on December 7 – two years to the day since the surprise attack on the Pacific Fleet. Following a brief stop at Pearl Harbor, the carrier was soon ordered to proceed to Puget Sound Naval Shipyard at Bremerton, in Washington state, to address the shaft vibration. To the dismay of CVLG-23 personnel hoping to get back stateside, the squadrons were put ashore in Hawaii to await the return of "Sweet P" from Bremerton. All aircraft were offloaded at NAS Ford Island and then flown to NAS Puunene, on the island of Maui, where the lush pineapple and sugar cane fields had recently been interspersed with military installations. To compensate for the missed trip home, CVLG-23 was given the opportunity to visit the ranch of Mr and Mrs John E. Russell, where they could ride horses and hike the lava-red Maui hills when they were not busy with routine training at the naval air station.

After three weeks of work on a top priority basis, *Princeton* left Bremerton on January 3, 1944 with its shaft repaired and additional antiaircraft weaponry topside in the form of additional 20mm and 40mm guns. The wartime US Navy of the 1940s was no different from any other navy past or present in respect to sailors "jumping ship." On this occasion, *Princeton* sailed short-handed by no fewer than 67 crew who had either mistakenly overstayed their shore leave or intentionally gone absent without leave.

The carrier had certainly been busy over the previous six months, for as *Princeton* steamed westward, its log showed that in the 225 days since the start of the shakedown cruise on June 2, 1943, it had been at sea for 147 of them.

Ships with broader beams in relation to their length are inclined to pitch in heavy weather, bobbing up and down on their longitudinal axis, while vessels with greater relative length tend to roll from side to side. Independence-class carriers were "rollers," and *Princeton* did not disappoint in this respect as it sailed into heavy weather while headed back to Pearl Harbor. Occasionally rolling as much as 33 degrees, and taking water over the flightdeck, the carrier still performed well and made landfall on January 8.

The two courageous missions carried out by TF 38 against Rabaul in early November 1943 proved many things that US Navy's planners thought would be tested during the subsequent invasion of the Gilbert Islands. Halsey's landing force at Torokina had been spared destruction by carriers undertaking simultaneous offensive operations against a major enemy fleet and air base. Additionally, without battleships and cruisers by their side, the multicarrier formation had withstood a heavy air attack, repelling a sizable land-based enemy force.

Halsey's calculated risk had paid off when *Saratoga* and *Princeton* were then joined by three more carriers to add further damage to Rabaul. US Navy pilots and aircrew had proven themselves in battle, as had the weapons systems that had been designed and built for this very purpose. Shortly thereafter, the Gilberts had been taken, although at a cost in men and materiel, despite there being no legitimate opposition from the air since Adm Koga had lost half of his fighters and nearly all of his attack aircraft in the ill-fated protection of Rabaul.

Truk-based IJN vessels had been left exposed to attack from the air after the significant losses suffered by the IJNAF in the final months of 1943. The tables had now emphatically turned in the US Navy's favor, with the Pacific Fleet full of fight and growing more powerful literally by the day.

4
Task Force 58

While *Princeton* was making its way back to Pearl Harbor in early December, preparations for the capture of the Marshall Islands were underway. In November 1943, war planners had had no choice but to move forward with the amphibious assault on the Gilberts, for one of the numerous harsh realities of armed conflict was that the only way to learn how to wage war was by waging war.

Post-*Galvanic*, Rear Adm Turner completed a lessons-learned statement, along with recommendations upon direction from Adm Nimitz. He also compiled a list of requirements for the impending attack in the Marshalls. Turner had determined from accurate intelligence that the key island in the Tarawa Atoll, Betio, had been greatly reinforced in the three months leading up to *Galvanic* following the IJN's deduction that it was to be attacked before year-end. Speed of action, therefore, was essential to the success of upcoming operations, for the enemy needed to be kept off balance.

Back in September 1943, the US Navy's fast carriers had struck the Gilberts in conjunction with Seventh Air Force bombers, carrying out the first large-scale attacks of the Central Pacific campaign and causing a great deal of damage, although the pilots involved did not initially realize this. The strikes benefitted the Americans in a number of ways. They destroyed an IJNAF advanced airfield, prompted Adm Koga to sortie the Combined Fleet from Truk in anticipation of an American invasion there, produced good aerial photographs of the area and forced the IJN to expend thousands of 13mm rounds in aerial defense that would have otherwise been used against the US Marine Corps when the amphibious assault took place two months later.

As a result of Adm King's "whipsaw strategy," the Imperial General Headquarters could not decide with any certainty whether the next American amphibious landing would take place in the Central or South Pacific. It never imagined that two major invasions would take place within three weeks of each other.

Another flurry of intelligence signals reporting US Navy ship movements left Adm Koga struggling to cover all approaches to vitally important islands in the Central Pacific. In mid-October he sortied a significant task force to the Marshalls, where the vessels found nothing but open ocean. Concluding that the reported activity in the Central Pacific was little more than a ruse, Koga fatefully dispatched nearly 200 aircraft from 1st Carrier Division to Rabaul, followed by several cruisers. As previously noted, these forces were hit hard by aircraft from TF 38, which *Princeton* was a part of, when they carried out their daring raids on November 5 and 11. The losses they inflicted on the IJNAF during these engagements only revealed their significance to senior US Navy commanders involved in *Galvanic* after the conclusion of the latter operation.

While IJN submarines made their presence felt, as did IJNAF aircraft during night raids, the mighty Combined Fleet would not attempt a confrontation with the US Navy without the strike capability of its carrier-based aviators or the protection provided by its cruisers.

Galvanic was the opening campaign in the offensive against the Japanese in the Central Pacific, and in November 1943 fast carrier operations and an amphibious assault on a fortified target were both brand new and unproven. Fleet Training Publication No. 167, titled *Landing Operations Doctrine*, was barely five years old in 1943, yet it had gone through three major changes by then. Finally, the 2nd Marine Division, which adhered to the doctrine espoused in Fleet Training Publication No. 167 during the Tarawa landings, had only been founded in February 1941.

Despite effectively implementing its training, the US Marine Corps suffered terrible losses at Betio primarily because its landing vessels got caught out by the unpredictably low tides on November 20. Amphibious landing planners and staff meteorologists knew nothing about harmonic analysis or apogean neap tides in late 1943. The Central

Pacific Force was given no alternative landing date, with the Gilberts operation having already been postponed five days by the 20th. Any further delay would possibly compromise the more strategically located Marshall Islands campaign.

Although the *Landing Operations Doctrine* had proven adquate in a handful of landings in both the Pacific and Mediterranean theaters prior to *Galvanic*, it had never been fully tested under heavy enemy fire, let alone against the most heavily fortified base (Betio) in the Pacific at that time. By contrast, the 1st Marine Division had walked ashore unopposed at Guadalcanal on August 6–7, 1942, having taken the enemy totally by surprise. It would not meet any serious resistance from the IJA's 17th Army until counterattacks were launched on August 21.

Spruance and his admirals had confidence in the Central Pacific Force, but they still respected the capabilities of the IJN's Combined Fleet and fully expected it to strike the clusters of transports and cargo ships at anchor off the contested landing beaches while they were vulnerable, as the submarine *I-175* had done in the Gilberts. Additionally, Spruance was concerned about the timing and intensity of what he believed would be an inevitable IJNAF long-range counterattack, unaware that the Rabaul strikes had effectively neutralized Koga's forces to the point where the Japanese were essentially retreating.

The IJNAF had been neutered both by the recent attacks on Rabaul and the devastating war of attrition that had taken place since the 1st Marine Division had set foot on Guadalcanal and seized the newly built airfield there. Furthermore, the intense carrier air battles of 1942 had also inflicted heavy casualties on the IJNAF, with the loss of experienced pilots and aircrew being particularly hard to make good. Sensing that the tide of war had very much turned in-theater, Adm Nimitz commented after the Rabaul strike on November 13 that, "Henceforth, we propose to give the Jap no rest."

The operational tempo was indeed increasing, and in November 1943 the US Navy suffered the loss of 73 aircraft in non-combat-related accidents from a fleet of 831 machines assigned to units in the Central Pacific. This statistic pointed to the simple fact that most pilots then in the Central Pacific Force lacked operational experience. Amphibious landings carried out by a large assault force against a well dug-in enemy combined with complex fleet operations involving multiple aircraft carriers was no simple task. Adm Nimitz stuck with the principle that the way to gain combat experience was through combat, and he wasted no time in ordering a series of fast carrier strikes on the Marshalls shortly after the fall of Tarawa and Makin.

In early December 1943 the combined Allied planners concluded that an air and sea blockade of Japan would be the ultimate objective of all operations in the Pacific. Both MacArthur's Southwest and Nimitz's Central Pacific Forces would continue advancing separately toward a common objective in the Formosa–Luzon–China region, where a major assault would take place in the spring of 1945.

Although it was realized that the IJN fleet had to be destroyed at an early date if a blockade was to be achieved, flexibility would be the keynote of Allied strategy, with an emphasis placed on the importance of additional aircraft carriers in-theater to allow the Pacific Fleet to carry out future operations against the enemy. The strategy also stressed that preparations be made to take all manner of "short cuts" in accordance with the developing situation in the frontline, and this would be facilitated by the mobility and striking power of the fast carriers.

Once northern Luzon, in the Philippines, had been seized, the indirect blockade of Japan would commence, for its raw materials passed by sea from the East Indies to Japan through the restrictive ocean passages of the region.

An adjustment in the Pacific War timetable called for the seizure of the Marshalls sometime in January 1944, which would then be followed by Ponape Island, near Truk, on May 1. Its capture would allow land-based aircraft from the island to then soften up the fortress at Truk. One month later, Nimitz would assist MacArthur in taking Hollandia, on the northern coast of New Guinea, and then the Central Pacific Force would attack Truk on July 20. Landings in the Marianas would commence on October 1, enabling Boeing B-29 Superfortress strikes from bases hurriedly built there by year-end.

With the Marshalls clearly in their sights, strategists were still pondering which of the islands to take first by early December 1943. Before *Galvanic*, the plan for Operation *Flintlock* outlined the seizure by the Central Pacific Force of the three Marshall Islands closest to Pearl Harbor – Kwajalein, Wotje and Maloelap. The remaining two key islands in the south, Mili and Jaluit, could be neutralized by air strikes.

The Marshall Islands (29 coral atolls and five islands) sit atop ancient, submerged volcanoes rising from the ocean floor, and they are made

The Cleveland-class light cruiser USS *Tallahassee* (CL-61), which subsequently became the Independence-class light carrier USS *Princeton* (CV-23), under construction at the New York Shipbuilding Corporation's yard in Camden, New Jersey, on July 1, 1941. (Naval History and Heritage Command)

Workmen bolt down main deck plating, prior to riveting, aft from frame 69 at the Camden shipyard on April 1, 1942. The vessel's name had been changed from *Tallahassee* to *Princeton* just 24 hours prior to this photograph being taken. (Naval History and Heritage Command)

Princeton being prepared for launching at the Camden shipyard on October 16, 1942. It slid down the slipway into the Delaware River two days later. (Naval History and Heritage Command)

The imposing stern section of *Princeton*, photographed at the Camden shipyard on October 16, 1942. Much of this area would be blown off on October 24, 1944. (Naval History and Heritage Command)

Princeton slides down the slipway into the Delaware River on October 18, 1942, its progress being watched by hundreds of workers in the Camden shipyard. (Naval History and Heritage Command)

The ship's sponsor, Margaret Dodds (wife of the president of Princeton University) with Lillian Brakeley and Rear Adm Milo F. Draemel, Commandant, Fourth Naval District, at *Princeton*'s launching on October 18, 1942. (Naval History and Heritage Command)

Adm Frederick C. Sherman and Rear Adms Harold M. Martin and George R. Henderson on board the Essex-class carrier USS *Princeton* (CV-37) in 1951 during the Korean War. Both Martin and Henderson had commanded light carriers in the Central Pacific in 1943–44, with Henderson being the first skipper of *Princeton*. (Naval History and Heritage Command)

Newly fitted out, *Princeton* sits anchored in the Delaware River off the Philadelphia Naval Shipyard on March 28, 1943. By then, the ship's initial complement of 450 sailors had been on board for a month following the carrier's commissioning on February 25. (Naval History and Heritage Command)

Princeton heads down the Delaware River during a test sailing from the Philadelphia Naval Shipyard in late March 1943. A series of underway trials without any aircraft embarked were completed by the carrier prior to it reporting for duty on May 18 and heading into Chesapeake Bay, bound for the Atlantic.
(Naval History and Heritage Command)

Underway during its shakedown cruise, *Princeton* prepares for the day's flight operations as the carrier heads for the Gulf of Paria, between Venezuela and Trinidad, on May 31, 1943. (Naval History and Heritage Command)

A stern-to-bow photograph of *Princeton* sailing down the eastern seaboard, bound for the Gulf of Paria. From this angle, the vessel's stern-mounted dual 20mm and single 40mm gun sponsons are clearly visible. (Naval History and Heritage Command)

A bow-to-stern photograph of *Princeton* on May 31, 1943. The three forward gun sponsons on the bow are clearly visible, as are nine SBD Dauntless dive-bombers and 12 F4F-4 Wildcats of CVLG-23 parked tightly aft.
(Naval History and Heritage Command)

Lt Cdr Henry L. Miller (seen here as a rear admiral post-war) "double hatted" as both the CAG of CVLG-23 and the CO of VF-23 in 1943–44. (Naval History and Heritage Command)

Adm Ernest J. King, Commander-in-Chief, United States Fleet and Chief of Naval Operations, implemented leadership principles that emphasized "tell your men what to do" not "how to do it." This bucked micromanagement and led to a superior US Navy that allowed King's subordinates freedom to take initiative. (Naval History and Heritage Command)

Rear Adm Charles A. Pownall, commander of TF 50, was plagued by irritability and indecision in the combat zone. He lost his command to Rear Adm Marc A. Mitscher in January 1944. (Naval History and Heritage Command)

CINCPACFLT Adm Chester W. Nimitz and Vice Adm William F. Halsey, then commander of TF 16, on board the seaplane tender, flagship and repair and supply vessel USS *Curtiss* (AV-4) during Nimitz's visit to Espiritu Santo on January 20, 1943. (Naval History and Heritage Command)

Vice Adm Halsey poses with his TF 16 staff on the bridge of USS *Enterprise* (CV-6) in early 1942. *Princeton*'s future commanding officer, Cdr (later Capt) William H. Buracker, is standing in the front row second from right, wearing a fur-collared flying jacket. (Naval History and Heritage Command)

Although not a Naval Aviator, Vice Adm Raymond A. Spruance took the reins of the Central Pacific Fleet (later redesignated Fifth Fleet) and implemented excellent planning and tactics that led to monumental victories at the battles of Midway and the Philippine Sea. He was clearly one of the US Navy's finest ever admirals.
(Naval History and Heritage Command)

The pilot of this F6F-3 Hellcat from VF-6, attached to *Princeton*'s CVLG-23, gets a late wave off on September 9, 1943. Twelve Naval Aviators, and their aircraft, from "Fighting Six" were briefly assigned to CVLG-23 in August–October 1943. (Tony Holmes Collection)

On September 3, 1943, VF-6 pilot Lt(jg) Thaddeus Coleman claimed only the second victory to fall to a fighter flying from *Princeton* when he and his wingman, Ens Edward Phillipe, downed an "Emily" flying boat. Coleman subsequently became a double ace and a Navy Cross recipient. (Tony Holmes Collection)

VF-23 registered its first victory on September 8, 1943 when future ace Lt Harold Funk (of VF-6) and Lt(jg) Leslie Kerr (of VF-23) downed another "Emily" while conducting the Baker Island raids. (Tony Holmes Collection)

Armorers prepare incendiary bombs for loading into the bomb-bays of TBM-1Cs tasked with attacking Tarawa in November 1943 in support of Operation *Galvanic*. VC/VT-23 dropped these weapons during missions flown from *Princeton* in 1943, as did VT-27 in 1944. (Tony Holmes Collection)

A TBM-1C lands back aboard a light carrier in 1943. Arguably the most versatile piston-engined bomber to ever fly from a flightdeck, the Avenger could carry four 500lb bombs or a single 2,000lb bomb, multiple incendiary bombs, a single aerial-launched Mk 13 torpedo or five-inch rockets. Typically, *Princeton* would embark nine Avengers when on operations in the Central Pacific. (Tony Holmes Collection)

The original print of this photograph, which shows *Princeton* at anchor off the Puget Sound Naval Shipyard in Bremerton, Washington state, on January 1, 1944, was annotated with the location of the vessel's various radar antennas.
(Naval History and Heritage Command)

Princeton steams at 20 knots off Seattle, Washington state, on January 3, 1944 after having had its shaft vibration issues rectified. The carrier set sail for Pearl Harbor, and TF 58, shortly after this photograph was taken. (Naval History and Heritage Command)

Lt Cdr Ernest W. Wood (seen here in his US Naval Academy graduation photograph from 1938) commanded CVLG-27 and VF-27 until he lost his life when his Hellcat suffered structural failure at the very start of the "Marianas Turkey Shoot" on June 19, 1944. (US Navy)

Lt Cdr Frederick A. Bardshar (also seen here in his US Naval Academy graduation photograph from 1938 – he was in the same class as Lt Cdr Wood at Annapolis) took command of CVLG-27 and VF-27 after Lt Cdr Wood's death. Bardshar ended the war as an eight-victory ace. (US Navy)

VF-27's pilot cadre pose with one of their uniquely marked F6F-3s while at Maui awaiting *Princeton*'s return to Pearl Harbor from Seattle. No fewer than 22 of these Naval Aviators would subsequently be credited with aerial victories (and seven of them achieved ace status) while assigned to the unit and embarked in *Princeton*. (Tony Holmes Collection)

Left Vice Adm Jisaburo Ozawa held several important commands at sea throughout the duration of World War II that included Southern Expeditionary Fleet, 3rd Fleet, 1st Mobile Fleet and Combined Fleet. He survived the war and died at the age of 80. (Tony Holmes Collection)

Below Vice Adm Marc A. Mitscher, Commander, TF 58, on board his flagship, USS *Lexington* (CV-16), at the time of the Marianas campaign in June 1944. (Naval History and Heritage Command)

Opposite Fifth Fleet vessels sit at anchor in Majuro Atoll in between operations in 1944. Visible, among many other ships, are three Independence-class light carriers (one of which is possibly *Princeton*), four Essex-class carriers, *Enterprise* (right front) and South Dakota- and Iowa-class battleships. (US Navy)

Left Armorers carefully load a Mk 13 torpedo into a TBM-1 – a dangerous, time-consuming and labor-intensive process. VT-27 never got the chance to drop torpedoes against enemy vessels while embarked in *Princeton*. (Tony Holmes Collection)

Below An F6F-5 Hellcat of VF-27 makes a heavy landing aboard *Princeton* shortly after the Marianas operation, the fighter's tail section having been detached from the rest of the aircraft when its tailhook caught one of the carrier's arrestor cables. (Tony Holmes Collection)

up of two island chains. To the east is Ratak (sunrise) and to the west is Ralik (sunset), with the atolls running parallel to each other in a northwest to southeast direction. The two chains cover approximately 180,000 square miles of the Pacific, with only a tiny fraction of that being land mass. Each chain includes 15 to 18 islands and atolls, making up roughly 70 square miles of land mass, with Kwajalein Island, in the western chain, being the largest area at just 6.3 square miles – it is in turn surrounded by one of the world's largest lagoons, which covers an area of 839 square miles.

Maj Gen Smith recommended that Wotje and Maloelap in the eastern chain be taken first, followed by Kwajalein to the west of those two. Fearing that an attack on three islands simultaneously would pose too great a risk, and with the casualties of Tarawa still fresh in their minds, Smith and Turner agreed that such an assault plan would not be prudent. If American forces were to capture only one of the initial three target islands, their lines of communication could be threatened by aircraft flying from enemy airfields on Jaluit and Mili to the south. Strategic reasoning dictated that complete bomber airfields had to be captured in order to allow the southern islands in the Marshalls to be neutralized by newly flown in land-based aircraft operating from the northern islands. This move required the capture of Wotje and Maloelap, for Kwajalein had no large bomber airfield.

The fast carriers in the Kwajalein strike enjoyed their first real flexibility since the beginning of the Gilberts operation as Spruance put TF 50 on the move. He ordered Pownall to leave two carriers (*Bunker Hill* and *Monterey*) under Sherman's control north of the Gilberts for "insurance," should the IJNAF launch a retaliatory attack, and take the rest around the Marshalls for a large-scale strike on Kwajalein as preparation for the upcoming amphibious landings.

The planning for these strikes had to be done on board ship, which aggravated the methodical and precise Spruance. Strategic planning had dictated that the Pacific Fleet would give its enemy no time to rest, and tactical initiative and operational flexibility would allow the fast carriers to range far and wide in the coming months.

The six-carrier striking force rendezvoused far to the east of the Marshalls on December 1, 1943, ready to undertake Pownall's mission of neutralizing enemy air power at Kwajalein and obtain photographs of the atoll for the landings there. Rear Adm Pownall commanded

TG 50.1 with *Yorktown*, *Lexington* and the light carrier *Cowpens*. TG 50.3, commanded by Rear Adm Montgomery with *Essex*, *Enterprise* and the light carrier *Belleau Wood*, rounded out TF 50. The task force would be accompanied by five heavy cruisers, two light cruisers and two light antiaircraft cruisers, plus destroyers. The combined force fielded 386 aircraft in total, consisting of 193 Hellcats, 104 Dauntlesses and 89 Avengers. Carrier air groups had recently been altered on the Essex-class carriers to give them more fighters – 38 in total – while reducing the number of dive-bombers embarked to 28.

At 0600 hrs on December 4 – the day before *Princeton* would begin its journey back to Pearl Harbor – TF 50 commenced launching aircraft from the northeast, with an estimated time over target of 0750 hrs. The attack surprised the Japanese, who were accustomed to strikes from the south, and from that point on a succession of errors due to a lack of aggressive leadership and initiative plagued Pownall.

Strikes were planned at Roi, on the north side of the atoll, and Kwajalein Island, at the southeastern tip, instigating a response from the IJNAF in the form of 50 fighters, plus heavy antiaircraft fire over the target. The strike on Roi by *Essex* and *Lexington* aircraft did not go smoothly due to weak intelligence concerning the target and communication issues between aircrew. Although little damage was inflicted on key targets when just 12 fighters descended for strafing passes, Hellcats and Dauntlesses involved in the attack were credited with downing 18 IJNAF fighters and ten bombers in aerial combat.

Concurrently, *Enterprise* and *Yorktown* attacked the principal IJN naval and submarine base on Kwajalein, along with roughly 30 vessels in the atoll. Supply ships were sunk, along with damage done to a light cruiser, and 18 floatplanes were also destroyed. In summary, the strikes on Roi and Kwajalein resulted in the destruction of approximately 55 IJNAF aircraft, in exchange for five fighters and bombers shot down and several more damaged beyond repair. Most of the Japanese merchant ships, all the naval vessels and 30 to 40 "Betty" bombers on the airfield at Roi escaped destruction.

The land-based twin-engined G4M "Betty" had an extraordinary range of 3,000 miles – twice that of any American carrier-based aircraft. Capable of carrying bombs or torpedoes, it had been a thorn in the US Navy's side since the start of the war. The IJNAF's go-to aircraft for night torpedo attacks, it had frequently targeted warships of the Pacific Fleet.

The fast carrier strike plan called for a second wave of aircraft to be launched at 1200 hrs, and the senior Naval Aviators involved expected this attack to destroy the IJNAF bombers at Roi. However, Pownall, ever cautious, decided to withdraw. Concerned that the fully alerted IJNAF posed a threat to his carriers, the rear admiral had no desire to remain in the waters surrounding the Marshalls any longer. On board *Yorktown* (the force flagship), the carrier's CO, Capt Joseph J. "Jocko" Clark, and the squadron commanders of CVG-5 pleaded with Pownall to launch a second strike, but he refused.

Although the enemy did indeed respond to the raid, the attack consisted of just three elderly "Kate" torpedo-bombers from Roi or Maloelap that targeted *Lexington* and were quickly shot down by antiaircraft fire. At 1248 hrs, as *Yorktown* was launching a strike on Wotje Island in the southern Marshalls, four more "Kates" penetrated fighter CAP and attempted to attack the carrier. Three were shot down and the fourth escaped.

After recovering the Wotje strike, TF 50 headed for friendly waters, although heavy seas slowed the retreat. Cruising at 18 knots, the task force braced for a night attack, and shortly after 2000 hrs it came. Under a bright moon, 40 to 50 "Bettys," guided by a lone reconnaissance aircraft that had been shadowing the task force, struck. The two task groups separated, with Pownall relying on independent evasive ship maneuvers and antiaircraft fire to evade an erratic attack. This close shave prompted *Yorktown*'s Capt Clark to boldly holler "Goddammit, you can't run away from airplanes with ships!" while fleeing Wotje at maximum speed.

At 2330 hrs, parachute flares silhouetted *Lexington*, and ten minutes later the carrier was struck by a torpedo near its stern on the starboard side. The resulting explosion destroyed its steering engine and jammed the rudder hard left. Settling five feet by the stern, *Lexington* began circling to port as dense clouds of smoke poured from ruptured tanks aft. Damage control personnel went to work and were able to center the rudder, which enabled *Lexington* to steer with its engines, while fighting off more attacks. The last "Bettys" were repulsed by a combination of antiaircraft fire and a darkening sky as the moon set at around 0130 hrs on December 5, allowing the remaining vessels of TF 50 to withdraw undamaged.

An emergency hand-operated steering unit was quickly devised on board *Lexington*, and the carrier made it to Pearl Harbor for emergency repairs a few days before *Princeton*'s return from Washington state in early December 1943. The damaged Essex-class vessel would then sail for Bremerton, just as *Princeton* had done, to undergo extensive repairs.

Rear Adm Pownall's career had also been seriously damaged. Previously, the US Navy's carrier doctrine had been based on "hit and run" tactics, with the thought of trading blows with a land-based air threat being considered a bad idea. However, as he retreated, Pownall found himself dead center of a paradigm shift. As was shown at Rabaul, the Fast Carrier Task Force had the capability to fend off attacks from shore-based aircraft through a combination of superior fighters and lethal antiaircraft batteries on board its ships. Despite the latter, Pownall was worried about his lack of night intercept capability, which convinced him to withdraw when he did in the ultimately forlorn hope his carriers could outrun such attacks.

Pownall had completed only part of his mission with the destruction of some enemy aircraft, the sinking of a few merchant ships and photographic coverage of Kwajalein. He had failed to neutralize *all* IJNAF aircraft in the Marshalls – specifically the 40-plus "Betty" bombers at Roi, which naval intelligence soon reported had been withdrawn to Nauru, southwest of the Marshalls. Leaving the torpedo-bomber force unscathed meant Pownall had placed his carriers in serious jeopardy, and the IJNAF duly targeted the vessels at night in Japanese-held waters. The fact that TF 50 escaped intact was the direct result of the maneuvering skill of Pownall and his ships' captains and superb gunnery by antiaircraft battery crews.

The fleet that had attacked Kwajalein went into battle with a combined force of 386 aircraft, 193 of them Hellcats. Additionally, the antiaircraft weapons on board TF 50's cruisers had proven themselves time and again in recent engagements with Japanese aircraft.

Rear Adm Charles A. "Baldy" Pownall's lack of aggression on December 4, 1943 and occasional nervousness and skittish behavior during combat operations prior to this date landed him a desk job at Pearl Harbor for the duration of the war.

The Kwajalein attack was not a total bust, for crews captured some quality photographs of the eventual objectives for *Flintlock*. When sifting through the many images provided to them, photo interpreters were able to discover a nearly completed bomber runway.

WHERE TO INVADE?

The invasion of the Marshalls would be a true test of Adm Nimitz's leadership, with a number of senior planners urging caution due to the heavy losses suffered at Tarawa and Makin. The fallout from *Galvanic* influenced the decision as to which atolls in the Marshalls would be captured first. The islands of obvious importance were the ones that boasted airfields. An atoll had to be large enough, flat enough and oriented to the prevailing east–west winds to be deemed suitable to house a runway. It was these islands that were occupied by the Japanese, rapidly developed into operational military bases that included airstrips and then fought over once the Pacific Fleet launched its war-winning offensive.

The US Navy planners now had to choose which one of these islands to invade first – whether to take a bold step and invade Kwajalein directly or take a stepping-stone approach and hit one or more of the islands in the southern Marshalls first. With the latter tactic, there were several options that could be targeted including Wotje, Maloelap or Jaluit, all of which had airfields and, like Kwajalein, were heavily defended.

As part of his new role as Nimitz's deputy chief of staff, Rear Adm Sherman headed up mission planning for CINCPACFLT. He immediately suggested a direct assault on Kwajalein, bypassing Wotje and Maloelap. The amphibious commanders, led by Spruance, objected. Kwajalein, they asserted, was encircled by airfields at Wotje and Maloelap to the east and at Mili and Jaluit to the south. These airfields would allow attacking aircraft to quickly stage in from Japan through Eniwetok to the west. The amphibious commanders could not forget the horrors of Marshall-based night air attacks off the Gilberts, which had come from only one direction. After Kwajalein was occupied, the invading troops would be virtually surrounded.

The November strikes against Rabaul and the undisputed command of the air during *Galvanic* gave Nimitz all the confidence he needed to bypass all the Marshall Islands but Kwajalein, and he wasted no time. Calling together his top commanders two weeks before Christmas, he opened the floor for discussion. Spruance argued strenuously for landings at Wotje and Maloelap, which would keep Hawaii at his back and ensure secure lines of communication. Rear Adm Turner and Maj

Gen Smith wholeheartedly agreed. After each man had finished with his opinion, Nimitz boldly announced, "Well, gentlemen, we are going to Kwajalein." Spruance and Turner stayed behind after the meeting and continued to plead with Nimitz, stating that going directly to Kwajalein was "dangerous and reckless" to the point that Nimitz resorted to threatening them with their jobs, and told them that if they did not want to do it, he would find someone else who would.

The Joint Chiefs of Staff quickly approved Nimitz's decision, and on December 14 *Flintlock*'s aim was changed to the capture of Kwajalein only. Twelve days later, Spruance asked and obtained permission to include the seizure of Majuro Atoll, with its fine anchorage between Maloelap and Mili, as part of the operation.

Spruance and Turner had routinely defaulted toward caution prior to *Galvanic*, and Nimitz concurred with the overall strategy of placing the carriers in a defensive role. Now, the persuasive Sherman had Nimitz's ear, and as he listened to the intellectual young Naval Aviator he fully realized that the carrier task forces had developed into powerful, offensive weapons. Air power would neutralize all the islands around Kwajalein. Additionally, Hoover's land-based aircraft from the Gilberts and later from Kwajalein itself could bomb them regularly, while the growing Fast Carrier Task Force would eliminate fresh threats from Truk, the Marianas or Japan.

The assault on Kwajalein from both ends of the atoll would require the fielding of two infantry divisions. However, there were not enough transport vessels available to carry them, resulting in two delays until a final invasion date was set – January 31, 1944. While this did give the IJN time to reinforce and improve upon its positions in the Marshalls, what the troops on Kwajalein were not aware of was the fact that they were on their own. The Japanese Imperial General Headquarters had given up on trying to defend the outer ring of islands in the Pacific, which included the Gilberts, Marshalls, Solomons and eastern Carolines, which included Truk. Tokyo was now focused on the inner ring of islands much closer to home that included the Marianas, the western Carolines and the western end of New Guinea.

While *Princeton* was fighting through rough seas in early January en route to Hawaii, the picture changed completely on the 5th of the month with the arrival of Rear Adm Marc "Pete" Mitscher at Pearl Harbor. He relieved Pownall that morning, and the following day the fast carriers were designated TF 58, with Mitscher in command. By war's end, he had been engaged in every major naval battle in the Pacific Ocean during World War II with the exception of the Battle of the Coral Sea.

Considered a brilliant tactician, Mitscher would introduce or support most of the revolutionary new operating procedures and tactics used by the Fast Carrier Task Force in its drive toward Japan. Unlike some of his peers, and very much like Spruance, he would shun the spotlight and avoid speeches at all costs. To some, he appeared remote and hard to understand, but to those who served under him, Mitscher was truly a fighting admiral with courage, skill and, most importantly, human understanding.

Down to 115lbs in weight and still recovering from malaria acquired in the South Pacific, Mitscher hoisted his flag on board *Yorktown* as Commander, TF 58. An early Naval Aviator, he had been captain of the old *Hornet* during the Doolittle Raid in April 1942 and at the Battle of Midway two months later. After the loss of *Hornet* at the Battle of the Santa Cruz Islands, Mitscher took over as Halsey's land-based air commander in the Solomons. He was very much welcomed at the helm of TF 58.

After returning to Hawaii, *Princeton*'s first order of business was a two-day joint operation with sister ship *Langley*, whose key officers had been counselled and trained by "Sweet P's" counterparts before it had left Philadelphia for the Pacific six months earlier. The operational plan for this event had two objectives – give both crews the opportunity to practice working as a team and to deck qualify new pilots. On January 11, one of *Princeton*'s torpedo-bombers (now flying with the redesignated VT-23), flown by Ens Elwyn P. Eubank, struck the carrier's mast in taking a wave-off from the LSO. Eubank was lost when the Avenger crashed into the sea, but the two crewmen on board the aircraft managed to escape the sinking TBF and were rescued.

TF 58 sortied from Pearl Harbor on January 19 in support of Central Pacific Force operations in the Marshalls, and its departure marked the last time the fast carriers would operate from Hawaii – it had now become a rear area base. Mitscher commanded 12 fast carriers embarking 650 aircraft, with eight fast battleships, cruisers and destroyers adding to the muscle. As a part of TF 58, *Princeton* was operating with TG 58.4, commanded by former *Enterprise* CO Rear Adm Samuel P. Ginder.

This task group alone boasted an impressive array of warships. In addition to *Princeton*, the roster included *Saratoga*, *Langley* and the Baltimore-class heavy cruisers USS *Baltimore* (CA-68), USS *Boston* (CA-69) and USS *Canberra* (CA-70), along with an array of destroyers. These vessels were assigned the job of protecting the northern flank of the main task force by neutralizing enemy airfields at Wotje and Taroa while US troops carried out amphibious landings at Kwajalein and Majuro.

Although the overall command of Operation *Flintlock* rested with Adm Nimitz, CINCPACFLT, the operation would be executed by Vice Adm Spruance embarked in the heavy cruiser *Indianapolis*. Rear Adm Turner would lead TF 51 – the Joint Expeditionary Force – embarked in Appalachian-class command ship USS *Rocky Mount* (AGC-3), and TF 56 was led by the Commander, Expeditionary Troops, Maj Gen Smith. *Rocky Mount* was a new type of specially configured amphibious command, control and communications vessel based on USS *Ancon* (AGC-4), which had been successfully employed in Mediterranean operations from September 1943.

TF 56 consisted of 297 ships, its transport vessels carrying 54,000 assault troops from the US Marine Corps and the US Army. Designated the Southern Attack Force, TF 56 would land the US Army's 7th Infantry Division (TG 56.1), under the command of Maj Gen Charles Corlett, on the island of Kwajalein at the southern end of Kwajalein Atoll.

TF 53, led by Rear Adm Richard L. Conolly, embarked in Appalachian-class command ship USS *Appalachian* (AGC-1), would land Maj Gen Harry Schmidt's 4th Marine Division on the islands of Roi–Namur, the two joined by a small sand spit and a causeway, at the northern end of Kwajalein Atoll.

Majuro was to be attacked by the Majuro Attack Group (TG 51.2), under Rear Adm Hill, with the Majuro Landing Force consisting of the US Army's 2nd Battalion, 106th Infantry led by Lt Col Frederick B. Sheldon. TG 51.1, with the 22nd Marine Regiment embarked under the command of Capt D. W. Loomis, was the designated reserve force.

The campaign to seize Kwajalein began on January 29 when TF 58 made its run into the waters surrounding the Marshalls. Sixteen Hellcats launched from *Princeton* at dawn to participate in the first of three bombing and strafing attacks on Wotje that day, D-Day Minus Two. The four task groups had different targets, with TG 58.1 (*Enterprise*,

Yorktown and *Belleau Wood*) and TG 58.4 (*Saratoga, Langley* and *Princeton*) attacking Taroa, Maloelap Atoll's largest island, and Wotje to neutralize the dangerous airfields there. TG 58.2 (*Essex, Intrepid* and *Cabot*) targeted Roi–Namur, where the IJNAF still had 92 aircraft, and TG 58.3 (*Bunker Hill, Cowpens* and *Monterey*) attacked Kwajalein Island itself. Antiaircraft fire was not as heavy as had been anticipated, and it became even lighter after the first mission. In between the bombing and strafing sorties, VF-23 provided CAP for the task group, although no enemy aircraft appeared to challenge them.

The following morning (January 30), *Princeton*'s crew had a hearty "battle breakfast" of steak, eggs, fruit and coffee and commenced launching aircraft at 0545 hrs to revisit Wotje and Taroa, with an emphasis placed on Japanese installations on the latter atoll. Before the day had ended, *Princeton*'s pilots had flown six missions over Wotje airfield and four strikes on Taroa to ensure no enemy aircraft could pose a threat to the fleet. One four-aircraft division from VF-23, on the last flight of the afternoon, provided spotting guidance for the three Baltimore-class heavy cruisers while they shelled Taroa.

As the landings on Kwajalein were being carried out on January 31, air strikes raked both Wotje and Taroa in coordination with intense surface bombardment by the heavy cruisers. CVLG-23 CAG Lt Cdr Miller, who spotted for the warships during his final mission of the day, brought back reports that both Wotje and Taroa were "a shambles."

Sadly, on this day CVLG-23 lost one of its senior pilots, Lt(jg) William G. Buckalew, during an attack on Wotje. According to CAG Miller:

> Lt.(jg) Buckalew, while carrying out daring strafing runs against an enemy gun emplacement he had spotted, was struck by antiaircraft fire which disabled his plane and forced him to make a water landing. Buck, himself, apparently was not hit. He told his wingman by radio that he planned to ditch his plane. When he landed, the Hellcat disappeared almost immediately and for some reason Buck wasn't able to get out. Our planes circled the area for as long as possible, but without success.

Buckalew made his water landing approximately ten miles east of Wotje, and several Hellcats and Avengers circled anxiously over the crash site waiting for him to surface. Seeing no sign of him, and eventually running short of fuel, they had to return to the carrier.

After a day of refueling at sea, which gave the pilots a chance to catch up on some much-needed sleep, the task group headed for Eniwetok, the westernmost atoll in the Marshall Islands. During the first three days of February, the carrier air groups from Sherman's TG 58.3 attacked IJNAF aircraft and airfields on Eniwetok Atoll's Engebi Island. Additional landings had also taken place on Kwajalein, Namur and Roi on February 1.

In a brief shift in assignments, aircraft from *Princeton* had photographed the next assault target, Eniwetok, on February 2. The following day, CVLG-23 had also commenced three days of attacks on the airfields on Engebi. CAG Miller subsequently noted:

> There were no enemy planes in the air [over Engebi], so a systematic destruction of their airfield was carried out. Sorties were conducted every day. The antiaircraft fire was reduced to nothing and, as a matter of fact, the torpedo planes were taking passengers, in the form of non-flying personnel, toward the end to watch the bombing and get a look at an enemy target under attack.

Although enemy resistance to aerial attacks on Engebi had totally collapsed by February 5, the dangers of carrier operations remained ever present. At 0945 hrs that day, a Hellcat flown by Ens Boyd attempted to land aboard *Princeton*'s pitching flightdeck. The aircraft bounced over the crash barriers as the tailhook cleared them by about 6in. Boyd gave his aircraft full throttle, allowing it to clear three other fighters parked at the forward end of the flightdeck. One of the Hellcats had just taxied toward the ship's bow after landing, and its turning propeller cut the tailhook off Boyd's fighter as it passed overhead. Managing to keep his aircraft airborne, Boyd gained altitude, dropped the Hellcat's belly tank and expended all of its ammunition prior to making a successful barrier crash-landing aboard *Saratoga*.

By February 7, US Army and US Marine Corps forces had come ashore on 30 different islets surrounding Kwajalein Atoll's huge lagoon. The landings had been a resounding success, demonstrating the flexibility of American armed forces in joint operations. Aside from the rapid introduction of new warships to the Pacific Theater, the US

Navy's command and control of these vessels was also clearly maturing. From January 31 to February 3, the aircraft involved in the Kwajalein campaign had taken directions from air support commanders on board command ships offshore to ensure the enemy's defensive positions were effectively attacked in a timely manner. The innovative employment of such vessels had worked as planned, contributing a great deal to *Flintlock*'s overwhelming success.

As previously noted, Mitscher's TF 58 had commenced attacking IJNAF airfields and installations in the Marshalls on January 29. Unlike on the December 4 raids, the squadrons involved in *Flintlock* had access to more detailed photo intelligence and received guidance from precise strike plans. This in turn made them far more effective when it came to knocking out both the airfields and their aircraft. When the air strikes began on January 29, the IJNAF had an estimated 150 operational aircraft in the Marshalls. Within 48 hours there were none left. The last enemy fighter seen in the skies over Kwajalein Atoll had been shot down 20 miles northeast of Taroa at 1130 hrs on the 30th.

Japanese shipping also took a beating, with all vessels found in the lagoon being either sunk or heavily damaged. No major warships were destroyed, however, as they had all departed prior to TF 58's arrival. Such was the superiority of the Central Pacific Force involved, not a single US Navy vessel was attacked from the air during the week-long campaign in the Marshalls. The numbers in respect to carrier air group operations speak for themselves. TF 58 flew more than 6,200 sorties, with 4,021 seeing aircraft directly over the target. US Navy aircraft losses totaled 17 Hellcats and five Avengers to enemy fire and ten Hellcats, 14 Avengers and three Helldivers to operational accidents. The task force had 24 pilots and 24 aircrew killed.

Remembering what *I-175* had done during *Galvanic*, the Central Pacific Force was determined not to let IJN submarines get anywhere near the fleet. Proving to be equally as effective as TF 58's carrier air groups, submarine-hunting destroyers sunk four Japanese vessels throughout the operation. One of them was *I-175*, which was attacked 120 miles northwest of Jaluit Atoll on the night of February 4.

Incorporating another "lesson learned" from Tarawa, at daybreak on February 1, prior to the landings on Kwajalein, the battleship bombardment had been lifted long enough for a reconnaissance by underwater demolition teams led by Lt Cdr John Koehler. They quickly confirmed that the landing beaches were clear of obstacles.

With Engebi now "out of business," *Princeton* and its task group steamed to the newly captured base at Roi on February 7 for some time off. The waters off Roi Island, part of the Kwajalein Atoll, had been turned into a mammoth US Navy anchorage and staging area literally overnight. "As we approached," recalled CAG Miller, "we could see many ships in the lagoon. They were of all types and sizes. As we drew closer to shore, we also spotted evidence of our landings, with the remains of our tanks and landing craft, as well as destroyed enemy gun emplacements. Marines were everywhere, souvenir hunting."

At Roi, three members of CVLG-23 were given permission to go ashore to look over the badly damaged Japanese fortifications. The trio consisted of Lt C. C. Schmidt and Lt(jg)s Kerr and Crockett, the latter being the VF-23 pilot who had bravely defended Cdr Caldwell during the Rabaul strikes, downing an enemy aircraft in the process. CAG Miller recalled:

> They came back loaded with souvenirs and colossal stories. It seems the Marines had cornered the market on Japanese property, and demanded terrific exchanges for a flag or sword. What the Marines wanted most of all was one of our .45-caliber revolvers. For that you could get a Japanese sword. Next on their list was whiskey. For a bottle you could get practically anything they had. Money meant absolutely nothing in that marketplace.

While there at Roi, *Princeton* underwent a change of command. Capt Henderson, who had been in charge of the carrier since its commissioning, was relieved by Capt William H. Buracker, who had been on board the vessel during the Marshall Islands operation observing and preparing to take over. Henderson, who had started his US Navy career as an enlisted man, was promoted to the rank of commodore. He was very well-liked among *Princeton*'s crew, as noted by the ship's navigation officer, Lt Vic Moitoret:

> When Hank Miller flew aboard with Air Group 23, he came up to the bridge to chat with the skipper. He began by apologizing for the fact that some of his fliers didn't have a full bag of uniforms, and

that for lack of laundry or dry-cleaning at the Parris Island Marine base, the uniforms they did have might not pass Captain's inspection. Henderson smiled and said, "Hank, I expect you and your boys to do a helluva lot of flying aboard this ship, and I am not going to be too much concerned about how your uniforms look."

Capt Buracker relieved Henderson of command of *Princeton* on February 7, 1944. He had graduated from the Naval Academy in June 1919 and served successfully in a number of ships, and completed shore assignments, during the interwar period. As war clouds loomed in Europe, Buracker was serving on board *Enterprise*, first as the carrier's navigator (June 1939–June 1940) and then as Vice Adm Halsey's tactics officer until July 1941. Following that assignment, he became the admiral's operations officer through to July 1942. Buracker then participated in the early carrier raids against the enemy-held mandated Pacific Islands, the Doolittle Raid on the Japanese home islands and the Battle of Midway, receiving the Silver Star for his "conspicuous gallantry and intrepidity" during those battles.

ENIWETOK

Surprised by the overwhelming victory at Kwajalein, Vice Adm Spruance and Rear Adm Turner quickly began lobbying Adm Nimitz for a follow-up landing at Eniwetok before the enemy could send in reinforcements.

Like Kwajalein, Eniwetok is an atoll in the Marshalls that consists of a number of small, low-lying islands ringing a central lagoon about 50 miles in circumference. Part of the Ralik chain of atolls, it lies 325 miles west-northwest of Kwajalein and 1,000 miles east of the Marianas. At the northern end lay Engebi Island, which housed an airfield, and at the southern end was Eniwetok. There were only two passages into the lagoon, with one of them being the "wide passage" at the southern end that featured significant shoals and, as it turned out, mines – the first minefield to be discovered in the Marshalls, its detection being thanks to IJN charts inadvertently captured at Kwajalein.

While conducting landing operations on one of the many smaller islands during *Flintlock*, US Army troops were set down on the wrong island. The snafu put aside, the soldiers ventured into a beached IJN vessel and found a trove of 75 secret charts and maps of lagoons and harbors across the Pacific. This valuable information quickly made its way to naval intelligence personnel, and it paid immediate dividends with the discovery of the minefield.

Spruance and Turner planned to use the 8,000-man Marine reserve force that had not been needed for the Kwajalein assault and was still afloat to seize Eniwetok. Designated Operation *Catchpole*, the plan was quickly approved and D-Day pushed up to February 17, as opposed to the original date of May 1. Through the interception of coded messages from the Imperial General Headquarters to various outposts in the Central Pacific, glaring weakness in the vicinity of the Gilberts and Marshalls had been revealed following Japan's change of strategy that the Americans had previously been unaware of. The Allies' original timetable had called for the capture of Kavieng and then the encirclement of Rabaul as part of the South Pacific campaign. Reacting to the Central Pacific Force's overwhelming success in the Marshalls, Spruance preferred to move immediately against Eniwetok, as it was closer to Kwajalein and had a good airfield.

Rabaul was currently being encircled by Halsey's South Pacific forces, even though Japan continued to bolster its defenses. At about the same time that *Flintlock* was commencing, aircraft of the IJN's 2nd Carrier Division had arrived there, only to be subsequently destroyed by overwhelming Allied air power. The annihilation of the IJNAF's fighters and dive- and torpedo-bombers in the South Pacific convinced Allied planners that Halsey had sealed the fate of Rabaul, whose focus then turned to Truk. The Pacific War timetable had originally called for the invasion and occupation of the Marshalls *after* Truk had been attacked on July 20, 1944. However, Adm Nimitz agreed to swiftly move against Eniwetok as soon as Kwajalein had fallen. He also contemplated a carrier strike on Truk in the hope of provoking a decisive fleet engagement with the IJN.

The original date for capturing Eniwetok Atoll had been May 1, 1944, with Truk not to be targeted by an air raid before late March. Kwajalein had changed all that, with Spruance taking Nimitz's proposal to his amphibious commanders, Turner and Smith. Turner endorsed the idea immediately, while Smith produced an operational plan that he had already drawn up in case of such rapid strategic change. As for TF 58 hitting Truk early too, Mitscher was totally in agreement. Spruance duly received Nimitz's approval to attack Eniwetok and Truk on February 10.

The Eniwetok Expeditionary Group (TG 51.11) was commanded by Rear Adm Hill, embarked in the Bayfield-class transport USS *Cambria* (APA-36) which had been fitted with additional communications equipment to also serve as a flagship. The primary component of the force was the nine transports of the former Kwajalein Reserve Force, commanded by Capt Loomis, embarked in the attack transport USS *Leonard Wood* (APA-12). The 22nd Marine Regiment was embarked in five of the transports, while two battalions of the 106th Regimental Combat Team of the US Army's 27th Infantry Division were embarked in four other vessels. They were then accompanied by three old battleships making up the fire support group, along with three heavy cruisers and 15 destroyers. CAS was provided by TG 53.6's Sangamon-class escort carriers USS *Sangamon* (CVE-26), USS *Suwannee* (CVE-27) and USS *Chenango* (CVE-28), with three escorting destroyers of their own.

TF 58 sortied from Majuro on February 12–13, 1944, having been ordered to undertake the largest independent carrier strike of the Pacific War to date. Nine carriers set sail, these being split between TGs 58.1, 58.2 and 58.3. To reduce the ability of the IJN's powerful Combined Fleet to interfere with the landings in the Marshalls, these three task groups would strike Truk while Rear Adm Ginder's TG 58.4 covered the Eniwetok landings, scheduled for February 17.

Princeton weighed anchor and put out to sea from Roi on February 15 in support of Operation *Flintlock*, CVLG-23's two squadrons being manned by 25 Hellcat pilots and 12 Avenger pilots. On February 16–17, aircraft from TG 58.4's carriers (*Saratoga*, *Princeton* and *Langley*), along with F6Fs and TBFs from the three "baby" flattops of TG 53.6 supported landings on Eniwetok and Parry Islands. Six divisions of Hellcats from the carriers strafed enemy trenches on Engebi, at the northern end of the atoll, on the 16th, along with piers and more trenches on Eniwetok. Tanks and fighting positions were struck on Parry Island, and military facilities set on fire on Japtan Island as well. A total of 16 Avengers flew strikes that dropped 124 100lb bombs on trenches and foxholes on Engebi and 36 100lb bombs on similar targets across Eniwetok.

While carrying out strike 1A, Ens Cox of VF-23 was struck in the lower jaw by a single bullet as he pulled up over Engebi following a strafing run. Despite losing a considerable amount of blood, he brought his fighter back to *Princeton* and landed safely. In another incident that culminated in a water landing, Lt(jg) G. W. Spear of VT-23 suffered engine problems with his Avenger while acting as the air coordinator on an afternoon strike on February 20. Not having enough power to return to the ship, and noticing that the runway on Engebi appeared to be too badly damaged to risk a landing, he chose to set the torpedo-bomber down in the water close to the Fletcher-class destroyer USS *Hazelwood* (DD-531). The destroyer lowered a boat and rescued the three-man crew.

By this point in the war, VF-23 was starting to feel the effects of prolonged operations and the wear and tear of continuous flight time. On more than one occasion, the squadron flew 12-aircraft patrols followed, after a brief period, by another 12-aircraft patrol. Of course all of these flights ended with a landing on a small carrier flightdeck. Pilots were flying 11-plus hours a day with very little rest between sorties, and it contributed greatly to their lack of motivation and growing fatigue.

CAG Miller was quite critical of his younger pilots, commenting on the morale of his men in a separate report on the strikes against Eniwetok:

> The older pilots, and those with experience always had to substitute for the youth and inexperienced who cracked first when the going got tough. This refutes the theory which is advocated by a great many that all one needs in this fighting game is a youngster with spirit and enthusiasm. Combat flying requires the same amount of experience and common sense as a professional ball club. The pilot who is matured and has the will to win always holds up where youth and enthusiasm fail.

Mitscher was not pleased with Ginder's handling of TG 58.4 during the Eniwetok landings, and he left the Task Group behind while the rest of TF 58 headed for Truk and then an initial raid on the Marianas. Everything "rolls downhill," and that could possibly explain the hammering received by CVLG-23's nuggets from Lt Cdr Miller.

Fatigue and weariness could be expected as *Princeton*'s Hellcats and Avengers flew 118 sorties from the carrier's flightdeck, dropping 23 tons of bombs and expending 13,000 rounds of machine-gun ammunition in strafing attacks that contributed to very successful amphibious landings and a quick seizure of the Marshalls. CVLG-23 had supported the 22nd Marine Regiment and the 106th Regimental Combat Team as they came ashore on the first atoll at Eniwetok on February 17 and pushed across the islets until Japanese resistance ceased five days later. The carriers stood by until February 28.

Flintlock and *Catchpole* went very well for the American forces, with no enemy surface vessels, submarines or aircraft opposing the landings on Eniwetok, while air strikes by Seventh Air Force heavy bombers flying from Tarawa, some 900 miles to the southeast, contributed a great deal as well. The United States was now firmly in control of the Marshalls with the capture of Majuro, Kwajalein and Eniwetok – key islands that would ensure further advances across the Central Pacific. The islands of Jaluit, Mili, Maloelap, Wotje and Nauru were bypassed, along with the destruction of their aircraft and airfields. Unable to be resupplied with men and materiel due to their remote locations, they were left to simply "wither on the vine," with what was left there being regularly bombed by carrier air groups using them for target practice.

At the same time that the assault of Eniwetok was underway on February 17, TF 58 was striking the "Gibraltar of the Pacific" at Truk in Operation *Hailstone*, thus ensuring that no Japanese forces from there could threaten the Eniwetok landings or the other islands that had just been seized. Truk was on the receiving end of two days of continuous carrier air strikes from TF 58, and the devastating attack was a huge blow to Japanese morale. Allied commanders had not yet decided whether Truk would need to be invaded or bypassed at that point, and it was not until March 12, 1944 that Adm Nimitz chose the latter option. Truk would also "wither on the vine" along with the other islands recently deemed not worthy of fighting over.

Mitscher and TF 58 did not stop after their strikes on Truk. On the night of February 21–22, while en route to start preliminary strikes in the Marianas, the task force was spotted by a "Betty" bomber. Undeterred, Mitscher simply stated that "we'll fight our way in." Strikes were launched from 100 miles east of Saipan and Tinian before dawn, with the Hellcats shooting down most of the 74 IJNAF aircraft scrambled to intercept them. TF 58 then retired to Majuro on February 22.

Of the Marshalls campaign and the raid on Truk, naval historian Rear Adm Samuel Eliot Morrison would write:

> Courage and determination the Navy had shown from the first, but in the Marshalls, it demonstrated mastery of the art of amphibious warfare; of combining air, surface, submarine, and ground forces

to project fighting power irresistibly across the seas. The strike on Truk demonstrated a virtual revolution in naval warfare; the aircraft carrier emerged as the capital ship of the future, with unlimited potentialities.

MILESTONES

Princeton marked the first anniversary of its commissioning (February 25, 1944) by recording that the vessel had steamed 70,701 miles during the first year of service and launched 44 air strikes that had dropped 440,000lbs of bombs and torpedoes on the enemy. The carrier remained on station in the Marshalls until February 28, then was relieved and sent back to the newly established naval base at Majuro.

The ship's crew enjoyed a long overdue shore liberty at Majuro from March 1–16, receiving its first mail in more than six weeks. "There were 339 sacks for *Princeton*," Lt Cdr Miller recalled. "Little by little it arrived. The packages were in terrible condition, especially if they contained cakes or candy. No first-class mail was included, which meant no letters."

While the carrier was being refueled, rearmed and resupplied, the crew and personnel from CVLG-23 enjoyed a few hours of sun-bathing, athletics and letter writing while off-duty. A Catholic chaplin from another carrier came aboard and conducted services that included memorials to the pilots lost in action. Each evening, the carriers would leave the lagoon to prevent enemy submarines or aerial "snoopers" from catching them helpless at anchor. *Princeton* then sailed to Espiritu Santo to replenish and undertake carrier qualification landings for CVLG-23.

During early March a powerful US Navy force was mustered. The combined Allied seaborne and amphibious strength had been "consuming" enemy-held islands at a rapid pace in a relentless move west across the Pacific. It was now time for these vessels, which formed TF 58, to head north toward the core of the Japanese Empire.

After the shift was made from Majuro to Espiritu Santo in early March, *Princeton* had 29 Hellcat and 16 Avenger pilots embarked. Eleven F6F-3s and eight TBM-1Cs were flown in from Luganville Field on Espiritu Santo, raising the number of aircraft embarked as part of CVLG-23 to 25 Hellcats and nine Avengers.

On March 23 the carrier sailed as part of TG 58.3, with instructions to attack enemy installations and shipping in the Palau archipelago and at Ulithi, Woleai and Yap in the western Carolines. The task group also included the carriers *Yorktown*, *Lexington* and *Langley*, the heavy cruisers USS *Louisville* (CA-28), USS *Portland* (CA-33), *Indianapolis* and *San Juan* and 16 destroyers. For the Palau strike, Spruance was in overall command on board *Indianapolis*, leaving tactical command of the carriers to Mitscher.

Two of the task groups making up TF 58 had four carriers, and the personnel on board *Princeton* were quick to notice the size of the growing fleet. Lt Cdr James Large, a transplanted Philadelphia banker serving as the carrier's air plot officer, was among those impressed by the tremendous display of naval strength: "Ours was only one of three task groups involved. The overall task force included so much sea power that at one time it was possible to see 67 major combat vessels from *Princeton*'s bridge."

CAG Miller had a similar impression: "The operations plans had come aboard. We were headed for Palau and Yap. When you got up on the flightdeck and looked around, you had a strong feeling of security. The greatest fleet in the world lay before your eyes; and we were going out to give the enemy hell."

Although TF 58 headed south after departing Espiritu Santo to avoid Truk-based reconnaissance aircraft, the IJNAF had "snoopers" out, and on March 26 they spotted the fleet without being intercepted. All was quiet until noon on March 29, when one of the pilots on a CAP intercepted a lone "Betty" torpedo-bomber approaching the task force low on the water and finished it off. Later that afternoon, as the sun was starting to go down, two more "Bettys" were "tally-hoed" and shot down, and just before dusk a third was added to the score.

While the CAP was engaged, several more G4M torpedo-bombers attacked the task group and another ship "splashed" one of the intruders – burning fiercely, the aircraft hit the water 3,500 yards off *Princeton*'s starboard quarter. A "Betty" attacked the carrier immediately thereafter, approaching from its port quarter and prompting nearby ships to open fire. Antiaircraft fire set the G4M's right engine ablaze, and the torpedo-bomber then plunged in *Princeton*'s direction as if to carry out a suicide dive. The carrier's aft 20mm and 40mm guns succeeded in shooting the "Betty" down in flames barely 400 yards from the vessel. Two enemy aircraft were now burning on the surface of the water, illuminating the carrier against the dark sky and presenting it as a target to other enemy torpedo-bombers.

The FDO failed to detect a third incoming "Betty" prior to it attacking *Princeton* from the vessel's port quarter. As the aircraft passed along the carrier's port side and crossed the bow, a single 40mm mount and seven 20mm cannon opened fire. They missed the G4M as it streaked by, the torpedo-bomber's crew shooting a burst of machine-gun fire at parked aircraft on the flightdeck in retaliation before then disappearing into the night sky.

Having been fully alerted that a major task force was headed its way, the IJN had moved all of its warships at Palau well out of the area by the time Mitscher attacked at dawn on March 30. Eleven carriers of TF 58 would launch a series of strikes intended to eliminate Japanese opposition to the upcoming landings at Hollandia, in northern New Guinea, and to gather photographic intelligence for future battles. In a first for carrier-based aircraft, Avengers from *Bunker Hill*, *Hornet* and *Lexington* sowed extensive minefields in the approaches to the Palau archipelago.

Princeton and *Lexington* sent Hellcats aloft in the pre-dawn darkness for a combined fighter sweep over the airfield on Peleliu. *Yorktown*'s fighters were also slated to join the group, but having failed to rendezvous they proceeded independently to the target. The F6F pilots spotted five "Zekes" airborne and shot down two of them (the first of 41 victories claimed that day), with the remaining three disappearing into a cloud as the US Navy fighters switched to strafing aircraft parked along the runways and in revetments. The attacks continued throughout the day, without incident, other than the loss of one *Princeton* Hellcat that was forced to ditch due to engine trouble. Its pilot was retrieved unhurt.

With all the carrier aircraft recovered and darkness having settled in, the IJNAF turned to its usual night attacks. Approaching the task force low on the water, thus confusing the ships' gunners, the enemy torpedo-bombers skimmed the wave tops as they made their runs. "With hundreds of our guns firing, no Fourth of July ever looked like that scene," said Lt Cdr James Large, *Princeton*'s air operations officer. "The tracers were flying everywhere." The attackers were beaten back and the task group survived the night unscathed.

Princeton launched its own "fireworks" the next day (March 31) when it sent 12 Hellcats aloft at 0730 hrs for a fighter sweep over Peleliu. The weather was three-tenths cloud cover with unlimited visibility as Lt Cdr Miller led his charges aloft. Two of the fighters suffered engine trouble and had to return to the ship, but the remaining ten pressed on with their mission, encountering a lone "Betty" on the way to the target and swiftly dispatching it.

"Over the target," Miller later recalled, "there were Zeros all over the sky, and VF-23 waded in with guns blazing." Miller led Division 1 with his wingman, Ens Lawrence McWilliams, as they reached Peleliu airfield at 0840 hrs and dived in to attack from 11,000ft in cloudless skies. Lt(jg) J. W. Syme and Ens F. James shared in the destruction of a "Betty" as they bounced it from above, shooting up the bomber's engines and wing root while Division 1 proceeded to strafe the airfield.

Division 2, led by Lt C. C. Schmidt, then sighted a flight of 15–20 "Zekes" flying low at around 3,000ft roughly five miles away. Schmidt reported the sighting to Miller by radio, and the Hellcats of Division 1 broke off their strafing runs and climbed to engage. Upon intercepting the IJNAF fighters, Lt(jg) Syme maneuvered into position to make a firing pass on a division of four "Zekes." Having failed to spot other enemy aircraft close by, Syme quickly had a "Zeke" slide in to position behind him. Fortunately for him, Schmidt's division was alert to the threat and shot the fighter off Syme's tail.

During the fiercely fought clash that lasted 35 minutes, Lt(jg) F. B. Muhlfeld was wounded in the head by shell fragments that also broke his leg, while Lt(jg) Syme finally ran out of luck and was shot down. Bailing out of his stricken Hellcat over the southwest part of Palau lagoon near Peleliu airfield, Syme was attacked by an enemy fighter while descending beneath the canopy of his parachute – his brutal demise was witnessed by one of his squadronmates.

VF-23 was credited with downing 15 enemy aircraft (from a total of 68 claimed by TG 58.3 on March 31), plus one probable, with two more destroyed on the ground. Ens J. R. Hill led the way with claims for three "Zekes," followed by with Ens James with one and one shared (a "Betty") in the air and one destroyed on the ground. Lt(jg) J. M. Abell claimed one in the air and one destroyed on the ground, and Lt C. C. Schmidt and Lt(jg) L. H. Kerr were each credited with two aerial victories.

While VF-23 had been carrying out its strafing attacks, antiaircraft fire struck two Hellcats. The pilots of these aircraft, along with three others that were running low on fuel, experienced some very anxious moments as they headed back to the task force. Unable to reach

Princeton, all five Naval Aviators landed aboard *Bunker Hill*. By then, the two damaged F6Fs had just 11 gallons of fuel remaining between them. Despite having lost a significant quantity of blood due to his head and leg wounds, Lt(jg) Muhlfeld managed to make it back to *Princeton* and slam his shot-up fighter into a crash barrier.

The downed Lt(jg) Syme had not been forgotten, with four Hellcats scrambled from *Princeton* as quickly as possible following news of his demise. These aircraft escorted a pair of Vought OS2U-3 Kingfisher floatplanes from Observation Squadron (VO) 6 catapulted from the stern of the South Dakota-class battleship USS *Alabama* (BB-60). There was still hope that Syme had survived his descent, but the search came up empty. "The promptness with which the OS2Us were dispatched on this search," Miller reported, "and the fact that the search was conducted both within and outside Palau Lagoon, has had a most beneficial effect on pilot morale."

No enemy low-level attacks occurred that night, giving thankful aircrews some much-needed sleep. Flight operations continued the next day (April 1), with a fighter sweep launched to attack Woleai, east of Palau. Radar produced reports of unidentified aircraft in the area that, upon checking, proved to be spurious and resulted in additional fuel consumption. The latter prevented VF-23 from reaching their planned target.

While carrying out strikes on Palau, aircraft from CVLG-23 had dropped 11.5 tons of bombs. The task group overall had claimed the destruction of 157 Japanese aircraft, sunk the destroyer *Wakatake*, the repair ship *Akashi*, the aircraft transport *Goshu Maru* and 38 other vessels and denied the IJN access to Palau harbor for an estimated six weeks.

Despite Miller's earlier scolding of the younger men under his command, following the Palau strike he had decidedly changed his tune. CAG reported that the "performance of Air Group 23 throughout this operation has been of an exceptionally high order, both in combat and in routine operations."

Shortly after TF 58 turned away from Palau to resupply at Majuro, a dispatch reached *Princeton* detaching Lt Cdr Miller as CAG and CO of VF-23 and promoting him to air officer of an escort carrier. These orders had come through two months earlier, and "playing a ghost" for some time now, Miller had been dodging the posting for as long as possible in order to stay in the fight with his boys. When *Princeton* dropped anchor at Majuro on April 6, CAG was still trying to figure out how much longer he could delay reporting in for the escort carrier assignment.

Three days later was Easter Sunday. Sunrise services were held on *Princeton*'s flightdeck at 0630 hrs and a Catholic Mass was celebrated in the hangar bay at 0800 hrs. Many members of CVLG-23 and some of the ship's crew had the opportunity in the afternoon to go ashore for a swim and a can or two of beer. Little did these men know that ten weeks earlier, Australian soldiers of the 9th Infantry Division, while out on patrol and on the heels of the IJA's 20th Division in New Guinea, had stumbled upon an intelligence gold mine. A Japanese signals officer had collected IJA code books and other related material that was too soggy to burn because of the continuous monsoon rains, packed it all into a heavy steel box and thrown it into a swampy bog.

The Australian soldiers found the box on 19 January 1944 and realized that they had discovered precious intelligence material. The box was forwarded to the Central Bureau (one of two Allied signals intelligence organizations in the South West Pacific Area) in Australia so MacArthur's cryptanalytic personnel could get to work on its contents. Although the documents were stained with mud and sodden, they were dried out using commercial cooking ovens and most of the codes deciphered. The latter gave the Allies a detailed look at the IJA's status in New Guinea, which in turn had an immediate effect on future planning.

MacArthur's intelligence personnel discovered that his next move, a landing at Hansa Bay, on the north coast of New Guinea, would have amounted to US forces walking into a massive ambush. MacArthur pivoted and decided to jump 200 miles further west and outflank the IJA with a landing at Hollandia. This bold move would rule USAAF fighters out when it came to protecting the landings, as none of the land-based aircraft in-theater had the range to reach Hollandia. Having been informed of the new plan Halsey ordered TF 58 to set sail for the north coast of New Guinea.

While the strikes against Palau had gone smoothly, Mitscher was subsequently confronted with the first major crisis over task group command. Following the death of his chief of staff in a flying accident in March, Rear Adm Sam Ginder had suffered a mental breakdown that confined him to his cabin during the Palau operation and rendered him completely ineffective as a task group commander. This behavior, coupled with his unsatisfactory handling of his task group off Eniwetok, led to Ginder being replaced as the commander of TG 58.3 by Rear Adm John W. "Black Jack" Reeves.

The decision at the highest levels whether to bypass Truk and/or the Marianas rested on the outcome of the Marshalls operation. If the Japanese had resisted strongly and turned the Marshalls landings into protracted operations, then the Fast Carrier Task Force would have been unable to support MacArthur's offensive in New Guinea. However, the Central Pacific Force had performed in the way that US Navy planners had expected, thus allowing TF 58 to support MacArthur as he endeavored to maintain the two-pronged offensive toward the Luzon bottleneck.

Shortly after the Truk raid, the fighting in the South Pacific Theater had been declared over in March 1944, so there was no reason for Nimitz to split his operations into South and Central Pacific – all were now Central. On April 26 he abolished the title of the Central Pacific Force and replaced it with Fifth Fleet, the title by which the fleet had been known administratively for some time. Simultaneously, all forces under Halsey became known as Third Fleet, with both fleets falling under Nimitz's authority. That same day, Spruance shifted his flag to Pearl Harbor to begin planning the Marianas campaign, leaving Mitscher on his own until June.

Four days of heightened preparation made *Princeton* ready to sail, and on April 13 the vessel steamed out of Majuro lagoon with a fleet-sized task group that included four carriers, five battleships, three heavy cruisers and 17 destroyers. Each flattop left a pilot contingent ashore to fly out new aircraft once the fleet was underway, and Lt Cdr Miller led three other VF-23 pilots from Majuro to *Princeton* several hours after the carrier had sailed.

TF 58 was tasked with supporting the US Army's I Corps in its assault on Humboldt Bay, near Hollandia, codenamed Operation *Reckless*, and the landings at Aitape and Tanahmerah Bay (Operation *Persecution*), also on the north coast of New Guinea. Rear Adms Montgomery and Reeves headed the two task groups (58.2 and 58.3) responsible for providing aircraft for raids and CAS, along with CAP and antisubmarine patrols. As the fleet sailed toward its objective, senior officers developed their strategy for the air attack on New Guinea. Each carrier air group and squadron commander took turns visiting their counterparts on the other carriers, making detailed plans for the invasion. Pilots and aircrew were briefed on their intended targets, the enemy strength anticipated and the operational schedule. While en route, *Princeton* crossed the equator for the 45th time.

MacArthur's invasion forces had departed Finschhafen, in eastern New Guinea, and nearby Goodenough Island on April 16–18 and proceeded to rendezvous with the carriers from TF 58 on the morning of April 20. The group sailed westward, reaching a mark about 80 miles north of the New Guinea coast and then changed course to the southwest at dusk bound for Hollandia. TG 77.3 detached from the larger force after dark and made its way to Aitape for *Persecution*, while the rest of the force sailed on to Hollandia for the larger operation of the two, *Reckless*.

While still two days from New Guinea, an unidentified aircraft had been detected on fleet radar, sending all hands to general quarters until the "bogey" disappeared from the screens. During the early morning hours of the following day (April 20), TF 58 met up with a tanker for some much-needed fuel. At 1313 hrs that same day, a *Princeton* fighter division led by Lt(jg) L. H. Kerr intercepted another enemy "snooper" while on CAP. Their quarry turned out to be a "Betty," which was quickly dispatched by Kerr's division after being spotted.

At 0700 hrs on April 21, US Army units commenced coming ashore at Humboldt Bay, and 45 minutes later troops reached Tanahmerah Bay. VF-23 was assigned three strikes against IJAAF airfields at Hollandia, Cyclops and Sentani to the west of Humboldt Bay. In all, five heavy and seven light carriers launched preliminary strikes through adverse weather conditions on IJAAF airfields around Hollandia, Sawar and Wadke. Led by CAG Miller, the ship's strike group raked aircraft on the ground during strafing runs and added fragmentation clusters, incendiaries and 100lb bombs to the destruction of airfield installations.

Having completed two strikes, CVLG-23 was prevented from participating in the third strike of the day when *Princeton*'s forward elevator became jammed with a Hellcat spotted on it. There was a good chance CVLG-23 did not miss much in any case, as USAAF medium bombers had also hit the area prior to the US Navy strikes. The latter had started fires that produced sufficient smoke to prevent accurate post-mission battle damage assessment of the targets that had been attacked.

The landings at Aitape commenced at 0645 hrs on April 22, and *Princeton*, along with the other carriers, sent up CAPs to cover the landing areas but they were not called upon for assistance. "The Japanese evidently had moved into the hills," CAG Miller said, "from which they could venture forth later." As the Hellcats began to return to their carriers, the US Army's landings appeared to be virtually completed. The foul weather, which had not gone away, closed in to near zero ceiling conditions as Miller and his squadron landed back on *Princeton* just in time.

It had been a long day aloft for CVLG-23. "Our planes got back to *Princeton* after sundown," Miller said. "The landing signal officer had to resort to lighted wands as darkness closed in. Just as the last of our fighters were retrieved, the Japs appeared over the task group, and we went to general quarters again. Our nightfighters from the bigger carriers shot down one bogey, but others got into Hollandia to bomb our forces there."

The action continued for VF-23 on April 23 when pilots strafed two enemy barges and a 125 ft boat at Matterer Bay. They also pursued the occasional enemy aircraft when it made a fleeting appearance, although no victories were achieved. Providing effective CAS, three Avengers from VT-23 bombed and a pair of Hellcats strafed a concentration of IJA troops and vehicles on the Pim–Hollandia Road. D-Day Plus Two for Operation *Persecution* saw the task force and the eight escort carriers supporting the advance ashore at Aitape, with aircraft flying cover and antisubmarine patrols.

After three days of CAPs and attack missions, the task group retired for refueling. While the operation was underway, a lone Japanese bomber approached the formation and was quickly shot down. Survivors were plucked from the sea, transported to *Enterprise* and interrogated by intelligence officers on Rear Adm Reeves' staff.

On the morning of April 26, two four-aircraft divisions of Hellcats were launched from *Princeton* to fly a routine CAP over the task group. One division was led by Lt(jg) J. M. Webb and the other by Lt(jg) R. S. Tyner, neither of whom had a confirmed victory. A "snooper" appeared shortly after the fighters had been launched, and it so happened that the enemy aircraft was closer to Webb's division than to Tyner's. Webb led Ens I. T. Bledsoe, Ens J. R. Hill and Ens W. E. Packer into the interception and shared in the destruction of a "Betty."

Meanwhile, Tyner's division was flying directly above the task group, hoping another opportunity would arise. Any chance they had of seeing action disappeared when Webb's division was vectored onto another "snooper." After receiving the call from the FDO, the chase was on. Webb and his fellow pilots pursued the enemy aircraft for 70 miles before finally catching up to it. The "snooper" was identified as a twin-engined Kawasaki Ki-45 "Nick" heavy fighter of the IJAAF. A new type to VF-23, the aircraft was appreciably faster than the "Betty" downed earlier in the mission, hence the long chase. Nevertheless, it was not quite quick enough to escape the Hellcats, and Webb's division chalked up its second victory of the mission.

As the "Nick" plunged toward the sea, the F6F pilots looked at their fuel gauges and quickly realized that they were dangerously low. Still roughly 100 miles from *Princeton*, Webb immediately radioed the carrier to report their status. Showing his true mettle, new skipper Capt Bill Buracker wasted no time in acting to save his pilots, as CAG Miller recalled:

> Capt Buracker immediately requested permission from the Admiral to be detached from the task group in order to speed to the assistance of the distant and nearly fuelless planes. Permission was granted, and the captain ordered the carrier crew to pour on the coal. He really produced when our boys needed help. When *Princeton* met the returning fighters, one Hellcat's fuel gauge indicated empty. Luckily, the ship was already headed into the wind and that pilot came straight in, followed by the others, without any wave offs or nervous landings. When all four were safely aboard, everyone on the flightdeck and bridge let out a loud cheer.

Later in the day, three more "snooping" "Bettys" were shot down near the task group perimeter, although their demise was credited to fighters from other carriers flying CAP at the time.

As evening settled over the western Pacific, Nimitz radioed his "congratulations on another job well done." Mitscher also added a "well done." And from his task group command on *Enterprise*, Reeves told *Princeton* "Good work. Your boys are right on the job."

In the six weeks that followed the successful flanking maneuver on the IJN in New Guinea, American soldiers completed mopping-up operations against their Japanese counterparts in the area. "Pioneer troops" of the US Army Corps of Engineers and Seebees from US

Naval Construction Battalions, with help from Allied engineers, began developing bases in and around Hollandia from early June. Humboldt Bay was soon home to a naval base that boasted supply and ammunition depots and ship repair and unloading facilities. Other support installations were also built at Tanahmerah Bay, including a new fuel depot. These bases, along with airfields in the Lake Sentani area nearby, soon became an invaluable staging area for the upcoming campaign to retake the Philippines.

Spirits were high on *Princeton* after another successful operation, and the men on board were all expecting a few days of shore leave and maybe a bottle or two of beer on the beach at Majuro, but it was not to be. New orders had arrived calling for another raid on Truk. Crossing the International Date Line once again, pilots and aircrew returned to their ready rooms in order to formulate strike plans. For the final two days of April, VF-23 carried out strafing runs against land targets on Truk, while VT-23 attacked shipping in the nearby harbor. Concentrating on the Japanese seaplane base on the southern tip of Moen Island, CVLG-23 destroyed three floatplanes on the ramp and damaged some of the buildings.

Despite the operational tempo, the pilots stayed sharp. CAG Miller and his wingman, Ens L. F. McWilliams, shared in the destruction of a fighter over Moen Island. Not to be left out, Avenger turret gunners AMO2c R. L. Pennock and AMM3c A. S. Andress also shared a fighter between them while defending their respective TBMs as they carried out their bombing runs on the seaplane base on Moen Island.

Miller's squadron was not the only one engaged on April 29 during the first day of operations against Truk. Eight Hellcats of VF-32, led by "double hatted" CVLG-32 CAG and squadron CO Lt Cdr E. C. Outlaw, flying from *Langley*, downed 21 Japanese aircraft in less than ten minutes, with Outlaw's division accounting for 15 alone – CAG claimed five of them. A total of 58 victories were credited to Naval Aviators and aircrew following the Truk attack that day.

This brief melee over the once feared IJN bastion on April 29, 1944 could very well act as an indicator of things to come in the not-too-distant future. While the enemy presence was still felt in the form of moderate to heavy antiaircraft fire, and an attempt was made by the IJNAF to challenge US Navy aircraft in the air, Truk was being reduced to rubble by TF 58. The efficiency and skill of carrier-based

Naval Aviators in-theater was now fully matured, allowing Fifth Fleet to literally blow through the Marshalls. Ominously for the Japanese Empire in the Central Pacific, TF 58 would soon be able field 15 fast carriers.

With a job well done once again, Mitscher detached his heavy surface ships to bombard Satawan Island on April 30 while Lee's battleships shelled Ponape the following day. TGs 58.2 and 58.3 set a course for Majuro, while Clark's TG 58.1 provided air cover for the battleships.

Princeton, never shirking its duties during this period, launched 548 sorties between April 14 and May 3. Its aircraft dropped 29 tons of bombs and fired more than 22,000 rounds of 0.50-cal. between these dates.

A glorious one-month breather followed the Hollandia–Truk operations, giving Mitscher the time he needed to make final preparations for the upcoming Marianas campaign. In January 1944 air command in Pearl Harbor had established a rotation schedule for carrier air groups on a basis of six to nine months of combat operations, but that was deemed too long in April. The intensive pace of the Central Pacific offensive indicated that this tour needed to be shortened to six months. Under this directive, six carrier air groups were rotated home in May for rest, re-equipment and reassignment. *Princeton*'s CVLG-23 was one of them.

5

"Fighting 27"

Princeton arrived at Majuro and dropped anchor on May 4, with a departure date for Pearl Harbor of the 6th. Accompanied by *Yorktown* and *Monterey*, the carrier would take aboard new squadrons and undergo minor repairs once in Hawaii. Before "Sweet P" departed, an epic farewell party was thrown for the pilots and personnel of CVLG-23. This affair was, in the words of Lt Cdr Edward Clifford, aide to *Princeton*'s executive officer, "the type of party you could expect under the circumstances."

Two bottles of beer were the normal issue given to members of the ship's company and the carrier air group when they had an opportunity to go ashore between combat operations. On *Princeton*, the beer supply became an object of unusual interest, along with some questions as to exactly how much was actually consumed during the farewell party.

The ship, which had originally been laid down as a light cruiser and was converted into a carrier, featured some design innovations. The main deck of a cruiser slopes from the bow toward the stern while an aircraft carrier's top deck is the flightdeck and, obviously, to receive and launch aircraft this must be level. Consequently, the basic cruiser hull was topped by the necessary superstructure to make it an aircraft carrier, and this created a vacant space that on *Princeton* was used for storage.

"The beer was in a compartment in this void between the first deck and the hangar bay," said water tender Larry Brown, a survivor of the *Hornet* sinking:

> The cases of bottles were stacked in one area maybe five feet high, with a hatch on one side so that the Marine guard could look in to make sure the beer was still there. What somebody did was get into the space near the beer compartment and then cut a hole with an acetylene torch so cases of beer could be taken out from the back of the pile. When the Marine checked, he saw cases still stacked near the hatch, so he closed the hatch and locked up.

Brown said he was under the impression there were thousands of cases of beer in the storage compartment to begin with. Essentially, *Princeton* had become a floating alcoholic beverage warehouse. With the "withdrawals" continuing for months, Brown could not be sure how much disappeared in all.

One thing was for sure – *Princeton* threw one hell of a bash for a carrier air group and personnel that had earned every bit of it. During the period from May 19, 1943 to May 26, 1944, *Princeton* had been at sea for 243 days, or two-thirds of that year. During that time, the carrier had steamed some 95,000 miles over the vast expanse of the Pacific. Flying from its flightdeck, CVLG-23 had played a prominent role in 12 major operations as the US Navy closed in on the Japanese home islands. VF-23 and VT-23 were instrumental in establishing the innovative Independence-class flattops as worthy participants in the sea-oriented counter offensive against an enemy which had used its own massive carrier force and navy to occupy a large chunk of the Pacific Theater.

CVLG-23's log showed more than 9,000 hours of combat flying. Its fighter pilots listed 325 strikes against the enemy and nearly 300 hours of CAPs. They had been credited with downing 34.5 enemy aircraft in aerial combat, with four more as probables and eight damaged. At least 11 aircraft had also been destroyed or damaged by strafing on the ground. In return, five pilots had been posted as missing in action, one was killed in action and one perished in an operational accident.

The torpedo squadron, VT-23, had accounted for a further four Japanese aircraft shot down. Additionally, VT-23 pilots scored torpedo hits on two enemy heavy cruisers and one destroyer, with 12 other vessels and a score of smaller craft reported as being destroyed or damaged in the 52 strikes carried out by that squadron. Five pilots and aircrewmen were lost or missing in action.

Princeton arrived back at Pearl Harbor on May 11 and immediately prepared to receive CVLG-27, which had been in training on the island of Maui. As CVLG-23 disembarked, more than one member of the ship's company wondered whether their replacements would be as good under fire. All hands agreed that it would be a tough act to follow. The men of CVLG-23 embarked aboard USS *Altamaha* (CVE-18) two days later and sailed the 2,104 miles to NAS Alameda, California, where they took "rehabilitation leave" before moving on to various stations for further training and assignments.

VF-27

Like a number of US Navy squadrons during World War II, VF-27 was formed at NAS Norfolk in April 1942. It was initially commissioned as VGF-27, with VGF indicating that the fighter squadron was assigned to an escort carrier. The first deployment that marked this squadron as one of the most traveled of all US Navy fighter units of the war was when it found itself operating from the escort carrier *Suwannee* as part of CVLG-27. The vessel was in turn assigned to the Western Task Force in the Mediterranean Sea as a part of Operation *Torch* – the Allied landings in French North Africa in November 1942.

Four American carriers were tasked with providing support for the US Army in its first offensive against Germany, with landings taking place at three different points along the Moroccan coast and six locations in neighboring Algeria. USS *Ranger* (CV-4) and *Suwannee* (then designated ACV-27) would cover the main landings at Casablanca, with *Sangamon* and USS *Santee* (ACV-29) protecting the flanks at the northern and southern beaches. Between them, the four escort carriers embarked 109 F4F-4s, plus SBD-3 dive-bombers and TBF-1 Avenger torpedo-bombers.

While the Free French government in exile was aligned with the Allies, the Vichy French in North Africa were not. When US Army troops came ashore on November 8, they encountered relatively weak opposition on the ground. The *Armée de l'air de Vichy* (Air Force of

Vichy), on the other hand, put up a fight. The more experienced French pilots flying Dewoitine D.520 and Curtiss Hawk H-75 fighters readily engaged US Navy aircraft that were, in the main, flown by pilots seeing combat for the first time. The heaviest fighting occurred on November 8, with carrier pilots claiming 18 aerial victories. Lt Cdr C. T. Booth's VF-41, embarked in *Ranger*, claimed 13 kills in a single dogfight north of Cazes airfield in Casablanca. The CO of *Ranger*'s VF-9, Lt Cdr John Raby, added one more, while the pilots of VGF-26, embarked in *Sangamon*, claimed four victories. During the eight days of *Torch*, 25 French aircraft were shot down, although no fewer than 31 US Navy aircraft (including three F4F-4s from VGF-27) were lost to antiaircraft fire, French fighters or in operational accidents.

VF-41 had enjoyed the most success in the skies over French North Africa, with six of its pilots claiming two victories each. One of those Naval Aviators was Lt Ernest W. Wood, the future commanding officer of VF-27. A US Naval Academy graduate in the class of 1938, he had been born on January 31, 1916 and hailed from Garden City, New York. "Woodie," as he was known to his academy classmates, was:

> Gifted with an easy-goin' nature. He is always willing to oblige with his own arrangements of popular music. You can find Woodie almost any night contentedly smoking his pipe, composing or arranging music for our musical club show or perhaps watching photographs "come out" in his darkroom. In four years, we have come to know Woodie as a happy-go-lucky fellow with a heart of gold – always a true friend and ever the gentleman.

Wood was assigned to various commands upon graduation until he reported to flight training. On March 10, 1941 Ens Wood was transferred to NAS Pensacola, Florida, and he was promoted to lieutenant (junior grade) on July 1, 1941 and designated Naval Aviator No. 8199 later that same month. When Pearl Harbor was attacked, Lt(jg) Wood was assigned to Wildcat-equipped VF-41 embarked in *Ranger*. On July 1, 1942 he was promoted to lieutenant, and four months later participated in the fighting over North Africa while still serving with VF-41.

Following *Torch*, VGF-27 remained embarked in *Suwannee* for the next eight months. On January 18, 1943, the carrier arrived in the South Pacific after departing Norfolk on December 5, 1942.

The squadron was redesignated VF-27 on March 1, 1943, and it would operate Wildcats ashore from Henderson Field, on Guadalcanal, from March 10. "Fighting 27" would be accompanied on this deployment by sister squadrons VF-26 and VF-28. On April 25, all three squadrons were transferred out of Guadalcanal and VF-27 would again be assigned to *Suwannee*, before returning to Guadalcanal on June 26. It would fly from Henderson Field until being pulled out for the final time on August 5, 1943.

During the four-month period spanning April through July, VF-27 would tally 12 aerial victories. One of these successes was claimed by Lt(jg) Cecil E. Harris on April 1, and he would go on to score multiple kills during single missions with VF-18 between September 13 and November 25, 1944 while embarked in the Essex-class carrier USS *Intrepid* (CV-11). In a rare display of gunnery and fighting skill, Lt Harris would score 16 of his aerial victories on four different days, downing four enemy aircraft on each occasion. To add to his aura, not once during the course of his 88-day tour with VF-18 did a bullet hit his aircraft. It has been said that Harris "was arguably the most consistently exceptional fighter pilot in the US Navy." He ended the war as the US Navy's second highest scoring ace with 24 victories after Cdr David McCampbell with 34, earning Harris a Navy Cross.

Having returned to California in September 1943 for reorganization and reequipment following their spell in the South Pacific both ashore and embarked in *Suwannee*, CVLG-27's VF-27 and VT-27 were officially reformed on October 15 at NAS Alameda. Pilots, aircrew and other personnel reported in on a day-to-day basis, with CVLG-27 and VF-27 being briefly led by Lt Cdr J. Roudebush. One of the first pilots to report was Lt William "Bill" Lamb, a dark-haired, softly spoken Annapolis graduate who temporarily became VF-27's senior officer after Roudebush was reassigned. Lamb was soon joined by both squadrons' air combat intelligence officers, Lts Thomas Bradshaw and Bill Kerr, who were recent graduates of the Naval Indoctrination and Air Combat Intelligence Schools at NAS Quonset Point, Rhode Island.

Future ace Lt Frederick Bardshar arrived just before CVLG-27 was ordered to move to Naval Auxiliary Air Station (NAAS) Watsonville, approximately 90 miles south of Alameda. It was one of a number of former civilian airfields dotted all along the west coast that had been acquired by the US Navy in 1942–43 to support the burgeoning demand for new squadrons in the Pacific Theater. Also an Annapolis graduate, and a veteran of the Pearl Harbor attack, Bardshar assumed command upon reporting in at VF-27, with Lamb becoming his executive officer.

The unit took its newly received F6F-3 Hellcats with it when sent to Watsonville, while TBF-1-equipped VT-27 was posted from Alameda to NAAS Hollister, a few miles inland from Monterey Bay. The pilots assigned to VF-27 were very happy to receive Grumman's newest fighter, with Bardshar being particularly pleased because his long frame was ill-suited to the cramped cockpit of a Wildcat.

Some members of the squadron were none too pleased with the move to Watsonville, which meant exchanging the off-duty nightclubs, bars and restaurants of San Francisco and Oakland for a small town where the attractions were a movie theater, a hamburger joint and two bars, one of which was the *White Swan*. Naval Aviators renamed it the "Dirty Duck."

However, being literally stationed on Pacific Coast Highway One (completed in 1937), and just a few short miles from Monterey Bay, pilots and aircrew enjoyed a stunning view of California's central coast when aloft. Flying north, they would have had the Pacific Ocean to their left, with the cliffs and winding highway that had been cut into the coastal mountain range in sight as well. Continuing north, the skyline of San Francisco would have eventually come into view. Not long after takeoff, if a pilot elected to turn south, he could literally buzz right over the quaint little town of Carmel-by-the-Sea and one of the most famous golf courses in the world, Pebble Beach. Large forests of California redwoods dotted the landscape, while the coastline was literally untouched by suburban sprawl in the fall of 1943.

A few of VF-27's married pilots were lucky enough to rent houses for their families at nearby Rio Del Mar, on Monterey Bay, while the less fortunate settled for rooms on base, including those in the Bachelor Officer Quarters. The few buildings at NAAS Watsonville were constructed of California redwood, creating the impression of a bizarre wild west or frontier settlement clustered along the two runways, with modern Hellcats parked in neat rows nearby.

Now moved into its new home at NAAS Hollister, VT-27, under command of new skipper Lt S. M. Hadley, engaged in ground training at the base and flight exercises over the rolling hills to the east, as well as the offshore areas to the west. Meanwhile, Lt Bardshar assessed his individual pilot's previous experience and talent as each new member of VF-27 reported for duty. From this process, he assigned the men to their divisions. A US Navy fighter division consisted of a pair of two-aircraft sections. After the division leader, the most important member of this team was the section leader. He and the division leader each had an accompanying wingman. In combat, the division was frequently forced to break formation, but the leader and his wingman made every effort to stay together, protecting each other from surprise side, rear or overhead attack.

Among those selected as a division leader was former Pensacola instructor and future ranking ace of VF-27, Lt(jg) James A. "Red" Shirley, who had had operational experience of early four-aircraft division tactics prior to the US Navy adopting the two-aircraft section as its optimal air tactical unit. The division leader, in addition to bringing out the flying potential of his section leaders, was also responsible for carrying out the training process within his group of pilots. In Shirley, and others like him, it was soon discovered that "Fighting 27" was stacked with talent.

Also chosen to lead fighter divisions were Lt(jg) Carl A. Brown, who, like Shirley, was to establish a remarkable combat record while becoming an ace; Lt(jg) Robert B. Grove, a softly spoken but serious type who quietly guided his more exuberant "nuggets"; and Lt(jg)s Richard E. Stambook (also a future ace) and John L. "Patty" McMahon, a pair of extraordinary fliers who completely enjoyed the profession they had chosen, and who took every opportunity to refer to each other as "Shorty."

A perfect example of the many ways in which pilots earned their Wings of Gold was Dick Stambook, a native Californian born on April 9, 1921 in Lancaster, which was at the time a small, isolated community roughly 70 miles northeast of Los Angeles. After finishing high school, he enrolled in the local junior college at Palmdale with the support of his father, who ran the oil pumping plant in town. Motivated by his uncle's experiences in World War I and his conversations with his father concerning the deepening unrest in the world, Stambook signed up for the Civilian Pilot Training (CPT) program when a local barnstormer won a contract to set up a course at the college.

The fledgling pilot logged 40 flight hours while attending Palmdale, but since there was no secondary CPT course being offered there, he transferred to Bakersfield Junior College for his sophomore year. The course was conducted in a Waco biplane, which was excellent for aerobatics training, and he logged 40 hours in the secondary course, for a total of 80 hours in the air, after which he received an invitation from the US Navy to attend flight training at Pensacola. Following two weeks of naval indoctrination at Naval Station Long Beach, California, three of the students from the Bakersfield CPT class traveled to Pensacola by train to enroll in Class 7A-41 in July 1941.

Stambook graduated as an ensign and a Naval Aviator in January 1942 with orders to report to the battleship USS *California* (BB-44). He and several new ensigns had become scout seaplane pilots assigned to the battleships *California*, USS *Utah* (BB-31) and USS *Arizona* (BB-39), all of which had been sunk in the Japanese attack on December 7, 1941. Now lacking ships to fly from, they joined a composite scouting unit equipped with OS2U Kingfishers that had had their floats replaced by a fixed undercarriage. These aircraft were used to undertake inshore patrols from NAS Pearl Harbor, Stambook and his squadronmates conducting sector searches seeking out IJN submarines. The young ensign later claimed that he saw plenty of "critters" and US Navy vessels, but not the enemy.

Subsequently posted to Scouting Squadron (VS) 3D-14 in March 1942, Stambook yearned to fly fighters. Feeling trapped in his current assignment, he badgered his CO for months until the latter relented. Stambook duly received tuition from pilots assigned to Lt "Butch" O'Hare's VF-3, which was based on Maui following the Coral Sea and Midway battles. He noted that training in the F4F Wildcat was relaxed here, with pilots from the unit tutoring him as he ran through a syllabus of flight tactics, gunnery and field-carrier landings. Stambook also had the privilege of working with Lt Cdr Jimmy Flatley's VF-10, which flew from the airstrip on Maui for several weeks before heading to the South Pacific on board *Enterprise*.

In July 1942, orders came in for Stambook to report to Lt Cdr Lou Bauer's VF-6, which was headed to the South Pacific embarked in *Saratoga*. The carrier eventually linked up with *Enterprise* and operated in the Coral Sea for several quiet months. *Enterprise* was then relieved by the Royal Navy carrier HMS *Victorious*. Still with VF-6, he twice flew into Guadalcanal's Henderson Field, only to find himself diving into fighting holes at night to avoid the errant bombs dropped by "washing machine Charlie" – the Japanese aircraft that flew over the airfield and did a fantastic job of thoroughly annoying them. In March 1943 Stambook was transferred to Wildcat-equipped VF-3, where he remained until he received orders to join VF-27 at NAS Alameda in September. Following leave at home in Southern California, he travelled to the San Francisco Bay area and reported in with his fellow fighter pilots.

As the fall of 1943 turned to winter, a new commander for both CVLG-27 and VF-27 reported in – Lt Ernest "Woodie" Wood. Short and slight of build, he and Lt Bardshar presented a contrast that earned them the nicknames "Mutt and Jeff" after the key characters in a long-running and popular American newspaper comic strip created by cartoonist Bud Fisher in 1907. The two lieutenants made an excellent team. "Woodie" – the name Wood preferred – could not say no to any request, and Bardshar frequently had to play "bad guy" to prevent him from being taken advantage of. Under Wood, Bardshar became VF-27's executive officer and Lt Lamb served as the operations officer.

Wood, who was an excellent pilot, soon proved his mastery of the 13,000lb Hellcat that seemed to dwarf him when he was sat in the cockpit. From various sources, members of CVLG-27 learned of Wood's Operation *Torch* exploits, which included the downing of two D.520s – a fighter type that was appreciably more agile than the Wildcat he was flying. Pilots from VF-27 soon discovered that their CAG/CO also played the piano the same way he flew. Sometimes it appeared to possess a "throttle," allowing the piano to be played both soft and low and swiftly and wildly.

One of the Rio Del Mar residents was VF-27's flight officer, Lt Herman J. Baker, who occupied a house along Monterey Bay with his wife and young son. Formerly a flight instructor prior to his assignment to the unit, Baker had logged more hours than most of "Fighting 27's" younger pilots put together. During the afternoon of December 29, 1943, four Naval Aviators from the squadron returned to the field early, long before their scheduled landing time. They reported that Lt Baker, whose Hellcat was rigged with a gunnery target sleeve, had failed to rendezvous with them over Monterey Bay.

As the hours ticked away on the squadron office clock, California's Central Coast weather began to close in and a low overcast forced a temporary end to the search. Further search efforts the following day turned up nothing, and finally a blimp was called in from a nearby lighter-than-air base. The slower craft located the wreckage of Baker's fighter high in the snow-dusted coastal mountain range, only a few minutes flying time from Watsonville. The next morning a ground party, guided from the air by the blimp, worked its way up the side of the mountain through dense underbrush and snow to the wreckage of the F6F and Baker's remains. It appeared that the tops of the towering, beautiful pines of the California coastal range had snagged the target sleeve (a 40ft-long by 4ft-wide banner attached to a 300ft-long cable towed by the aircraft) and pulled the aircraft into the ground.

The search party also discovered that the Hellcat's six 0.50-cal. wing guns and much of the ammunition had been taken out of their compartments and were not to be found. An intense search, which eventually involved the FBI, tracked down the missing weapons and belt-fed ammunition – they had been taken by several young locals and were quickly retrieved from various hiding spots. Baker's death cast a shadow over the final weeks of CVLG-27's stay in California, as preparations were now being made for its departure to Hawaii.

After completing carrier qualifications on the Bogue-class escort carrier USS *Copahee* (CVE-12) off San Francisco Bay in late February 1944, followed by three weeks of joint training at Hollister in March, VF-27 and VT-27 (which had by now received brand new TBM-3 Avengers) were deemed ready to head west. On March 22 both units returned to Alameda, where another Bogue-class escort carrier, USS *Barnes* (CVE-20), waited to transport the aircraft and personnel of CVLG-27 to Hawaii. The subsequent days at sea were occupied with what might be called shipboard ground school – briefings on the Hawaiian Islands, enemy aircraft identification tests, tactical discussions and even a first-hand account of the IJNAF attack on Pearl Harbor as witnessed by Lt Bardshar, who had been the gunnery officer on board *Pennsylvania* at the time.

Upon reaching Pearl Harbor, Wood passed along the word from Pacific Fleet Headquarters that CVLG-27 was to train on the island of Maui until *Princeton* returned to Hawaii. Some of the pilots ferried the fighters and torpedo-bombers from NAS Ford Island, on Oahu, to the US Navy auxiliary air stations at Kahului and Puunene, on Maui. Meanwhile, the remaining personnel from CVLG-27 made the trip to Maui on a minesweeper, with the highlight of the daylong voyage being a close look at the east coast of Molokai – site of the famed leper colony founded by Father Damien.

"FIGHTING 27"

Kahului and Puunene proved to be typically drab auxiliary air stations, although the natural beauty of Maui with its beaches and coconut palms could not be denied. The island boasted an extinct volcano at each end, and its two airfields were situated on either side of two bays at Maui's narrowest point.

As part of the ground training program, two experts came to Maui from the Bishop Museum in Honolulu to lecture on survival in the South Pacific. The impression was gained by the pilots that the lecturers could have been dropped off on almost any tiny island on the map and lived in relative comfort. On the stage at the Kahului auditorium, they constructed small waterproof huts from palm fronds, made shoes, cooking utensils, and eating bowls from coconuts and even started a fire from scratch. One of the fighter pilots, Ens Van Carter, attempted to get a fire going himself, but he could not quite produce a flame after several attempts. His failed efforts earned him the nickname "Castaway."

While at Maui Lt Wood permitted, if not encouraged, the painting of the now legendary "fierce faces" on VF-27's Hellcats. While this type of squadron identification had been used successfully, and with considerable fanfare, by the American Volunteer Group (AVG) in China from 1941, the US Navy and USAAF strictly prohibited it – although the 23rd Fighter Group, which received a small cadre of AVG personnel when the latter disbanded, also adopted the marking on its P-40 Warhawks.

Evidently, some of VF-27's pilots decided that the policy did not apply to them, as Lt(jg) Brown explained:

> When we were at Maui, prior to the Mariana Islands invasion, we arrived at this ugly face design on our Hellcats. It came about like this. When I was flying [Grumman] F3F-3s in training at Corpus Christi, one of the planes had two big eyes painted on the cowl. I remembered that and took a piece of chalk to draw a pair of eyes on my Hellcat at Kahului. I tried to arrive at a face, utilizing the braces on the air intake as teeth. I couldn't get anything worth a darn.
>
> The air station had an ACI [Air Combat Intelligence] officer, Lt Germain Glidden, who was a portrait painter as well as being a top-notch squash player [he was national champion both pre- and post-war]. A couple of my fellow pilots – Hugh Little, Bob Burnell

and one other – carved a wooden model of that part of the Hellcat forward of the cockpit. Then they took the model to Glidden, who designed a face and painted it on the carving. Then we painted one plane, and our CO, Lt Wood, said to go ahead and paint the rest of the Hellcats. Ours was the only Navy squadron with anything like that on its planes.

While the group was training on Maui, an admiral from Pearl Harbor came to Kahului for an inspection, putting the pilots and other VF-27 personnel in an "instant scramble" to get canvas covers on the painted faces before his arrival. After inquiring about the canvas covers, the admiral was told that because of the red volcanic dust that seemed to stir up due to the constant sea breeze, the covers were a necessity. It worked, and the faces stayed.

EXERCISE TRAGEDY

A joint exercise was scheduled involving both the fighter and torpedo-bomber squadrons in early May 1944. The idea of the drill was for the pilots to make a realistic combined dawn attack, simulating bombing and strafing runs without any live ordnance or ammunition being employed. The target was NAAS Barking Sands on the small island of Kauai, northwest of Oahu.

Lt Bardshar agreed to let one of VF-27's ACI officers ride along as an observer in an Avenger, the aircraft taking off and rendezvousing in the surprisingly crisp early morning air. With aircraft exhausts flashing, Hellcats and Avengers from CVLG-27 formed an organized pattern in the pre-dawn sky. The torpedo-bombers climbed slowly while the appreciably faster Hellcats "split-S" turned to stay with them. Arriving over their target while the horizon was still not quite edged with light, the fighters and bombers began their runs.

In the pre-flight briefing, the torpedo-bomber pilots had been instructed to come out of their attack dives at 2,500ft. However, as they reached 4,000ft, the Avengers pulled up abruptly and began circling. At the end of Barking Sands' north–south runway was a tremendous blaze, which could only mean one thing. VF-27's worst fears were confirmed on landing. Lt R. P. "Robin" Butler, a lanky Texan and one of the most popular members of the squadron, had collided with another Hellcat as the two fighters approached the airfield from slightly different angles. Although the pilot of the other aircraft involved in the collision managed to recover and land, Butler lost control of his fighter and crashed into trees near the airfield perimeter.

Fully aware that the accident had badly affected VF-27, Wood and Bardshar made sure that the remaining pilots were given plenty of time to relax at the beach near their Kahului base.

Despite this unfortunate accident, CVLG-27 was now ready for combat. VF-27 and VT-27 headed to Pearl Harbor on May 14, with pilots flying their aircraft back to NAS Ford Island. Twenty-four hours later, both units participated in a two-day exercise off the island of Oahu with the carriers *Princeton*, *Yorktown* and *Langley*. On *Princeton*, the reaction to the replacement squadrons was voiced by the assistant to the ship's executive officer, Lt Cdr Edward Clifford: "Air Group 27 proved at once that it was a superior outfit. All hands were satisfied at our good fortune." The carrier's air operations officer, Lt Cdr James Large, agreed: "We soon realized our new air group was 'hot.' They looked good, and future events were to prove them among the very best."

Upon returning to Pearl Harbor, *Princeton* was moved into the naval shipyard for nine days of repairs and the application, for the first time, of a black–white–gray paint pattern known as Measure 33/7a camouflage that was designed to break up the outline of the ship and confuse the enemy. The time in port at Pearl Harbor made it possible for the ship's company to implement rotating leaves. Fully aware that they would not be seeing Hawaii again for many months, the sailors made the most of their runs ashore.

The veteran, battle-hardened *Princeton*, with CVLG-27 embarked, headed out to sea from Pearl Harbor on May 29, 1944 bound for Majuro and a rendezvous with Mitscher's TF 58 once again.

6

Forager

Senior officers in the US Army and US Navy had carried on heated debates for months concerning the direct axis of attack against Japan. Finally, on March 12, 1944, the Joint Chiefs of Staff issued a directive calling for the occupation of Saipan, Tinian and Guam in the Marianas Island chain by June 15, followed by the invasion of the Palau archipelago from September 15. The directive also clearly stated their designs to neutralize, not capture, Truk and other islands in the Carolines – they would be bypassed and beaten down by air bombardment and cut off from their supplies by land-based aircraft and submarines.

Gen MacArthur had continuously argued that the main axis of advance should be westward along the northern coast of New Guinea to the Philippines, and that Adm Nimitz's forces, including the fast carriers, should be deployed in a supporting role, all under his command. MacArthur's concept was generally backed by the US Army, but the US Navy, under Adm King, pushed for an advance across the Central Pacific through the Caroline Islands, with forward bases rapidly established within massive atoll lagoons that could serve the growing fleet. King intended to establish such facilities either on Formosa (Taiwan) or along the coast of China to bring about the ultimate defeat of Japan, bypassing the Philippines in the process and avoiding a costly ground campaign.

The Marianas were not initially a part of King's strategy because they did not possess a sizable port or anchorage and they were considered to be heavily defended. For several months leading up to the March 12 directive the Joint Chiefs of Staff had avoided making a firm decision on either strategy, allowing both forces to proceed with their respective lines of advance – MacArthur along the New Guinea coast and Nimitz's forces through the atolls of the Gilberts and Marshalls.

The USAAF then sided with the US Navy and its Central Pacific campaign, with the understanding that the Marianas were to be taken. Once this had been achieved, it could deploy new long-range B-29 bombers from Saipan, which was the closest island to Japan at that time – it offered a 1,200-mile one-way flight to Tokyo.

A mighty armada of US Navy vessels departed Majuro on June 6, 1944, Marianas-bound. In preparation for the first strikes of what was codenamed Operation *Forager*, when pilots and aircrew were not flying or occupied with aircraft maintenance and up-keep, they attended briefing sessions. D-Day for the landings on Saipan had been set for June 15, and resistance was expected to be heavy, if not heavier than any objective experienced thus far in the Pacific. Enemy air strength in the Marianas was enough to create a major problem for the attacking task force, and there was a strong possibility that the IJN's Combined Fleet might deploy to engage the US Navy.

This did not concern Nimitz, for TF 58 possessed an overwhelming number of ships and aircraft that would allow it to simultaneously cover the landing at Saipan and engage the Combined Fleet. The recent campaigns spanning the Pacific had moulded TF 58 into a unique, combat-experienced fighting force ready for the test that would be *Forager*.

The operation called for Saipan to be taken first by a Northern Expeditionary Force, consisting of the 2nd and 4th Marine Divisions, with the US Army's 27th Infantry Division acting as a reserve. These same forces were then scheduled to land on Tinian after Saipan had been captured. Meanwhile, the Southern Expeditionary Force, consisting of the 3rd Marine Division and a US Army regimental combat team, would capture Guam.

Adm Nimitz, Commander-in-Chief, Pacific Ocean Areas and CINCPACFLT, was in overall charge of *Forager* from his Pearl Harbor headquarters. Fifth Fleet was commanded by Adm Spruance, embarked in *Indianapolis*, while TF 51 (Joint Expeditionary Force) was led by Vice Adm Turner, embarked in the specially configured command ship

Rocky Mount. Two fire support groups consisting of seven battleships, numerous heavy cruisers and destroyers would provide covering fire for the landings. Air power for the Saipan landings would be supplied by aircraft from escort carriers of two carrier support groups, with FM-2 Wildcats and Avengers tasked with both antisubmarine warfare and CAS for the troops ashore. TF 58.7 was formed in anticipation of fleet action with the IJN, and it consisted of seven new fast battleships, four heavy cruisers and 17 destroyers.

TF 58 was commanded by Vice Adm Mitscher from his flagship, *Lexington*, and it consisted of 15 carriers embarking just over 900 aircraft, with half of that number being Hellcats.

Operation Forager Pacific Fleet Organization, June 6, 1944
Commander-in-Chief, United States Fleet and Chief of Naval
   Operations – Adm E. J. King
Commander-in-Chief, Pacific Fleet – Adm C. W. Nimitz
Commander, Fifth Fleet – Adm R. A. Spruance
Commander, TF 51 (Joint Expeditionary Force) – Vice Adm
   R. K. Turner
Commander, TF 58 – Vice Adm M. A. Mitscher
Commander, TG 58.1 – Rear Adm J. J. Clark
   Hornet – Capt W. D. Sample (CVG-2 embarked)
   Yorktown – Capt R. E. Jennings (CVG-1 embarked)
   Belleau Wood – Capt J. A. Perry (CVLG-24 embarked)
   Bataan – Capt V. H. Schaeffer (CVLG-50 embarked)
Commander, TG 58.2 – Rear Adm A. E. Montgomery
   Bunker Hill – Capt T. P. Jeter (CVG-8 embarked)
   Wasp – Capt C. A. F. Sprague (CVG-14 embarked)
   Monterey – Capt S. H. Ingersoll (CVLG-28 embarked)
   Cabot – Capt S. J. Michael (CVLG-31 embarked)
Commander, TG 58.3 – Rear Adm J. M. Reeves
   Enterprise – Capt M. B. Gardner (CVG-10 embarked)
   Lexington – Capt E. W. Litch (CVG-16 embarked)
   San Jacinto – Capt H. M. Martin (CVLG-51 embarked)
   Princeton – Capt W. H. Buracker (CVLG-27 embarked)

Commander, TG 58.4 – Rear Adm W. K. Harrill
  Essex – Capt R. A. Ofstie (CVG-15 embarked)
  Langley – Capt W. M. Dillon (CVLG-32 embarked)
  Cowpens – Capt H. W. Taylor (CVLG-25 embarked)

America's commitment to total war was absolute. The same day TF 58 set sail for the Marianas, Allied forces on the opposite end of the Eurasian continental area committed more than 5,000 ships and landing craft to put ashore more than 150,000 troops on five invasion beaches at Normandy in Operation *Overlord*. Nine days later, American forces, consisting of 128,000 troops and more than 600 ships, would initially land two divisions of the US Marine Corps on the invasion beaches at Saipan. Adm King's shipbuilding program by this time was fully matured, and this allowed three reinforced, combat-loaded divisions to be transported across 3,500 miles of ocean from Pearl Harbor to their assault beaches by 37 troop transports and 47 LSTs.

As TF 58 approached the Marianas on June 11, Mitscher and his staff decided to put a wrinkle in the usual way of doing things. Instead of a dawn fighter sweep, which the enemy had grown accustomed to, before an amphibious invasion, they implemented a new schedule that would consist of an afternoon strike on the 11th as IJNAF "snoopers" flying from the Marianas became well aware that TF 58 was headed their way.

The initial strike was a complex plan that would see three of the large carriers each send off four divisions and the light carriers three divisions. The launching of 208 Hellcats commenced at 1300 hrs, with the aircraft taking off into a 14-knot headwind. Rear Adm Clark's TG 58.1 (*Hornet*, *Yorktown*, *Belleau Wood* and *Bataan*) was assigned targets on Guam. Rear Adm Montgomery's TG 58.2 and Rear Adm Reeves' TG 58.3 (which included *Princeton*) were given Saipan and Tinian, while Rear Adm Harrill's TG 58.4 (*Essex*, *Langley* and *Cowpens*) attacked Tinian and Pagan.

There were numerous, widespread dogfights on June 11 that saw TF 58 pilots and aircrew claim 98 victories (*Hornet*'s VF-2 was credited with 22 of them) for the loss of 12 Hellcats. Three pilots were recovered, including Lt Cdr Robert H. Price, CVLG-25 CAG and CO of VF-25 (embarked in *Cowpens*), who had been shot down by antiaircraft fire while attacking a convoy off Saipan. He ended up drifting in his little yellow raft for two excruciating weeks before finally being rescued.

"Fighting 27's" Lt Dick Stambook recalled the aerial engagements of that first day as follows:

> After my strafing run, which burned and exploded several airplanes on the ground, I climbed rapidly to 10,000ft to prepare for a riled-up Zero crowd. The only thing visible, however, was a Betty low on the water heading south away from Saipan toward nearby Tinian. I made a steep dive on the Betty from 10,000ft and almost overshot, even with the power off. A burst of about three seconds with all six rifles flamed the left engine, and the Betty crashed into the sea. Two other VF-27 pilots got kills that day – my comrade Lt Paddy McMahon got one Zeke on his own and shared one with Ens Hugh Lillie.

The next morning, while on a CAP, a division of four VF-27 Hellcats led by newly promoted Lt Cdr Bardshar splashed a lone "Nick" as the carriers began a rolling series of raids against enemy installations on Guam, Rota, Tinian, Pagan and Saipan. On June 13, VF-27 and VT-27 flew combined strikes in three missions against Aslito airfield on Saipan. On D-Day Minus One and again on D-Day itself (June 15), CVLG-27 helped soften up the enemy as Hellcats strafed targets ahead of the Avengers, which dropped 100lb general purpose (GP) and fragmentation bombs. Additional CAS was rendered as CVLG-27 made low-level attacks on gun positions and tanks found near Aslito airfield.

As the invasion unfolded, Hellcats strafed the beach ahead of the Marines as they battled ashore amid heavy resistance. Sixteen of *Princeton*'s fighters were directed by the support aircraft commander to attack a group of enemy tanks headed for the landing area from the town of Charon Kanoa. Pilots later reported a number of hits among the tanks, which were forced to take cover along the roadsides. They were not observed moving again as long as there were Hellcats in the sky above them. On their return flight to *Princeton*, fighter pilots again strafed aircraft on Aslito airfield.

With the battle raging on the invasion beaches, IJNAF aircraft launched from Guam attacked TF 58 that evening at about 1820 hrs in what proved to be the heaviest air onslaught *Princeton* had experienced thus far. Hellcats from VF-51, embarked in *San Jacinto*, were flying CAP at the time, and they splashed six of seven aircraft as they approached the carriers from high altitude. Although identified as IJAAF Kawasaki Ki-61 "Tony" fighters, they were more likely IJNAF Yokosuka D4Y1 "Judy" dive-bombers – unusually for Japanese aircraft, which, in the main, had radial engines, both the "Tony" and the "Judy" were powered by inline engines.

At 1909 hrs, seven "twin-engined bombers," erroneously identified as Yokosuka P1Y "Frances" (a type that did not enter service with the IJNAF until October 1944 – the aircraft were almost certainly "Bettys"), attacked from ahead. Some dropped torpedoes, with one weapon passing *Enterprise* close aboard to port. The aircraft took full advantage of the massive concentration of US Navy warships, coming in low on the water and flying between their intended targets to make countering them with antiaircraft fire more difficult. According to Lt Cdr James Large:

> The torpedo planes were flying low. They barely skimmed the surface. With every ship in the task force firing, it was a thousand Fourth of Julys in one. As we dodged and weaved at high speed, we had a ring of blazing and exploding enemy planes close aboard. The Japs raced down the columns of ships like great black bats, and the automatic fire from our own forces etched the sky in a crisscross of flame.
>
> We were caught momentarily in a crossfire and the 40mm projectiles produced a roman candle effect as the balls of fire seemed to be arching toward us in leisurely lobs. It was anything but harmless. We had nine people wounded and were holed below the surface. Miraculously, no ship was seriously damaged, and I doubt if any of the Japanese got home.

Carrier-based fighters intercepted the attackers and splashed a number of them. "I recall," Capt Buracker said, "that there were at least six flaming Japanese planes in our immediate vicinity at one time." One torpedo-bomber flew so close between *Princeton* and a nearby battleship that its pilot could be seen clearly outlined in the cockpit from the carrier by the bursting gunfire behind the aircraft. As the torpedo-bomber passed abreast of the carrier, it suddenly glowed like a giant neon sign, flamed spectacularly and then crashed astern of the ship. At the same time, a group of sailors standing on *Princeton*'s port catwalk clutched the railing with white knuckles as a torpedo wake streaked toward the carrier and passed under the ship's overhang barely astern.

Lt Frank Bell, the ship's assistant navigator, was at his battle station topside during the attack:

> I have never seen such a display of fireworks. The multi-colored tracers were going all over the place. One enemy plane went between us and two battlewagons, the *Indiana* and *North Carolina*, which were off our port bow about 1,500 yards. I could see by the tracers approaching that we were going to be hit by the fire from one or both of the battleships. I yelled to my crew "hit the deck." Almost immediately our ship was struck. A splinter shield near us saved our lives as a large hole was blown only 18 inches from me. Another shell hit the shield and splattered shrapnel, killing two men and wounding others directly aft of us at a gun sponson.

Later, after the ships had secured from general quarters, the alarm was again sounded because a submarine periscope reportedly had been sighted. Strangely, the "periscope" came closer and closer to *Princeton*. It turned out to be the upended handle of a mop, which somehow had gone overboard in the confusion surrounding the Japanese air attack.

According to Pharmacist's Mate George Pantages:

> The night engagement off Saipan was indelibly engraved on everyone's memory. During the heart of the action, which lasted less than 30 minutes, the sky was completely lit with thousands of tracers, shells exploding, and flares. This was our first experience with casualties aboard *Princeton* as a result of enemy fire. We were caught in a crossfire with our own ships, and one 40mm shell penetrated into the officers' wardroom.
>
> One of the wounded had a considerable amount of intestine torn by a huge piece of shrapnel. After hasty preliminary surgery, it turned out he needed a piece of medical equipment we didn't possess, namely a thing called a Waggonstein apparatus, which is designed to suck waste from the stomach through tubes in the patient's nostrils. Necessity being the mother of invention, we were not to be outdone by the emergency.

By joining two one-gallon coke bottles with a couple of feet of glass tubing and partially filling one bottle with water, a rapid inversion of the containers provided the necessary suction required to do the job, and fairly efficient at that.

IJN RESPONSE

On June 14, senior Pacific Fleet intelligence officer Cdr Edwin T. Layton briefed CINCPACFLT Adm Nimitz that the IJN was about to execute a modified version of Operation *Z* (the defensive plan for the Marianas Islands, and Saipan in particular), a copy of which had fallen into American hands via guerrillas several months earlier. Senior US Navy commanders were skeptical to a degree, as the IJN had not sent its carrier force out to confront the Americans since the Battle of the Santa Cruz Islands in October 1942.

Layton stuck to his guns and argued that the Commander-in-Chief of the Combined Fleet, Adm Soemu Toyoda, correctly interpreted the US Navy's current actions in the Marianas as a full-scale landing, not another carrier raid, which would set in motion IJN plans for the "decisive battle," stopping the Allied forward advance. Additionally, the loss of Saipan would put Tokyo, and the Emperor, within range of USAAF B-29s. The IJN had no choice but to fight.

Layton detailed that the Japanese force would include nine aircraft carriers, six battleships and other escorts, and predicted that the battle would commence on June 17 — ultimately, he was one battleship off and a day early in his prediction. This excellent assessment was based on extensive intelligence derived from Ultra code-breaking, communications traffic analysis and other intelligence over the previous months that had been presented to senior commanders. This summation of what was about to happen from an IJN standpoint was better intelligence than the US Navy had had at Midway, and it would lead to the largest carrier battle in history.

The IJN would enter the fray at the Marianas with several weaknesses in its Combined Fleet. One of the most critical was an extreme shortage of fuel that meant major elements of the fleet were restricted in range to the waters around Borneo and Singapore – where the fuel was. Another key weakness was the Japanese inability to replace losses of ships, aircraft and trained, experienced pilots. Over the previous two-and-a-half years of war, the IJNAF had lost a significant number of pilots during the battles at Midway and the Santa Cruz Islands. When the IJNAF put its carrier aircraft ashore at Rabaul and Bougainville in an attempt to thwart advancing US forces in the South Pacific, it suffered more heavy losses in senior pilots, especially squadron and flight leaders.

As a remedy, the IJNAF instituted a rapid training program, but it was too little too late for there was not enough time or fuel available to accomplish more than basic flight training. This left the IJNAF with a small number of extremely good, combat-seasoned pilots and a large number of novices who were simply no match for the highly trained and now-veteran US Navy pilots flying from an ever growing fleet of carriers.

A forced change in leadership at the top of the IJN also had a detrimental effect. Beloved and respected Adm Yamamoto was killed when the "Betty" transporting him on an inspection tour of the South Pacific was intercepted by USAAF P-38 Lightnings over Bougainville and shot down on April 18, 1943. Adm Mineichi Koga assumed command of the IJN until March 31, 1944, when the "Emily" flying boat on which he was a passenger went down in a typhoon off the Philippines. Koga had developed Operation *Z* that would lead to the "decisive battle" in defense of the Japanese inner defense line, which the Marianas were a part of.

Adm Soemu Toyoda became Commander-in-Chief of the Combined Fleet after Koga's death, and he developed Operation *A-Go* which was a variation of Operation *Z*. The United States considered Toyoda to be highly intelligent, but with an abrasive personality. Like Yamamoto, Toyoda had been strongly opposed to war with America.

Major air strikes on the western Carolines by TF 58 between March 22 and April 6, 1944 had prompted Adm Koga to withdraw the Imperial Fleet's headquarters from Palau. As previously noted, he was in the final stages of this move when his flying boat crashed after it flew into atrocious weather caused by a typhoon. A second aircraft, carrying Koga's chief of staff, Vice Adm Shigeru Fukudome, ditched off Cebu, in the Philippines. Fukudome survived the crash and was rescued by Filipino fishermen after an eight-hour swim. Documents that had been washed into the sea from the downed flying boat were also discovered just offshore and retrieved by local villagers.

Both Fukudome and the papers were turned over to guerillas led by Lt Col James Cushing of the US Army. Although the chief of staff was traded alive to the Japanese after the IJA promised to stop killing civilians on Cebu, the guerrillas kept the papers. The latter included detailed plans of Operation *Z*, which were turned over to the crew of Balao-class submarine USS *Crevalle* (SS-291) that had been dispatched specifically to collect the papers once their content had been briefly analyzed in the field. The plans were rushed back to MacArthur's headquarters in Brisbane, Australia, with copies then quickly sent to Pacific Fleet headquarters at Pearl Harbor. Here, Cdr Layton, along with other members of Nimitz's intelligence team, were able to study them extensively.

The IJN would commit 69 warships, mostly under the command of Vice Adm Jisaburo Ozawa's recently formed 1st Mobile Fleet, for Operation *A-Go* in its attempt to defend the Marianas. These ships included five fleet carriers, four light carriers, five battleships, 11 heavy cruisers, two light cruisers, 23 destroyers and 19 submarines. Ozawa, tapped by Toyoda to command the fleet, wore three hats – commander of 1st Mobile Fleet, 1st Carrier Division and A Force.

The latter consisted of the new IJN carrier *Taiho*, veteran *Shokaku* and its sister ship *Zuikaku*, two heavy cruisers, one light cruiser and nine destroyers. The three carriers had 209 aircraft embarked between them. B Force was comprised of 2nd Carrier Division under the command of Rear Adm Takaji Joshima, and it included the medium carriers *Junyo* and *Hiyo*, the light carrier *Ryuho* (with the three carriers having a total of 137 aircraft embarked), the battleship *Nagato*, one heavy cruiser, one light cruiser and ten destroyers.

Ozawa's plan had A and B Forces operating roughly 100 nautical miles behind a very powerful Van Force that included three light carriers (3rd Carrier Division), four battleships, eight heavy cruisers, one light cruiser and eight destroyers under the overall command of Vice Adm Takao Kurita. 3rd Carrier Division, under the command of Rear Adm Sueo Obayashi, included the light carriers *Chitose*, *Chiyoda* and *Zuiho* with 90 carrier aircraft embarked between them. Included in the Van Force were the two super-battleships *Musashi* and *Yamato* and the aging but fast battleships *Kongo* and *Haruna*, plus a contingent of the largest heavy cruisers in the world.

The IJN plan placed tremendous reliance on the powerful land-based 1st Air Fleet, under the command of Vice Adm Kakuji Kakuta headquartered at Tinian. 1st Air Fleet depended upon its mobility for success, and it could feasibly operate from a number of outlying airfields in the western Caroline Islands that included Truk, Yap and Palau. Its authorized strength was 630 aircraft in the region, including 500 in the Marianas, with those numbers varying depending upon losses and replacements. Actual numbers had dwindled to between 250–540 come the spring of 1944, and these figures were reduced to next to nothing by June because Kakuta had been reluctant to inform his superiors of how bad his losses had been from repeated US Navy carrier-based raids earlier in the year, leaving Ozawa in the dark at a critical operational juncture.

Additionally, Ozawa was relying heavily on the range of land-based IJNAF aircraft, which was now no greater than that of their US Navy counterparts. While maneuvering A and B Forces out of range of American carrier aircraft, Ozawa would launch strikes from maximum range against the enemy fleet. Should the US Navy choose to close the distance and launch an air strike, Ozawa's plan envisioned that the first IJN ships that they would encounter would be the battleships, cruisers and destroyers of the Van Force, throwing up a deadly curtain of antiaircraft fire.

IJN Operation A-Go Fleet Organization, June 13, 1944
Commander-in-Chief, Combined Fleet – Adm Soemu Toyoda
Chief of Staff – Vice Adm Jinichi Kusaka
Commander-in-Chief, 1st Air Fleet – Vice Adm Kakuji Kakuta
Commander-in-Chief, 3rd Fleet – Vice Adm Jisaburo Ozawa
Commander, 1st Carrier Division – Vice Adm Jisaburo Ozawa
   Taiho, Shokaku, Zuikaku
Commander, 2nd Carrier Division – Rear Adm Takaji Joshima
   Junyo, Hiyo, Ryuho
Commander, 3rd Carrier Division – Rear Adm Sueo Obayashi
   Chitose, Chiyoda, Zuiho

The Commander-in-Chief of the IJN's Combined Fleet, Adm Toyoda, issued the order "Prepare for *A-Go* decisive operations" on June 13, 1944 as Ozawa's carrier forces raised anchor at Tawi-Tawi in the southwest Philippines. *Musashi* and *Yamato*, having previously been assigned to another operation that was abruptly canceled following news of TF 58's attacks on the Marianas, were then ordered to rendezvous with Ozawa east of the Philippines after his fleet passed through the San Bernardino Strait. The vessels' progress had been monitored by the Gato-class submarine USS *Redfin* (SS-272), and while attempting, unsuccessfully, to attack Ozawa's fleet as it left Tawi-Tawi, the crew sent a contact report that turned out to be one of the most important of the entire battle.

On June 14, as the bombardment and attacks on targets in the Marianas continued, Mitscher's intelligence officer, Lt(jg) Charles A. Sims, briefed the vice admiral on IJN movements. He informed Mitscher that the Japanese were intending to route major air reinforcements through the Bonin Islands (Iwo and Chichi Jima). Deciding that he had enough time to send two carrier task groups northwest 1,000 miles to strike the Bonins, Mitscher assigned Rear Adms Clark (TG 58.1) and Harrill (TG 58.4) to the task. Clark was disappointed with the assignment, thinking he was going to miss out on the upcoming carrier engagement, with Harrill equally not enthused and overly concerned about a grim weather forecast in the Bonins.

By nightfall on D-Day, June 15, the US Marine Corps had a beachhead six miles wide and roughly 800 yards deep on Saipan. A large IJA counterattack that night failed to break through, and the Japanese suffered heavy losses. The IJNAF's reaction to the landings that day had not been as significant as had previously been feared, resulting in just 13 aircraft being shot down by carrier-based fighter pilots.

June 15 also saw Clark and Harrill hit the Bonins with aircraft from three fleet carriers and four light carriers in foul weather. Their target possessed a well-developed radar network that detected the carrier strike about 60 miles out, giving IJNAF fighter pilots time to rise and meet their US Navy counterparts. In the ensuing engagement, VF-1, VF-2 and VF-15 claimed a combined total of 40 victories – all "Zekes" – for the loss of eight Hellcats (some of which fell to antiaircraft fire), with a further 86 aircraft destroyed on the ground. Carrier-based bombers subsequently struck designated targets on the islands 30 minutes after the devastating fighter sweep, and 11 TBM-1Cs and SB2C-1Cs were downed.

Late in the afternoon of June 15, Gato-class submarine USS *Flying Fish* (SS-229) sighted a large group of warships exiting the San Bernardino Strait, further confirming that the IJN was heading for the Marianas. *Flying Fish* was unable to mount an attack because of low fuel, but again the contact report was critical. A further report came in from Balao-class submarine USS *Seahorse* (SS-304), whose crew had sighted an enemy force that included large surface ships heading north from the Moluccas archipelago, in the Dutch East Indies. *Seahorse* then suffered a mechanical problem that prevented it from pursuing *Musashi* and *Yamato*, and their escorts, who were heading north to rendezvous with Ozawa after the cancellation of Operation *Kon*, aimed at relieving the island of Biak, off the coast of northwestern New Guinea, following its invasion by Allied forces on May 27.

The identities of these ships were unknown to the Americans at this time, but between intelligence derived from Ultra code-breaking and submarine sightings, which were enabled by Ultra, Spruance now had a solid understanding that the IJN was intent on engaging TF 58. He then requested that Gen MacArthur extend the search range of the B-24 Liberators based in his area to maximum, while at the same time ordering six Martin PBM Mariner flying boats to deploy from Eniwetok and operate from the roadstead (a sheltered stretch of water) off Saipan, hoping to get eyes on the enemy vessels.

Clark and Harrill, still on station off the Bonins, were scheduled to launch another strike on June 16, but the weather was so bad that morning it prompted a cancellation of all flight operations. Just after noon, there was a slight break in the conditions, despite an approaching typhoon. Clark quickly launched a 54-aircraft strike on Iwo Jima, catching the enemy by surprise, since they thought no one in their right mind would sortie aircraft into that "muck."

US Navy submarines, meanwhile, stayed vigilant in tracking Ozawa's movements. This paid off when Gato-class vessel USS *Cavalla* (SS-244), undertaking its first war patrol, located oilers from the 2nd Supply Force. Pacific Fleet's submarine commander, Vice Adm Lockwood, ordered *Cavalla*'s CO, Lt Cdr Herman Kossler, to trail the oilers after he had initially broken off from the vessels to return to station, as he hoped they would lead the submarine directly to the Japanese carriers.

On D-Day Plus One (June 16), *Princeton*'s Hellcats strafed and set fire to two enemy aircraft parked at Ushi Point airfield on Tinian. They then turned their attention to gun emplacements in the town of Garapan, on Saipan, strafing IJA troops moving south from there toward Charon Kanoa. At the same time, Avengers from VT-27, undertaking precision CAS, laid a string of bombs 400 yards ahead of advancing US forces.

Lt Stambook recalled the CAP duty and CAS missions VF-27 flew in June:

> I was vectored from a CAP flight by the fighter direction officer to shoot down a P1Y Frances twin-engine medium bomber [his victim was actually a "Betty"]. And on two other occasions, I turned the flight lead over to my second section leader and my wingman so they could destroy similar targets. We all did the job, but I never found Navy records of these kills.
>
> In addition to regular CAP duty, we conducted strafing missions against Japanese defenses ahead of our Marines on Saipan. The most gratifying thing that came of this was a statement on the radio from the Marine ground controller who assigned strafing sectors that in essence said, "Well done."

During the attack on June 16, VF-27's Ens F. P. Kleffner was shot down over Guam. His narrow escape from his burning Hellcat earned him the nickname "Smokey Joe." Kleffner, who was flying as wingman for CAG Wood at the time, gave the following account of this memorable mission:

> "Woodie" didn't have any sense of the limitations of the plane, and so we made a screeching dive from about 9,000ft over Guam to look for camouflaged targets – just he and I. The rest of the air group stayed at altitude. We came across the Guam airfield at about 200ft and doing about 300 knots. As I tried to stay with him, I couldn't have seen any targets, camouflaged or not.

The two Hellcats drew intense ground fire from the enemy in the process, as Kleffner recalled:

> Every kind of weapon opened up and caught me instead of him. I don't know what caliber they were using, but there were probably some small arms. One shot the throttle quadrant off in my hand while I had it on "full." The plane started to burn rather well and the oil pressure went to zero. It wasn't long before there was a severe sudden stoppage. RPMs went to the peg on the gauge as there was no prop governor. I could read Hamilton Standard (the prop manufacturer's name) on the propeller blade.

Kleffner briefly considered the possibility of jumping, but "I could see the Japs were still shooting as I zoomed up for altitude." Instead of parachuting, he "stayed in the turkey and got out to sea about a mile before flopping in the water." In so doing, he said, "I probably set some kind of record for stretching a glide." Kleffner scrambled out of the aircraft, at which point he noted that its entire underbelly had melted away as water poured in through the hole caused by the fire. He broke out his emergency rubber boat and inflated his Mae West life jacket, and as he climbed into the tiny raft he spotted splashes in the water all around him.

"I figured these coordinated with puffs of smoke I could see on the beach," Kleffner said, "so I sank the boat and went into the water, leaving just my head sticking out. Sea conditions that close to the beach were not particularly rough." He was later told that one of his squadronmates contacted a destroyer and "threatened them with strafing if they didn't pick me up." Whether or not those threats were actually made was never confirmed.

A naval vessel appeared on the scene about an hour after Kleffner went into the water. "When it was still on the horizon and hull down, I couldn't tell whether it was one of ours or otherwise," he said. "It really felt good when I saw the Stars and Stripes on it." A member of the destroyer's crew let Kleffner know that they intended to try a running pickup because of their closeness to the enemy-held island. "They indicated they were not going to slow down too much, and would throw lots of life rings in my direction, and I had better catch one. I did, and damn near jerked my arms out by the roots. The crew ran up the deck and got me alongside without getting me tangled up in the [ship's] screws."

The vessel was the Farragut-class destroyer USS *Aylwin* (DD-355), a combat veteran that had survived the attack on Pearl Harbor and subsequently been involved in action ranging from the Aleutians to Guadalcanal. Kleffner was relieved to have been rescued so quickly:

> I was happy, and slept the clock around. I was in some sort of mild shock. There was a doctor aboard the ship. He couldn't find one mark on me, so I didn't get the Purple Heart. All in all, it was rather humiliating, as I hadn't done any harm to the enemy. My forced landing [in a burning Hellcat] had been spectacular, and that's how I got my nickname, "Smokey Joe." I had celebrated my 21st birthday on March 9 and got shot down on June 16.

Kleffner was returned to *Princeton* when TF 58 next dropped anchor after the Marianas operation had concluded.

Action intensified on June 17 as IJNAF reconnaissance flights kept trying to locate TF 58. FM-2 Wildcats from four escort carriers continued to shoot them down, claiming eight of ten victories scored during the course of the day. That evening, after trailing the oilers, *Cavalla* reported sighting a force of at least 15 ships. Passing up a chance to attack, the submarine's skipper correctly decided that getting the report sent was much more important. A significant element of Ozawa's *A-Go* force had been found.

At around the same time as *Cavalla* spotted the IJN warships, Ozawa held a meeting on board *Taiho* to discuss strategy with his senior commanders. IJN intelligence informed him that he would be facing Mitscher and Spruance, and he assessed, correctly, that the former would want to aggressively pursue him, but that Spruance would take a defensive stance and keep his carriers within 100–200 miles of Saipan in order to protect the landings.

Ozawa stated that he would keep his forces outside the maximum range of US carrier aircraft, adding that the location of them would be relatively fixed. He would use the range advantage to strike the American carriers, hopefully in a coordinated attack with land-based aircraft flying in from Guam in the opposite direction. His carrier aircraft would then have the option to land, refuel and re-arm on Guam before striking again and then returning to the carrier.

In theory, this was a great plan – strike TF 58 from opposite sides, and at the same time give carrier-based pilots the option to land at a shore-based facility from where they could possibly mount a second attack. Ozawa did not know, however, that his land-based air power had been badly mauled by carrier aircraft during the preceding months to the point where half of his planned strike force had been significantly reduced in number.

While CVLG-27 continued bombing and strafing missions against installations at Rota, 47 miles north of Guam, Clark and Harrill rejoined TF 58 following their strikes in the Bonins. The task force then broke off support of the beachhead on June 17, leaving the escort carriers to provide CAS to the troops ashore. Spruance ordered the vulnerable vessels of TF 51 (the Joint Expeditionary Force) to a position east of the landing area in anticipation of the arrival of the enemy fleet.

That night, another failed attempt to attack TF 58 with torpedo-bombers was carried out, with little damage resulting.

At 0400 hrs on June 18, Capt Arleigh Burke, Mitscher's chief of staff, informed him of the *Cavalla* sighting, concluding that Ozawa would be 660 miles west of Saipan at dawn. He reasoned that if TF 58 immediately began moving in the direction of the enemy force, it would be in range of US carrier aircraft by late afternoon. Mitscher then turned to Vice Adm Lee (CTG 58.7) and asked if he would seek a night engagement with the enemy, pitting his new battleships against their counterparts in the IJN. Lee responded with, "Do not, repeat do not believe we should seek night engagement."

During the Naval Battle of Guadalcanal (November 12–15, 1942), Lee had won an epic, bloody night surface battle after the South Dakota-class battleship USS *South Dakota* (BB-57) had been put out of action, three of his four destroyers sunk and the surviving vessel crippled. In the middle of all this, Lee stood fast on the bridge of the North Carolina-class battleship USS *Washington* (BB-56) and fought off roughly 14 IJN vessels while dodging a flurry of incoming torpedoes. He, along with a growing number of American naval officers, still had a tremendous amount of respect for the enemy's surface fleet and their deadly Long Lance torpedoes. Vividly remembering the nocturnal battle of November 14–15, 1942, the last thing Lee wanted was to take on Japanese capital ships again at night.

At 0600 hrs on June 18 the opposing fleets were roughly 420 miles apart, and both forces, starting early, launched reconnaissance aircraft at daybreak in an effort to precisely determine where they were in relation to one another. US Navy aircraft flew out to 325 nautical miles and found nothing but open ocean. The IJNAF's first search wave consisted of 16 aircraft launched from Van Force carriers. They also failed to make a sighting, and a single Nakajima B5N "Jill" torpedo-bomber flying as a reconnaissance aircraft was shot down by TF 58's CAP.

At noon, an IJNAF aircraft at last reported a sighting after Ozawa had launched an additional 15 machines. Scout No. 15 spotted US carriers, followed a few minutes later by Scout No. 13 sighting a force of surface ships without carriers, which was probably Lee's CTG 58.7.

In reaction to those reports, which were received by the Japanese at around 1500 hrs, the commander of 3rd Carrier Division, Rear Adm Obayashi, operating with the Van Force, aggressively and on his own initiative ordered the launch of a 67-aircraft strike. Reaching TF 58 after dark, the Van Force attack had the potential to cause great damage thanks to it having the element of surprise. However, the pilots and aircrew involved were, in the main, quite inexperienced, thus greatly reducing their chances of delivering a successful attack. Most of the strike was airborne when Ozawa, who was completely unaware aircraft had been launched, ordered a course change to the southwest to maintain his range advantage. Now fearful that his aircraft would run out of fuel when trying to make it back following the attack, Obayashi recalled the strike.

Spruance was playing his hand patiently. If he had permitted Mitscher to close with the enemy as he had wanted to do, the late afternoon strike on June 18 would have run straight into heavy antiaircraft fire from four IJN battleships and eight heavy cruisers while Ozawa's carriers remained safely out of range 100 nautical miles to the rear.

That evening, the Gato-class submarine USS *Finback* (SS-230) sighted searchlights in the distance, but it was too far away to engage. Vessels in Obayashi's 3rd Carrier Division had turned on their searchlights to assist in recovering straggling scout aircraft in the dark after the impromptu strike mission had been aborted. Mistakes like this one could have led to disastrous results for the IJN if the US Navy submarines had been working in wolfpack-type formations and were in a position to attack.

Ozawa added to the blunders that evening when he transmitted a radio message to Vice Adm Kakuta, commander of the remaining IJNAF land-based aircraft in the Marianas, to coordinate air strikes the next day. The intent was for Ozawa's carriers to attack from the west while Kakuta's land-based aircraft struck from the east. Kakuta got the message, as did the Pacific Fleet's high frequency direction finding network (HFDF), thus getting an accurate fix on Ozawa's position. This was quickly forwarded on to Spruance, who, after almost two years of inactivity by the IJN, was reluctant to believe that the enemy fleet was willing to come out and fight.

It was clear to him, however, that the IJN was willing to force a carrier action to counter the American presence in the Marianas. Deciding that he must keep the carriers close to the landings in order to protect them while they were still vulnerable, Spruance also deduced, correctly, that Ozawa would keep his forces at a distance. He then decided on a defensive posture, with roughly 450 Hellcats available to protect the fleet.

During the night of June 18–19, Mitscher repeatedly pestered Spruance to let him go after 1st Mobile Fleet with TF 58 according to the information they had received from the HFDF report. Spruance staunchly refused. The Naval Aviators in the carrier air groups were livid, not truly believing that they would be tied to the Marianas as opposed to doing what they were supposed to do. Their mantra was "the best defense was a good offense." Spruance would not budge, sticking to the overall mission of executing the successful invasion of the Marianas and seeing that operation through by not exposing his flank to a counterattacking, powerful, enemy force.

BATTLE OF THE PHILIPPINE SEA

Enemy activity on June 19 started early. At 0100 hrs, a Japanese aircraft, likely from Guam, dropped float flares in the vicinity of the carriers of TG 58.1, which was usually an indicator of a night torpedo attack, but nothing materialized.

At 0200 hrs, Spruance was informed of the *Finback* sighting of several hours earlier, but he was not aware of another radar detection made by one of the PBM Mariners near the original HFDF contact that confirmed 40 ships within 70 nautical miles of that position, thus validating the hit. The PBM's radio report was not received by anyone in TF 58, the failure in the transmission being chalked up to "atmospherics." Meanwhile, 14 radar-equipped Avengers from *Enterprise* launched a nocturnal search for the enemy carriers, and fell short by 60 miles.

Ozawa ordered his force onto an attack course to the northeast at 0300 hrs as the searches continued. At 0430 hrs the Van Force launched 16 Aichi E13A "Jake" floatplanes from their battleships and cruisers in a two-phase search. They would fly 350 miles and continue on a cross leg at 0700 hrs – only six of the 16 would return. Eight were shot down by TF 58 Hellcats, another was destroyed attempting to reach Guam and the tenth floatplane lost was never heard from again. The Van Force tried again at 0515 hrs when it launched 14 "Jill" torpedo-bombers as scouts, and of these half would be lost.

In a precursor for the action to come, the very first IJNAF aircraft to be downed were engaged at 0547 hrs by CAP Hellcats from VF-28 (embarked in *Princeton*'s sister ship, *Monterey*) and VF-16 (part of *Lexington*'s CVG-16). A "Judy" reconnaissance aircraft and an unidentified bomber were quickly dispatched, with a third aircraft being brought down by gunfire from a screening destroyer. The intruders did not appear to be from a carrier, having probably sortied from Guam as part of the search for TF 58.

By 0600 hours, Ozawa had 43 scout aircraft airborne, and at that time TF 58 was roughly 230 nautical miles west-southwest of Guam, and Ozawa was located more than 300 nautical miles beyond that. TF 58 carriers had also launched scout aircraft – five from *Lexington* and three from *Essex* – but still no sightings were made.

Their IJNAF counterparts were enjoying more success, however, with crews reporting contact with US Navy vessels at 0730 hrs. One of the "Jakes" from Kurita's Van Force spotted American warships, including two carriers, 160 nautical miles due west of Saipan, but it was not an accurate sighting. The report sent by the crew suggested that multiple carrier task groups were operating across a colossal 200-mile stretch of ocean. Then Scout No. 9 sighted a force with no carriers – more than likely Lee's battleships – and at 0734 hrs it also spotted the carriers of Harrill's TG 58.4, which were just to the north of Lee's TG 58.7.

Ozawa then received the most accurate sighting of the day (report 7I) when Scout No. 7 successfully plotted the position of TG 58.1 (Clark). Ozawa immediately turned south, away from the American fleet, to preserve distance, while ordering his carriers to commence launching aircraft.

Mitscher had arrayed his five task groups in two north–south lines by the morning of June 19. To the east, in the middle, was TG 58.3 (Reeves) centered on *Lexington*, which was both the task force and task group flagship with Mitscher and Reeves embarked – *Princeton* was also a part of TG 58.3. Operating 12 nautical miles to the north was TG 58.1 (Clark) and 12 nautical miles to the south was TG 58.2 (Montgomery), maintaining distances close enough to give mutual fighter support without each task group interfering in the flight operations of the others. About 12 nautical miles west of TG 58.1 was TG 58.4 (Harrill).

Mitscher placed Lee's seven fast battleships south of TG 58.4 and southwest of the other task groups. In this position, they operated as a sort of "van force" that would be the first thing the attacking IJNAF aircraft would encounter. These ships not only had the ability to put up a tremendous barrage of antiaircraft fire, they could absorb a lot more punishment than the carriers could.

Following the multiple sightings of TF 58, Vice Adm Kakuta desperately started launching everything under his command that could fly. Just after 0600 hrs 12 bomb-armed "Zekes" from Guam or Tinian attacked the battleship screen but scored no hits. Kakuta had also issued a call for reinforcements from 1st Air Fleet units based on neighboring Japanese-held islands in the Carolines, and roughly 17 aircraft took off for Guam.

It was at this point that Mitscher started receiving reports from CAPs over Guam of heavy enemy air activity around the island. Aircraft and shipboard radios crackled with excited transmissions as fighter pilots from *Belleau Wood*, manning the CAP over the island, reported a flight of enemy aircraft approaching from the southwest. It is believed that these were reinforcements from Truk. Fighters from *Cabot*, *Yorktown* and *Hornet* were quickly vectored toward the *Belleau Wood* group.

In a series of engagements that lasted almost four hours, more than 40 IJNAF aircraft were shot down and the airfields (specifically Orote Field) on Guam endured multiple strafing passes as TF 58 prevented the land-based aircraft on the island from participating in the impending carrier battle. The Naval Aviators of VF-27, assigned uneventful CAPs over their task group, could only sit tight and listen in with envy to the "tally-ho" calls and "splash" reports generated by the fighter squadrons over Guam.

At 0800 hrs, 3rd Carrier Division, consisting of the light carriers *Chitose*, *Chiyoda* and *Zuiho* operating with the Van Force, launched a 69-aircraft strike led by two "Kate" torpedo-bombers that had experienced navigators on board. These veteran aircraft would act as pathfinders, and they had the strike formed up and heading for TF 58 by 0845 hrs. This was Raid One of the Battle of the Philippine Sea, and crews were instructed to act independently after they carried out their attack, with the option of returning to the carrier or recovering on Guam. Mitscher had advanced warning of this strike, and the other raids that followed, because TF 58's radio intelligence teams had the ability to intercept IJNAF radio operators conducting pre-flight checks prior to launch and then in-flight checks while outbound. Additionally, rough estimates of the strikes' rate of closure could be made based on signal strength.

Raid Two, commencing at 0900 hrs and launched from fleet carriers *Taiho*, *Shokaku* and *Zuikaku*, consisted of 128 aircraft. It was Ozawa's main strike effort. While *Taiho* was in the middle of launching Raid

Two, the Gato-class submarine USS *Albacore* (SS-218), with Cdr James Blanchard in command, snuck through A Force's weak destroyer screen. This was Blanchard's first war patrol in command and *Albacore*'s ninth.

The submarine was in a perfect position based on Vice Adm Lockwood's assessment of Ultra intelligence, and Blanchard patiently passed up shots at *Shokaku* and *Zuikaku* for a better shot at *Taiho*. While lining up to fire his torpedoes, *Albacore*'s target data computer failed, forcing Blanchard to eyeball it as he emptied all six bow tubes. As three IJN destroyers converged on his position, he immediately dove as depth charges started to explode dangerously close.

One torpedo struck *Taiho*, and it would have been struck by a second had it not been for a selfless act by WO Sakio Komatsu and his gunner, who had just launched in a "Jill" torpedo-bomber. Sighting the incoming weapon, he deliberately dove his aircraft into the water directly in front of the torpedo, which detonated upon hitting the aircraft.

The torpedo struck *Taiho* on the starboard side just ahead of the forward aircraft elevator, cracking open an aviation fuel tank and flooding the lower well with fuel oil and seawater. The elevator was jammed a few feet below the flightdeck, and crews quickly planked over the hole so that flight operations could resume as the ship continued on its way at 26 knots. Blanchard reported the attack after escaping the depth charges, stating that he believed he had torpedoed a Shokaku-class carrier but he did not think he had sunk it.

At 0957 hrs the battleship *Alabama*, operating with Lee's TG 58.7 southwest of the carrier groups, detected incoming Raid One at a range of 150 nautical miles and an altitude of 18,000–20,000ft. The IJNAF aircraft had become disorganized en route, and it had taken precious time to regroup for a coordinated attack. This allowed Mitscher to transmit the "Hey Rube" code word that signaled all US fighters airborne over Guam to return to the area of the task force, giving the pilots time to prepare for the defense of their carriers against the impending attack.

As the fighters were returning to TF 58, all 15 carriers turned into the wind, along with their escorting vessels, and prepared to launch complete deck loads of fighters – predominantly Hellcats, but also a few Wildcats. At 1017 hrs, the order came from Mitscher – assemble all available fighters. Moments later, with briefing data hastily written on leg pads or clipboards and flight gear donned in record time, pilots dashed for their aircraft. Flightdeck crews worked under terrific strain to help fasten seat belts and guide aircraft as the revved-up engines sent blasts of prop wash across the deck. F6F-3s and FM-2s soon began streaming off the flightdecks of all task group carriers, each succeeding launch following just seconds after the one before.

June 19 brought beautiful weather at daybreak. It was warm and bright, with a ten-knot morning easterly breeze and unlimited ceiling and visibility. Conditions were perfect for fighter pilots tasked with defending the fleet, as they would have to spot their targets in the distance. Ominously for the approaching IJNAF Naval Aviators and aircrew, there were few scattered low clouds that they could use to mask their approach.

After an uneventful early morning CAP, Lt Cdr Bardshar was basking in the sun, taking advantage of the beautiful day, when *Princeton* ordered a scramble. He launched in such a hurry that it was only after he climbed through 10,000ft that he realized he had forgotten to attach his parachute pack to his harness. Fully aware of what was about to take place, VF-27's senior pilots, including Bardshar, had been desperate to get aloft so as not to miss out on the action. Ens Les Blyth (a future ace), Ens Robert Hill and some of the other younger pilots had already manned their aircraft on *Princeton*'s flightdeck when, as Blyth lamented, "Our executive officer [Bardshar] got his division together, came up on the flightdeck and relieved us in the planes. They took off on the 'Turkey Shoot' [as the June 19, 1944 engagement was subsequently dubbed]. We did fly that afternoon, but things were pretty well quieted down by then."

Princeton launched two four-aircraft divisions led by Bardshar and Stambook, which joined up with two divisions (led by CAG Wood and Lt Lamb) that were already on CAP. One of the eight Hellcats launched limped back to the carrier with engine trouble, leaving a total of 17 VF-27 Hellcats airborne. Flying with Wood were Lt(jgs) "Red" Shirley and Howie Gregg, and he gave them the "tally-ho" call when the first wave of incoming enemy aircraft was spotted.

Immediately prior to engaging Raid One, and under the guidance of *Princeton*'s FDO director, the Hellcats had climbed hard to 27,000ft. This had put the Naval Aviators in an ideal position to intercept the "Zekes" and "Judys" (some of which were misidentified as "Tonys" – all aircraft involved in the June 19 mission were exclusively from the IJNAF) that were inbound 2,000–3,000ft below them.

As he gave the jubilant "tally-ho," Wood pushed the throttle "past the firewall" and rolled over for the attack. Within seconds he had pulled away from his wingmen as he hurtled down at incredible speed, plunging into cloud in the process. He was lost from sight momentarily, and when his fighter emerged, a portion of the tail was missing and fragments of fabric and metal floated through the air. Wood went into a vertical dive, and while in the process of performing a rolling pull-out, his vertical stabilizer sheared off under the extreme stress. Wood's F6F continued on its path toward the sea, and his fellow fliers could not spot a hoped-for parachute canopy.

His wingmen, Shirley and Gregg, remained together until they were separated in the wild melee that developed as VF-27 engaged the enemy. Shirley shot down two "Zekes" and set a third fighter on fire but could not confirm its demise. Gregg also damaged two "Zekes," although he too could not confirm them as kills in the confused, fast-moving engagement.

On the decks of the TF 58 ships below, anxious observers watched for indications of what was taking place 20,000–30,000ft overhead. As the horizon-to-horizon aerial battle took shape, the clear blue Pacific sky became laced with a crazy, random pattern of vapor trails. Aircraft pursued each other in deadly individual duels as, periodically, a white streamer curved earthward and became a plume of black smoke before finally impacting the sea.

Lamb's division had quickly become separated from the rest of VF-27 when the unit dived after the enemy formation. Lamb found himself on the tail of a "Zeke" and repeatedly hit it with 0.50-cal. rounds. The enemy fighter refused to go down until nearly two-thirds of his ammunition had been expended. Finally, the aircraft produced a smoke trail and spiraled away in flames as Lamb then pulled up and flew into a formation of scattered clouds to assess his situation. When he came out into clearer skies, he found himself flying close beside a group of seven torpedo-bombers (Lamb identified them as "Kates," but they were almost certainly "Jills," the B6N having replaced virtually all carrier-based B5Ns by then). Each of the aircraft were armed with a Type 91 Mod 3 Air Torpedo to launch against the nearest US Navy ship.

Lamb radioed a report of the approaching danger and asked for help, for although the enemy pilots were making no aggressive movement in his direction, his guns were jammed after the encounter with the "Zeke." Working feverishly, he succeeded in getting all six 0.50-cal.

weapons operable again and turned them on the torpedo-bombers. Systematically, one by one, Lamb picked off his quarry until three of the seven had been destroyed. As he ran out of ammunition, other Hellcats arrived and shot down the remaining aircraft. This extraordinary action would earn Lt William Lamb a Navy Cross.

Flying with him were Lt Hank Brotherton and Lt(jg)s Hugh Loveland and Van 'Castaway' Carter. Brotherton, having shot down two enemy aircraft, was chasing a third when he was forced to return to *Princeton* for fuel. Loveland destroyed one and damaged several others. Carter was not seen again after the initial "tally-ho" and the frantic first moments of the aerial battle.

Raid Three commenced at 1000 hrs when 2nd Carrier Division launched a 47-aircraft strike. A few minutes later, *Lexington*'s radar detected incoming Raid Two. Repeating the mistake made by Raid One, the pilots of Raid Two wasted time trying to get reorganized to attack, allowing VF-27 and VF-15 (from *Essex*) to pounce about 40 nautical miles west of TG 58.7's battleships.

Bardshar, covered by his wingman Ens Art Munson, plowed into the "Judy" dive-bombers, while Ens Gordon Stanley and Ens Lief Erickson – the remaining two members of the division – attacked the covering "Zeke" fighters. In minutes, Bardshar had shot down two "Judys," Stanley two "Judys" and two "Tonys" (also "Judys") and Erickson a "Zeke" and a "Kate" (probably a "Jill"). Stanley had accounted for two of his victories in a single firing pass, shifting his focus to a second target just as his first victim exploded under a hail of 0.50-cal. bullets.

The one-sided clashes with IJNAF aircraft from Raids One and Two had resulted in VF-27 claiming 29 victories, six probables and five damaged for the loss of two aircraft and their pilots. Bardshar later reflected on how the interceptions had played out from his perspective:

> Air communication discipline had been emphasized in VF-27 and was evident in the engagement. Section integrity was, generally, maintained, and transmissions were limited and to the point. We learned, among other things, that the F6F belly tank was a critical recognition item. Those who jettisoned their tanks were subject to attack by US aircraft from other squadrons.
>
> The tactics of our principal intercept were not refined, and we were quite vulnerable to the escorting Zeros who had a usable

altitude advantage. Having no altitude advantage on the bombers ourselves, we initiated with flat side runs followed by tail chases. My shots were all no deflection, which I think was typical. The Japanese were unquestionably constrained by fuel limitations.

Launched at the same time as Bardshar, Lt Dick Stambook had led his division on a cover orbit at 20,000ft directly overhead the task group while another division from VF-27 was below the quartet of fighters at 10,000ft. They received a radio transmission from the *Lexington* FDO giving them instructions to "vector [steer] 280 degrees at angels 20 [an altitude of 20,000ft], speed buster [maximum speed]" to intercept and destroy a large enemy formation heading "100 degrees, angels 20 and closing at eight nautical miles." This was Raid Two, as Stambook recalled:

> I called "tally-ho" at about 1030 hrs when I spotted the Zero high cover for the enemy bombers above the horizon. The sight of these enemy fighters prompted me to climb a few thousand feet more to gain the altitude necessary to build up a performance advantage if I needed it for conversion to speed. I reported 16 to 18 fighters escorting 21 to 24 Judy dive-bombers.

The Zero-sens did not prove to be very aggressive as Stambook began the attack:

> I probably would have delayed the engagement a few seconds and made a quartering firing run on the Zeros, but the apparently unperturbed progress inclined me to first attack the leader from above at about 10 o'clock. This required a brief burst of all six rifles [machine guns] at a range well outside the boresight distance of about 300 yards. I was in luck, blowing up the Zero.

Stambook then turned left onto an easterly heading to parallel the flight of enemy fighters. By then, the Zero-sens were becoming a little more aggressive:

> I had swung a bit wide to the south during my first gunnery pass on account of my diving speed, so I was heading back with about a 30-degree angle on the Zero formation, when almost before I could position myself, a Hellcat crossed in front of me, with a Zero

closing from behind. Since all three of us were at the same altitude and descending slightly together, it was my good fortune to get in a firing position on the Zero by making only a slight left-wing dip. As I recovered with a small gunsight lead, and pulling only about 2gs, I fired a short burst that blew the Zero to pieces.

The fight continued to descend to around 12,000ft:

> I was deciding on my next target – the closest Zekes – when my second section leader came into view, leading a Zero across my flight path in a steep descent at about a 40-degree angle from my airplane. The Zeke was rapidly closing to firing range, but with the excess speed I had gained during my descent from altitude, I maneuvered rapidly to fire into it while pulling about 3gs. I saw my arcing tracers hit the target just before it exploded.

With his adrenaline flowing after downing three "Zekes," Stambook looked around at a now-empty sky for further targets. He soon spotted a solitary "Judy" several thousand feet below him – Stambook was flying at 8,000–9,000ft at the time. Having positioned himself behind the dive-bomber after some maneuvering, he then discovered that his guns were jammed. After breaking off his pursuit to clear his weapons, he then repositioned himself on the "Judy's" tail and opened fire. The aircraft soon fell away in flames, despite the rear gunner having done his best to put Stambook off his aim.

Scanning the sky for another target, he sighted a Zero-sen flying straight and level off in the distance. Making a 20-degree heading change in order to close the distance for an attack, Stambook soon became very aware that unlike the previous four aircraft he had shot down during the mission to date, this fighter was not being flown by a novice:

> As I was getting into position on the Zero, two Hellcats in close formation dived over me from almost 180 degrees behind and fired at the Zero, which at the right moment went into a violent left skid. It worked. I personally was relieved that my own plane had not been hit by spent cartridge casings from the overflying F6Fs. The casings might have fouled my engine.

Once again, two more F6Fs dove on the Zero-sen, showering Stambook's Hellcat with empty casings. These two also missed when the enemy pilot pulled up and conducted another left skid, which caused Stambook to pause his pursuit. While regaining his focus, a single Hellcat appeared and its pilot did not miss, dispatching the Zero-sen in a ball of flames. Shortly thereafter, Stambook got a reading on *Princeton*'s YE-ZB homing beacon and was invited back aboard. After "safing" his guns and completing the landing checklist, he successfully trapped back aboard the ship.

As squadron debriefing reports were completed and details relayed to the admiral's staff on the flagship, the full significance of the results emerged. It had been one of the most one-sided aerial victories ever, inflicting a telling blow on Japan's steadily dwindling air strength. Few aircraft of the IJNAF's strike force had penetrated TF 38's perimeter, causing very little damage.

Between 0830 hrs and 1130 hrs, Ozawa had launched 326 aircraft from his nine carriers in a total of four separate raids – almost as many aircraft as the six carriers involved in the attack on Pearl Harbor had launched in December 1941. This was everything the Mobile Fleet could muster in what was very much a maximum strike effort. The IJNAF carrier squadrons at that time were staffed in the main by Naval Aviators who had been taught little more than the basics, and were nowhere near the quality of their predecessors from the 1941–43 period. Nevertheless, the enemy strike groups, due to their large numbers and the aircrews' raw courage and grim determination to penetrate the US Navy CAP and target the carriers, were still a force to be reckoned with.

The attacking IJNAF aircraft never encountered the full force of TF 58's available Hellcats that day because of the nature of carrier warfare. There were ample reserves waiting on deck, aircraft refueling and rearming, and the usual mishaps that took place causing delays in launches that consequently ruled F6Fs out of the fight. Although the Hellcat pilots were outnumbered by the enemy throughout the large-scale raids of June 19, the far better trained US Navy fighter pilots, guided by a superior network of shipboard air, surface and fire control radars, and equipped with IFF transponders and new four-channel VHF radios, were always in an advantageous position to launch their attacks. All of these factors also enabled the FDOs operating from new Combat Information Centers (CICs) within the carriers to effectively orchestrate the largest carrier battle in history firmly in favor of TF 58.

A group of the IJNAF aircraft that had survived the fighter gauntlet then made the mistake of turning toward Lee's battleships, where they were miraculously able to damage *South Dakota* and sister ship USS *Indiana* (BB-58), as well as two heavy cruisers. In the midst of all of this action, a group of dive- and torpedo-bombers decided to target *Enterprise* and *Princeton*. The "Jills" split off and initially went after *Enterprise*, but only one B6N succeeded in dropping a torpedo that exploded in the carrier's wake. *Princeton*, meanwhile, successfully dodged bombs from three "Judys." Then two more "Jills" appeared off *Princeton*'s starboard beam, but its guns splashed both of them.

Shortly after noon, the action continued as a lone "Jill" again roared in from the starboard side and dropped a torpedo, prompting *Princeton* to turn hard right to reduce the target angle as its guns opened up. The weapon missed and the attacking aircraft quickly had one of its wings shot off, causing the "Jill" to roll onto its back before hitting the surface of the water inverted.

In the final attack of the day, Raid Four was an 84-aircraft strike comprised of machines from *Taiho* and *Zuikaku*. Its pilots were intent on carrying out the shuttle plan – attack TF 58, land on Guam to refuel and strike again on the way back to the carriers. However, Raid Four had trouble finding their targets, and, after a fruitless search, the inexperienced pilots split up, with *Zuikaku*'s aircraft heading back to their carrier and the rest heading for Guam.

SUBMARINE STRIKE

While IJNAF and US Navy aircraft fought it out in the skies above the Philippine Sea, American submarines had remained watchful on its surface. At around noon, *Cavalla* sighted the Japanese carrier *Shokaku* in the midst of recovering fighters. The submarine's CO, Lt Cdr Kossler, could not immediately identify the carrier as Japanese due to the fact that he was not fully aware of TF 58's exact location. Kossler took the surfaced *Cavalla* in close enough to get a positive identification on a Japanese flag, immediately after which he fired a spread of all six bow tubes at eight-second intervals.

The target data computer expected four hits according to the geometry of the torpedo spread. However, either just before or just after the first torpedo was fired, the Kagero-class destroyer *Urakaze* spotted *Cavalla* and charged toward it. Kossler immediately went into a crash dive as the fifth torpedo was being fired, while the sixth was fired at a down angle after being hung up for a few moments in the tube. The first depth charge from *Urakaze* exploded simultaneously with the first torpedo impact on *Shokaku*. Being unable to out-maneuver the incoming torpedoes, the carrier was hit twice more on its starboard side forward and aft, igniting large fuel fires in the hangar bay, knocking out the number one boiler room and blowing a screw offline.

The carrier initially continued to steam ahead as its crew fought growing fires, only to then begin to take on a list to starboard that subsequently shifted to port as counterflooding overcompensated. The fires in the hangar bay rapidly spread when oxygen bottles in aircraft started exploding and ammunition began to cook off. The shutter screens between the hangar bays that were supposed to be fireproof failed to stop the conflagration from spreading as bombs exploded, setting off fuel vapor that had been leaking from a cracked tank. This in turn induced several larger explosions.

After an hour of trying to save the ship, Capt Hiroshi Matsubara issued the order to prepare to abandon *Shokaku*. As the crew assembled on the flightdeck for an abandon ship ceremony, which is a Japanese custom, the vessel suddenly lurched and then rolled over, resulting in the deaths of 1,272 sailors.

Meanwhile, *Cavalla* was getting hammered by more than 100 depth charges from three IJN destroyers over a three-hour period, causing severe damage. While in its initial emergency dive, the submarine exceeded its test depth by a harrowing 100ft before recovering, but with several issues for the crew to deal with. The main air induction trunk had flooded, adding about 15 tons of water to the vessel, along with additional flooding in the forward torpedo room bilges which made *Cavalla* difficult to control. Three of the four sonar sets were flooded, leaving it barely able to track the enemy destroyers that were busy trying to split the submarine in two. This forced Kossler to risk increasing speed, which in turn heightened the chance of detection, in order to maintain depth so as to offset the noise made by the operation of pumps to clear the flooding. Ultimately, *Cavalla* survived the day, earning a Navy Cross for Kossler and a Presidential Unit Citation for the submarine.

By 1430 hrs, as the battle was now in its latter stages, Ozawa assumed that most of his aircraft had made it to Guam, since very few had come back to their ships. With two carriers damaged, one of which was in its death throes, and not enough fighters to protect his fleet, Ozawa decided it was time to egress and put some distance between himself and TF 58.

1st Carrier Division's troubles were not over, however, for at 1530 hrs a massive explosion wracked *Taiho*, buckling its armored flightdeck lengthwise, blowing holes out of the sides of the hangar bay and holing the underside of the ship's hull. Following *Albacore*'s torpedo hit in the morning *Taiho* had continued operations, for the damage seemed minimal. The damage control teams understood that they had a serious problem, however, with leaking fuel vapor. They tried to punch holes in the sides of the hangar bay (the Japanese carriers did not have the rolling "curtains" like their American counterparts), and other attempts had only succeeded in spreading the vapor throughout the entire ship.

What eventually triggered the explosion remains unknown. Although having suffered catastrophic damage, *Taiho* remained on an even keel throughout the ordeal and took more than an hour to go down. Firefighting parties managed to hold the flames in the bow, despite loss of power, and a destroyer was pulling into position to take the carrier under tow when additional flames broke out aft – the ship could not be saved. Ozawa wanted to go down with *Taiho*, but his chief of staff talked him out of it, convincing him that there was still a chance of winning the battle. The Japanese penchant for overexaggerated reports on damage they had inflicted on the enemy, combined with the optimism that many of his aircraft had reached Guam as per the original battle plan, gave Ozawa pause and some temporary optimism.

At 1630 hrs Spruance decided to leave Harrill's TG 58.4 close to Saipan and allow the rest of TF 58 to commence the pursuit of Ozawa in a long-range strike the next day after reports had flooded in detailing massive IJNAF losses.

In "Fighting 27's" ready room on *Princeton*, the exhilaration of victory was coupled with an acute awareness of the unit's losses following the events of June 19. Lt Cdr Wood had been a well-liked and respected leader, and Van Carter was a friend, a companion and a fellow warrior participating in a very dangerous business. VF-27 had shot down 30 enemy aircraft (the last of which had fallen to Lt Carl Brown at 1605 hrs when his division was vectored onto a contact over Rota airfield and he shot down a "Judy" he misidentified as a "Tony" that was attempting to land), making it the highest scoring light carrier squadron of the day. Lt Dick Stambook had become the unit's first ace following his four-victory haul, and a further five future aces had also registered kills.

TF 58 had survived the most concentrated attacks against US carriers of the entire Pacific War by the end of June 19, 1944. Only two flattops and two battleships suffered minor damage throughout the day, and all were fully operational. Some 31 US Navy aircraft had been lost during the course of the battle, this total including 17 Hellcats downed in combat and four lost to operational causes. Fourteen F6F pilots and 13 other Naval Aviators and aircrew were dead or missing.

The air battle over the Philippine Sea subsequently became known as the "Great Marianas Turkey Shoot," and it had devastated the IJNAF. US Navy pilots claimed 229 Japanese aircraft shot down while opposing the four carrier raids (actual numbers are closer to 220–224). Among the personnel lost were 22 of 35 IJNAF squadron commanders committed to the operation, plus many senior fighter pilots. The tally of victories claimed by US Navy pilots on June 19 totals 380 when kills over land-based aircraft flying from Guam and Tinian are taken into account. A further 19 were credited to shipboard gunners. Finally, *Taiho* and *Shokaku* took 27 aircraft down with them and a further 60-plus were destroyed on the ground on Guam and Tinian. The units of the three carrier divisions and 1st Air Fleet had haemorrhaged aircraft and crews to the extent that the IJNAF was now a spent force in the Central Pacific.

On this day, Adm Spruance had participated in a hardcore game of poker and played his hand perfectly. One of the deadliest tactics employed in combat is ambush warfare, whether it be on land or at sea, and that is precisely how he positioned his forces. A good commander fully understands the capabilities of his troops and weapons systems, as well as that of his enemy. He also knows there are two things that almost always influence the outcome of every military operation – terrain and weather.

In this case, Spruance let the inherent aggressiveness of the IJN, along with the range advantage enjoyed by its aircraft, play into a scenario that literally wiped the IJNAF out. The terrain was simple – an open ocean that put a tremendous amount of space between TF 58 and IJN warships. Instead of closing the distance between his vessels and those of the enemy, Spruance stayed patient and let his prey venture into the "kill zone" that he had prepared. Then he simply unleashed the tremendous firepower that his fleet possessed – 450 Hellcats with highly trained pilots at the controls. They were Spruance's equivalent of the English longbowmen at the Battle of Agincourt.

Additionally, by letting the IJNAF come to them, rather than engaging enemy aircraft over IJN warships, many of the US Navy pilots that were shot down were successfully rescued and returned to their units. This would not have been the case had they been forced to bail out or ditch hundreds of miles from TF 58. Lastly, the IJN's powerful force of capital ships and heavy cruisers were not given the opportunity to engage their US Navy counterparts in a surface fleet battle that would have again exposed American vessels to the deadly Type 93 Long Lance torpedo – a weapon that contributed to the sinking of 22 Allied warships in World War II.

THE CHASE

Having neutralized the aerial threat posed by Ozawa's task force on June 19, TF 58 now set off in pursuit of the Combined Fleet in the second, and final, day of the Battle of the Philippine Sea. With the tail chase on in earnest, the US Navy vessels were pounded relentlessly by the prevailing westerly wind as they attempted to close a 320-mile gap.

Rear Adm Harrill's mishandling of refueling TG 58.4 dictated that it be left behind on station off Saipan while the rest of TF 58 commenced the stern chase. At 1359 hrs on June 20, a reconnaissance aircraft from *Enterprise* spotted the enemy carriers, and at 1715 hrs a "Jake" floatplane from the Takao-class heavy cruiser *Maya* sighted and reported TF 58, leaving Ozawa in no doubt that the US Navy was still not finished.

On board the American carriers, mission planners determined that the distance to the IJN fleet was about 230 miles – just at the outer limit for US Navy strike aircraft. An immediate launch would result in a night recovery. Fully aware of a looming fuel shortage among his vessels, Mitscher gave the "Launch 'em" order. At 1624 hrs, with 12 carriers in TGs 58.1, 58.2 and 58.3 contributing, 240 aircraft (of which 226 attacked) manned by 411 pilots and aircrew roared off the flightdecks, bound for the remnants of the Combined Fleet.

For CVLG-27, the day was a disappointment. Its aircraft had been assigned the chore of flying routine CAPs over TF 58, and this meant that neither VF-27 or VT-27 took part in the strike. This may have been a deliberate decision by higher command following the loss of CAG Wood the previous day.

After a successful strike against the retreating IJN fleet that had seen the light carrier *Hiyo* sunk and *Zuikaku*, *Junyo* and *Chiyoda* damaged (the battleship *Haruna* was also hit), the return flight was a challenge, even for the most experienced pilots. It was an exceptionally dark night with a new moon and an overcast, all of which increased the possibility of vertigo. Furthermore, some pilots, a number of them wounded, were flying damaged aircraft. Every last one of them was critically low on fuel. The YE-ZB homing beacon on the carriers was good out to 70 nautical miles when working properly, but that still left more than 150 nautical miles to navigate blind. The good news was that TF 58 had managed to close the distance by about 90 nautical miles during the outbound flight.

Sunset was just before 1900 hrs, with US Navy warships making radar contact on the returning strike at 2015 hrs. Most of the aircraft were to the west, but a number of them were off track to the north and south. At 2020 hrs, Mitscher gave the order for every vessel in the task force to turn on their lights. The returning pilots closest to the fleet were astonished, but definitely grateful, to see TF 58 lit up like New York City. The fleet soon attracted aircraft to it, resulting in a very chaotic recovery period. The lights were turned off when it became apparent that no more struggling aircraft would be returning to the task force.

Carrier crews worked throughout the night to clear the flightdecks of debris and wreckage, and to salvage any aircraft deemed to be worth saving. As dawn broke, a massive recovery effort got underway to search for the many missing Naval Aviators and their aircrew. For three days, TF 58 and its carrier aircraft scoured thousands of square miles of ocean for downed airmen. Dozens of life rafts and dye markers were spotted, followed by a radio report that brought a ray of hope that a friend, a fellow shipmate, had managed to survive this ordeal. Miraculously, most of those who had gone down in that black sea were indeed rescued.

Of the 172 pilots and aircrew who either bailed out or ditched into the dark Pacific Ocean on the night of June 20, 90 were soon rescued in the vicinity of the carriers. Eventually, all bar 16 pilots and 33 aircrew were pulled from the sea. Combined with 14 Hellcat pilots killed during the "Turkey Shoot" and 13 other pilots and aircrew lost during searches or in action over Guam on June 19, 76 Naval Aviators and aircrew had been killed and 42 aircraft lost in combat during the two-day Battle of the Philippine Sea. On board the ships of TF 58, 33 sailors had been killed either by Japanese bombs or fratricidal antiaircraft fire.

Prior to engaging in the battle, Vice Adm Ozawa had nine carriers with 430 carrier aircraft embarked. His capital ships and cruisers could also muster 43 floatplanes between them. Once the two fleets had disengaged, he had six carriers, 35 operational carrier aircraft and 12 floatplanes. Including Guam-based aircraft, the IJNAF had lost 476 aircraft and 445 pilots and aircrew. The largest carrier battle in history had turned into the most lopsided naval defeat in history.

While the US Navy had clearly won the Battle of the Philippine Sea, the occupation of the Marianas pressed on, with *Princeton*'s CVLG-27 continuing to support troops ashore. Organized resistance ended on Saipan on July 9, with the Marianas operation officially ceasing on August 10. From June 11 through to August 10, VF-27 had been the tenth highest scoring squadron of the campaign.

The most breathtaking naval force in history dropped anchor at Eniwetok on August 2. *Princeton*'s machinist's mates tended to its boilers as the ship was resupplied and rearmed, while the crew was given the opportunity to go ashore for rest and recreation. This proved to be a mixed blessing for some, as the sun in the Central Pacific was intense and particularly brutal for sailors who had not seen much in the way of daylight while working below decks. Exhausted from months at sea, many men simply fell asleep on the beach and returned to the ship with terrible sunburn – a hard lesson learned while trying to get a "tan." Simply touching a bed sheet to any flaming-red portion of their body was extremely painful, and virtually every sickbay on board the ships of the task force worked overtime treating sailors with sunburn.

The hot tropical sun was not the only recreational hazard awaiting those that explored the Marshall Islands lagoon. The varieties of fish were endless and fascinating, and servicemen wandering about on these beaches found them hard to ignore. If the fisherman was lucky, he had been educated on the differences between the safe species and those to avoid like the plague. Some were edible at certain times of the year, but fatal if eaten during the wrong season.

Many spent hours collecting seashells. Among those most sought after were cat eyes, which got their name from the colored pattern on the shell. After a good cleaning and polishing, they could be fashioned into attractive necklaces and bracelets for trading in port or for taking home as a souvenir.

Varied recreation programs were available during task force interludes at Majuro, Eniwetok, Ulithi and other atolls or islands that had been established as forward bases and fleet supply points after being taken from the Japanese. According to Aviation Machinist's Mate Lyle Giddle:

> When we got liberty, we'd go ashore for a bottle of beer, a swim and to hunt shells. At Eniwetok, they had one place fixed up pretty good for liberty parties. There was an old Japanese ammunition ship that had sunk there. Part of it stuck up above the water, and guys would swim out to it, although they weren't supposed to. There was some swimming off the side of the ships too, as well as the occasional movie in the hangar bay at night.

Organized sports ranged from volleyball to boxing (which was usually limited to those with prior experience), and many more besides, depending upon preference. The star of *Princeton*'s volleyball team was 2Lt Sam Jaskilka, who commanded the carrier's US Marine Corps detachment. While in the service, Jaskilka rose from the rank of second lieutenant to four-star general, eventually serving as deputy commandant of the US Marine Corps prior to his retirement.

Giddle recalled some particularly memorable sporting events that took place while *Princeton* was anchored at Eniwetok:

> Sailors from the *San Jacinto*, sister ship to *Princeton*, were invited over for the first competition outside their own property. They brought their volleyball teams, their boxers and also their orchestra. They had

better volleyball teams, but our boys won five of the nine boxing bouts. There was a turkey dinner that day with all the trimmings, and the *San Jacinto* orchestra played. Later, we went to the *Cabot*, another CVL, won the boxing card, and broke even in volleyball. Another time, our boxing team beat the guys from the *Langley*. We had in our crew one fighter who, before his induction in the Navy, had a chance at the middleweight title back home. His name was Buddy O'Dell.

One would-be boxer was held in considerable awe by his crewmates because of his impressive physique and his boastings of the damage he was planning to do to his opponents. This all changed shortly after he climbed into the ring for the first time. His opponent landed a flurry of blows in the first round, much to "Mr Big's" shock and surprise. Before the bell sounded at the end of the round, he climbed back through the ropes and let everyone know that he didn't want any more of that. His stock among his fellow sailors fell drastically, particularly with those who had put a wager on the bout's outcome.

One group of pilots from CVLG-27, after tiring of target shooting with their sidearms, discovered an Eniwetok octopus. VT-27 pilot Lt(jg) Tom Mooney tells the tale:

> When our ammunition was gone, we got some cans of beer and went back to the beach, where somehow we came across a large metal wash tub several feet in diameter and maybe ten or twelve inches high. We filled it with ice for the beer and started wading around in the surf.
>
> Octopuses were common in the lagoon, and we were careful around any coral outcroppings where we might come across one. I'm not sure where we found the damn thing, but it was my idea to unload the wash tub and try to scoop him up in the knee-deep water, which was so clear you could see for 50ft. He wasn't very big, maybe ten to twenty inches across his body when the tentacles weren't extended. He was pretty docile, and it seemed easy just to slip the tub under him, lift it up and carry the tub and octopus 30ft or so above the high-water line.
>
> It was really exciting just to watch him lobbing up and down for a while, not doing much of anything. It occurred to us that he needed a change of water periodically, so we'd carry the tub into the surf, let a wave break over it, and carry him back. He attracted a lot of attention

from other guys in the area; and I'm sure we had pretty good stories of how we had been deep diving when we caught him in 20–30ft of reef water!

As the afternoon wore on it got to be a drag to carry the tub back and forth to the surf to refresh the creature's water supply. The beer we had been issued wasn't the greatest. I decided to empty the last several cans into the wash tub. I wasn't even looking at him. With no warning at all, that little devil went crazy. Two or more tentacles were wrapped around my left arm.

In one millisecond all the grade "B" movies I had ever seen about divers being dragged to their deaths by an eight-foot-in-diameter octopus flashed before my eyes. I have no clear recollection as to how I got rid of him, but I do know that he had me flailing and pulling with my free hand, using all the strength I had. Somehow, I pulled the tentacles off. There was a hunting knife in my belt, but I knew I couldn't use it without cutting my own arm. Once out of his grip, I made an instant decision – get rid of that octopus. We carried the tub carefully down to the surf and threw him out of it. Moral – never give an octopus cheap beer.

7

"Uncle Sam's Cyclone"

A clever process of handing the ever-growing fleet off between the two commanders, Adms Spruance and Halsey, was devised by Adms King and Nimitz during World War II. The fleet and task force designation changed when the command changed hands. While under Fifth Fleet control, its commander was Adm Spruance, and the Fast Carrier Task Force was TF 58, while the invasion force was called the Fifth Amphibious Force. While under Third Fleet control, its commander was Adm Halsey and the Fast Carrier Task Force was TF 38, while the invasion force was designated the Third Amphibious Force.

The original TF 38 came into existence in August 1943, being built around the aging *Saratoga* and with Rear Adm Sherman in command. TF 58 was created on January 6, 1944 with Rear Adm Mitscher commanding, serving under the leadership of Adm Spruance in Fifth Fleet. TF 38 continued to exist, but as a command structure only, while TF 58 carried out multiple operations across the Central Pacific, starting with the Gilberts. The fleet never changed, just the commander – a concept that the Japanese became wise to in the latter stages of the war. Indeed, the enemy thought that the US Navy possessed two tremendous fleets, each with their own commander. Spruance handed the fleet off to Adm Halsey on August 26, 1944, after which he headed back to Pearl Harbor to plan the Iwo Jima and Okinawa invasions.

Mitscher requested that he retain command of the Fast Carrier Task Force until his replacement, Vice Adm John S. McCain, had had time to become more familiar with its operation. Halsey, like Spruance, sailed with the Fast Carrier Task Force, which was then composed of nine fleet carriers and eight light carriers.

To prepare for the western Carolines and Philippines operations, TF 38 consisted of four task groups. TG 38.1 was commanded by Vice Adm John S. McCain, with its previous commander, Rear Adm Joseph J. Clark, remaining on as an advisor. TG 38.2 was commanded by Rear Adm Gerald F. Bogan, TG 38.3 was commanded by Rear Adm Frederick C. Sherman and TG 38.4 was commanded by Rear Adm Ralph E. Davison.

Halsey was raring for a fight. After being hospitalized with a serious case of psoriasis upon completion of the Doolittle Raid, and thus missing Coral Sea and Midway, it was now time to command from the bridge of a warship after "driving a desk" in the South Pacific since late 1942. Then Vice Adm Halsey had been appointed Commander, South Pacific Force and South Pacific Area on October 18, 1942. The forces under his command went into action exactly one week later when the hard fought Battle of the Santa Cruz Islands commenced on October 25, and the following month Halsey also oversaw the Naval Battle of Guadalcanal. Success in the latter campaign effectively secured an Allied victory in the Solomons.

Over the next 16 months, Halsey would command all Allied armed forces in-theater, which remained on the offensive, attacked enemy bases in the Bismarck Archipelago and oversaw successful central and northern Solomons invasions that culminated in the isolation of Rabaul.

Now, as the fall of 1944 approached, Halsey and Mitscher had 16 carriers for the sweep westward. The Fast Carrier Task Force would be operating at full strength for the first time since going into battle with the Mobile Fleet in mid-1944.

TF 38 Organization, Carolines and Philippines, August 28, 1944
Commander-in-Chief, United States Fleet and Chief of Naval
    Operations – Adm E. J. King
Commander-in-Chief, Pacific Fleet – Adm C. W. Nimitz
Commander, Third Fleet – Adm W. F. Halsey
Commander, TF 38 – Vice Adm M. A. Mitscher

Commander, TG 38.1 – Vice Adm J. S. McCain
    Hornet – Capt A. K. Doyle (CVG-2 embarked)
    Wasp – Capt O. A. Weller (CVG-14 embarked)
    Belleau Wood – Capt J. A. Perry (CVLG-21 embarked)
    Cowpens – Capt H. W. Taylor (CVLG-22 embarked)
    Monterey – Capt S. I. Ingersoll (CVLG-28 embarked)
Commander, TG 38.2 – Rear Adm G.F. Bogan
    Intrepid – Capt J. F. Bolger (CVG-18 embarked)
    Bunker Hill – Capt M. R. Greer (CVG-8 embarked)
    Cabot – Capt S. J. Michael (CVLG-31 embarked)
    Independence – Capt E. C. Ewen (CVLG(N)-41 embarked)
Commander, TG 38.3 – Rear Adm F. C. Sherman
    Essex – Capt C. W. Wieber (CVG-15 embarked)
    Lexington – Capt E. W. Litch (CVG-19 embarked)
    Princeton – Capt W. H. Buracker (CVLG-27 embarked)
    Langley – Capt W. M. Dillon (CVLG-32 embarked)
Commander, TG 38.4 – Rear Adm R. E. Davison
    Franklin – Capt J. M. Shoemaker (CVG-13 embarked)
    Enterprise – Capt C. D. Glover (CVG-20 embarked)
    San Jacinto – Capt M. H. Kernodle (CVLG-51 embarked)

Princeton, commanded by Capt Buracker, sortied from Eniwetok with TG 38.3 as a part of TF 38 for Philippine waters on August 29, 1944. Lt Cdr Bardshar, now promoted to CAG of CVLG-27 and CO of VF-27, had 25 F6F-3 Hellcats and nine TBM-3 Avengers of VT-27 (led by Lt Cdr Sebron Haley, who had been an OS2U pilot assigned to the battleship *California* when Pearl Harbor was attacked) under his command.

Halsey, leading Third Fleet from the Iowa-class battleship USS *New Jersey* (BB-62), set out to do battle with the enemy. According to Allied plans, his vessels would support simultaneous landings at Morotai, in the Dutch East Indies, and Peleliu, in the Palau archipelago, on September 15, Mindanao, in the southern Philippines, on November 15, and Leyte, in the central Philippines, on December 26. Halsey was carrying out a two-fold mission: first, support the landings at Morotai and Peleliu; and second, whittle down the approximately 650 IJNAF and IJAAF aircraft spread over 63 airfields in or near the Philippines. Third Fleet had a ten-week window to get this mission accomplished prior to the start of the Mindanao operation.

The action commenced with Davison's TG 38.4 striking Iwo Jima and Chichi Jima from August 31 to September 2, before moving on to attack Yap on September 6 – *Monterey* had targeted Wake Island the previous day. *Princeton* had crossed the equator on September 1, with its primary target being a familiar island from past operations, Peleliu – the site of an upcoming amphibious invasion by the 1st Marine Division in Operation *Stalemate II*. On September 6 TGs 38.1, 38.2 and 38.3 struck the Palau Islands, and after several bombing and strafing attacks the fast carriers pulled away on the 8th and turned the CAS over to a force of "baby" flattops and older battleships.

Ranging further west on September 9–10, carrier-based squadrons attacked installations in northern Mindanao. Del Monte, on the southernmost island of Mindanao, was attacked by aircraft from *Princeton* (VT-27 only), *Lexington* and *Enterprise*, while VF-27 undertook CAP and antisubmarine patrols for the task group. That day, guerillas in their jungle hideouts were able to see US forces attacking the enemy they had been resisting for more than two years. With the strikes being virtually unopposed and, therefore, very successful, Halsey "poured on the coal" and headed north.

On September 11, *Enterprise*, *Lexington* and *Princeton* launched aircraft that pounded the Visayan Islands in the central Philippines. Both VT-27 and VF-27 struck targets as far west as Iloilo, on Panay Island, as well as airfields and other targets on Negros, Cebu and Mactan. The Avengers and Hellcats destroyed enemy aircraft on the ground and set fire to barracks, repair facilities and oil storage tanks.

Halsey simply could not believe the relative lack of Philippine-based Japanese air strength during these operations. Nevertheless, TF 38's fighter and dive-bomber units claimed 82 aerial victories on September 12 over Cebu and Negros, and a further 94 kills over Negros the following day. More aircraft were destroyed on the ground and a number of small vessels sunk.

A stroke of good luck then came Halsey's way in the form of Ens Thomas C. Tillar from CVG-2's VF-2, embarked in *Hornet*. Shot down over Mactan Island, in the Visayas, on September 12 shortly after downing a "Zeke," he was sheltered by local Filipinos who informed him of the weak Japanese defenses in the central Philippines. Tillar was soon picked up by a Consolidated PBY flying boat and returned to his ship, where a report on his encounter with the locals was passed up to Rear Adm Clark on *Hornet*. This information soon reached Halsey, reaffirming his suspicions that the enemy's air defenses in the region were effectively a hollow shell.

With TF 38 having achieved aerial superiority in the western Pacific, there would be no need to invade Mindanao. Halsey now also believed that there was no need to whittle away Japanese air defenses in the Philippines for ten weeks prior to putting troops ashore. At noon on September 13, following a morning of aerial action over airfields on Negros, Halsey boldly recommended to Nimitz that MacArthur's Sixth Army could bypass Mindanao and head straight to Leyte, supported by TF 38.

Nimitz and MacArthur agreed on the plan the next day and passed on Halsey's recommendation to the Allied heads of state and combined planners who were then at a meeting in Quebec. Within 90 minutes the strategists had also approved the recommendation, and this changed everything. Troops that were gathering for three various landings at Yap, the Talaud Islands and Mindanao were shifted to the Leyte operation, which was in turn moved forward by two months to October 20, 1944.

Meanwhile, showing no signs of slowing down, TF 38 launched devastating attacks on Mindanao and the Visayas on September 14 and 21. *Princeton*'s VF-27 joined the Hellcat squadrons from other fast carriers in initial sweeps over Manila and the nearby Japanese airfields on the latter date. Lt Cdr Bardshar led one of two fighter sweeps generated by no fewer than six light carriers, 48 Hellcats striking the principal IJNAF airfield at Nichols Field as well as nearby Nielsen Field. These missions were heavily opposed by both IJNAF and IJAAF fighters, with a series of swirling dogfights initially being fought in the skies directly over the airfield and then heading out over Manila Harbor and Cavite Island, before reaching their climax over Laguna province, to the southeast of Manila.

The pilots of VF-27 did not miss a beat after their stellar performance in the "Turkey Shoot." In the ensuing melee, *Princeton*'s 16 fighters accounted for 38 enemy aircraft shot down – a tally that made VF-27 the most successful light carrier-based fighter squadron. It would retain this title through to war's end. Lt Stambook took his score to eight that day when he shot down a "Zeke" and two IJAAF Ki-61 "Tonys." The unit's top scorer on the 21st was Lt John R. Rodgers with 4.5 "Tonys" destroyed.

Bardshar also achieved aerial success that day:

> My group attacked Nichols and Nielsen Fields at Manila with 48 F6Fs. We were stacked in three sub-groups – *Princeton*'s at 12,000ft, 16 others at 16,000ft and 16 more at 20,000ft. We arrived over the target without opposition, and my wingman and I initiated action by shooting down a Nick over Nielsen at about 10,000ft. We fired as a section from a high-side run. The Jap did not see us. The 12 .50-caliber machine guns registered on the first burst with sensational effect. Our targets included parked aircraft at Nichols and Nielsen and also on Dewey Boulevard. I had my right aileron and tailhook shot out and was diverted to a large deck carrier for a barrier arrestment.

Two pilots from VF-27 were downed by antiaircraft fire. One of them, Ens Oliver Scott, made a forced water landing near the island of Masbate, his controlled crash landing being observed by a guerilla unit on the nearby shore. They then went to his rescue in a Banca (a type of canoe), took him to their headquarters and were able to establish radio contact with the carrier force. Later that same day, a seaplane from the South Dakota-class battleship USS *Massachusetts* (BB-59) went to the area under fighter escort, picked up Scott and attacked a Japanese vessel while outbound. He made it back to *Princeton* just in time for evening chow.

Lt William Lamb, VF-27's executive officer and second ace (he had claimed his fifth success in the form of a lone "Judy" while on a CAP over TF 58 on June 29), also made a forced landing in a lake near Manila that same day. He too was retrieved by Filipino guerillas – literally from right under the noses of IJA search parties who had seen Lamb's fighter go down and were combing the area. The Naval Aviator was spirited away as his fellow pilots circled overhead. Lamb was hidden by the guerillas until they were able to establish radio contact with the US Navy, and after almost seven weeks in the bush, a submarine maneuvered close to shore and took him aboard. Having spent so long with Filipino guerilla fighters, he had had the chance to observe the enemy at close quarters. Lamb duly returned with important information for naval intelligence.

"UNCLE SAM'S CYCLONE"

The remaining pilots from VF-27 had returned to *Princeton* on September 21 well aware that both Scott and Lamb had gone down, and they received no news on the fate of the XO until he showed up in Pearl Harbor on November 18.

There was also a third pilot from "Fighting 27" that did not immediately make it back to "Sweet P" following the action on September 21. Ens Frederick D. "Fritz" Hautop was one of the new Naval Aviators that had joined the unit at Eniwetok, and he was making his first fighter sweep on the 21st. As he later recalled, it was almost his last:

> It was a pre-dawn hop. The weather was bad. When we got about halfway to the target, they started jamming our radios. By the time we got to the target it was daybreak, and the weather had cleared. The only thing we encountered, beside enemy flak, was one enemy twin-engine bomber in the traffic pattern at Nichols Field. Our Skipper and his wingman left the formation, went in to shoot it down, then rejoined, and we circled Nichols Field for half-an-hour at 10,000ft. There were many planes on the field, so the skipper had us go down and strafe them, which is exactly what they were waiting for us to do. When we came up, there they were, and we were engaged in one of the biggest dogfights I have seen in my life.

Hautop quickly got a "Zeke" in his sights:

> All I had to do was give him a few bursts and that blew him out of the air. Immediately after that I had a Tony on my tail, and to this day I don't know what type of maneuver I made, but when I came out of it I was on his. The only thing was I was slow, and it took a long time to close. I had to chase him all the way across Manila Bay before I could get him in my sights and open fire, after which he rolled over and went in.

Hautop then scanned the skies, which now appeared to be empty of enemy aircraft. However, as he set a course for the rendezvous point, prior to heading back to *Princeton*, Hautop and the Hellcats he had formed up with were bounced:

> Heading in the direction of the task group, all of a sudden, we were jumped by a couple of dozen Tonys. One got on me as I started

to turn into my division leader and blew my guns right out of my wings. I expected my division leader to turn into me to get him off my tail, but he had left to shoot another Tony off the skipper's tail. I had no alternative but to dive down for the ground.

The Ki-61 "Tony" was armed with a single Ho-5 20mm cannon in each wing and two Ho-103 12.7mm machine guns in the upper fuselage forward of the cockpit. Hautop knew full well his attacker was making optimum use of all of his weapons:

> During the entire time of his pursuit I could feel the force of bullets hitting the armor plate behind me. As I dove for the ground I grabbed my microphone, which was made of a type of plastic, and screamed "Get this bastard off my tail!" My fear was so intense that my microphone crumbled right in my hand. I continued to dive with my throttle wide open until I damn near flew into Lake Taal [on Luzon]. When I leveled off, there was a hill ahead of me, and as I went over it my prop pitch went out and dropped back to 1,700 rpm. This guy was on me all the way. Fortunately, there was ground fog, which I flew in and out of three times. He was on my tail all the way, blowing me apart every time I came out.

After what seemed to be an eternity, Hautop reached the sea, where the weather had again turned foul: "I went into a black, mean-looking cloud hanging right over the water, and when I came out he was gone – apparently into the sea."

Hautop immediately turned on his emergency IFF, hoping to receive word by radio as to his location:

> One of the carriers sent three planes out to pick me up and I followed them in. I couldn't slow the plane down below 120 knots or it would stall out on me. I couldn't land aboard *Princeton* at that speed because it was too small, so I had to land on *Hornet*. I had almost got into position, but an SB2C dive-bomber was also coming in at the same time, so I had to get out of there. I called *Hornet* and told them I couldn't slow it down – I had no prop control; 1,700 rpm – and I was very low on fuel.

Hautop felt he could not make another landing pass on the carrier, and asked if he could make a water landing beside *Hornet*. "They said, 'No, come aboard.' Fortunately, everything went well, and I landed safely." As soon as the deck crew released the Hellcat's tailhook from the arresting cable, the fighter's wings were folded and Hautop taxied forward on the flightdeck: "After I jumped off the wing, I collapsed and sat there looking at the plane. I couldn't believe how badly it was shot up. They just removed the radio equipment and things like that, then shoved it overboard."

The following morning Hautop was provided with a Hellcat from VF-2, which he used to fly back to *Princeton* to rejoin his squadron.

Squadronmate Lt Carl Brown also came close to not making it back on September 21 as well. Having downed a "Hamp" (a clipped-wing A6M3 Zero-sen) and a "Tony," the engine of his fighter was then stopped by an accurate burst from a "Zeke." Brown instantly maneuvered into a "split-S," lost his attacker and decided to bail out while he still had some altitude. He was ready to jump when, "I thought the better of it. I hit the primer and pumped the throttle. The damned thing roared."

When the Hellcat returned to *Princeton*, two 20mm holes were found in one propeller blade. The damage did not end there, however. Brown's plane captain, having called him back up to the flightdeck shortly after he had reported to the squadron ready room, showed the pilot his parachute. It had been shredded by a third 20mm shell that exploded in his seat pack. Upon seeing this, Brown commented, "had I bailed out, my descent would have been faster than I planned."

Following the concentrated series of attacks on targets in the Philippines, *Princeton*'s magazines had been seriously depleted. On September 27, in a unique supply-by-night operation, it swung around with the rest of TF 38 and anchored at Kossol Roads, just north of enemy-occupied Babelthuap island in the western Carolines. After a month at sea, during which time the task force had been credited with the destruction of no fewer than 893 Japanese aircraft both in the air and on the ground and the sinking of 67 ships totaling 224,000 tons, it was time for a comprehensive replenishment of bombs, ammunition and supplies. This evolution would last several days, with the vessels sailing out of Kossol Roads each night to avoid being static targets for submarines. Finally, TF 38 returned to open waters, much to the immense relief of Capt Buracker.

A short time later, *Princeton* dropped anchor in Ulithi again for logistical purposes. Aside from again taking on much-needed supplies, CVLG-27 also received 36 pilots, 18 F6F-3s and seven of the very latest F6F-5s. By then Ulithi was a key forward base for the US Navy thanks to work undertaken by the Seabees and the US Army Corps of Engineers, who had literally performed miracles both here and on other remote islands and atolls throughout the campaign in the Pacific. Having installed the necessary supply facilities, they had turned Ulithi into a bustling, modern port on a small spit of land in the middle of the Pacific Ocean. Where there had been the solitude of a remote island and the lapping of waves on a beach protected by a reef, there were now piers, forklifts and mountains of crates and storage containers filled with high explosives, medical supplies and foodstuffs for the growing fleet.

While *Princeton* was at anchorage in Ulithi, Capt John M. Hoskins boarded the carrier as its prospective commanding officer. He was scheduled to take over from Capt Buracker after he had spent several weeks observing the current CO at work during the upcoming operation. Hoskins, a native of Kentucky, brought with him extensive experience in naval aviation. Early in his career, he had served on board the Omaha-class light cruiser USS *Memphis* (CL-13) when it had brought Charles A. Lindbergh home following his famed Atlantic crossing in the Ryan NYP *Spirit of St Louis* in May 1927. A decade later, he took part in the search for aviatrix Amelia M. Earhart and her navigator, Frederick J. Noonan, after they were declared missing in the Pacific. Hoskins then served consecutively as the air officer and the executive officer on board *Ranger* during the early days of the Pacific campaign.

In early October, while the task force was moored at Ulithi, word was received that a typhoon was approaching. The carriers, battleships, cruisers and destroyers hurriedly weighed anchor and headed for the open sea, where they would ride out the storm, as opposed to being destroyed in a confined port. For two days the ships rose and plunged with every wave, and even the largest vessels took "green water" over their decks while the destroyers were tossed about like plastic toys in a bathtub as sailors who had been at sea for months, even years, were violently seasick for the first time. Trying to maintain a formation, as the task groups normally did, was impossible. The tops of the battleships' superstructure would disappear in the trough between huge waves, lost from view for a few seconds to those on the vessels nearby.

On board the smaller destroyers, for crews it was a matter of always keeping a tight grip onto something. Hot meals were out of the question for those who still had the stomach for eating, and sleep involved rolling from one side to another in bunks that left bruises. Objects that were not lashed down were in constant motion, and they could become extremely dangerous.

Princeton and its sister light carriers rolled with the massive waves, sometimes as much as 30 degrees or more from an even keel, with green seawater washing over the flightdecks. Despite this, and as strange as it may sound, a court-martial actually took place in the middle of the typhoon on board "Sweet P." Lt Cdr James Large was named president of the summary court-martial to hear evidence and preside over the trial. Evidently, alcohol consumption followed by sailors beating each other up with wrenches and other tools at hand was the reason behind the court proceedings. Large recalled, "Some of the shipfitters, usually a rough and ready rating, had broken into a supply of aviation alcohol. The resulting midnight party developed into a near riot as the shipfitters became embroiled and used the heavy tools of their trade as weapons. It was a real donnybrook, and our medics had a busy night."

Charges were brought, and the court-martial convened despite the typhoon. Large continued:

> What a trial it was. Members of the court, witnesses, and the accused were seated in chairs lashed to a table. There was some slack in my line, however, and as the ship rolled heavily, I occasionally slithered right out of the proceedings, to return majestically with the counter roll. Somehow, we reached a tortured verdict, which later was lost with the ship to the delight of the defendants.

BACK INTO ACTION

TF 38 had so far performed faultlessly with Halsey in command. Thanks to excellent leadership and superior aircraft, ships' personnel and logistics, it had carried on where TF 58 had left off. Despite the Pacific Fleet's overwhelming successes since late 1943, the US Navy insisted that its sailors had to remain fully prepared for what the enemy might throw at them as the fighting moved ever closer to Japan. As a sober warning of what lay ahead, it published an analysis in July 1944 that warned "Losses will be heavier. Overconfidence is not justified."

Princeton again set out with TG 38.3 on October 5, rendezvousing with the other three carrier task groups 375 miles west of the Marianas two days later. The four task groups that comprised TF 38 boasted a fast carrier task force of unprecedented strength. Between them, they could put more than 1,000 fighters, dive- and torpedo-bombers into the air. These aircraft would be tasked with delivering the opening blow of the campaign to liberate Leyte.

During the first two weeks of October, with the stalwart Vice Adm Mitscher at the helm, the fast carriers of TF 38 roamed the western Pacific at will. The diminished state of the IJN allowed carrier-based aircraft to carry out bold attacks against Okinawa, the principal island in the Ryukyu group. These strikes brought the US Navy closer to the Japanese home islands than at any date since the start of the war.

TF 38 achieved total surprise when aircraft from 17 carriers flew a series of missions targeting airfields on Okinawa and other nearby islands on October 10. A total of 23 aircraft were claimed to have been shot down and 29 vessels sunk. Although VF-27 participated in four of the strikes, only Ens Howard Supan made any aerial claims – he was credited with the destruction of two "Tonys" west of Okinawa's Yontan airfield. The following day, carrier aircraft struck airfields on northern Luzon in preparation for raids on the Japanese bastion of Formosa.

The summer of 1944 prompted the Japanese to make some changes within their inner defensive perimeter in which the Philippines and Formosa saw activity in preparation for Operation *Sho-Go* (Victory). The latter was split into *Sho-Go 1* for the defense of the Philippines and *Sho-Go 2* for the defense of Formosa. These plans were put into place knowing that the Americans would probably invade the Philippines and the Japanese would be in a position for that "decisive battle," where the IJN's battleships would finish off their enemy. The forces that were allotted for this action were essentially withdrawn from current combat to avoid them suffering excessive losses. It was also hoped that with some deception, the IJAAF and the IJNAF could convince the Americans that their fighting strengths appeared weaker than they actually were.

The carriers of TF 38 arrived at their launch positions off Formosa before dawn on October 12. At 0544 hrs, the first strike – a fighter sweep to clear the air over Formosa and the Pescadores – was launched. In perfect flying weather, the incoming aircraft were picked up by radar, and 230 Japanese fighters were scrambled to meet them. The dogfights that ensued were compared in severity to the first Truk raid in February. A handful of Hellcat squadrons were engaged throughout the day, with a total of 1,378 sorties being flown during the course of three waves from all four carrier groups on the 12th. A total of 244 enemy aircraft were claimed as shot down, although the only victory credited to VF-27 was a lone "Betty" downed by Lt Carl Brown. This solitary success was enough to make him an ace, however.

The sheer size of the approaching raids had convinced Adm Soemu Toyoda, commander of the Combined Fleet, that it signaled the start of an invasion. He prematurely launched *Sho-Go 1* and *Sho-Go 2* as a result, sending poorly trained pilots up against the veteran Naval Aviators of TF 38. One third of the Japanese fighters scrambled were lost trying to oppose the first wave, with the majority of the remaining aircraft falling victim to fighters in the second wave. The third wave that appeared over Formosa met virtually no opposition.

On October 13, a further 934 sorties were flown. Despite the losses inflicted on the IJNAF the previous day, a torpedo-bomber (probably a "Jill") succeeded in striking the heavy cruiser *Canberra*, which was operating just 90 miles off Formosa at the time. While the badly damaged vessel was rigged for towing, aircraft from *Cowpens* (TG 38.1) and *Cabot* (TG 38.2) took up CAP duty above the damaged cruiser. VF-27 claimed three Nakajima Ki-44 "Tojo" fighters destroyed ten miles west of Tainan, these aircraft being among 37 victories credited to Hellcats from TF 38 on the 13th.

The enemy mounted further attacks the following day as they tried to finish off *Canberra*. The task force estimated that almost 200 aircraft approached or attacked its ships, with a further 225 being driven off. TF 38 was targeted both day and night, with fighter units claiming 92 victories. More than half of this total was credited to VF-11, VF-18 and VF-27. Two divisions from the latter unit had been launched during the afternoon, the aircraft being led aloft by CAG Bardshar with eight of his charges tearing into a formation of 16 "Frances" torpedo-bombers (a type that had only been declared operational by the IJNAF days earlier) as they approached TG 38.3. VF-27 claimed 13 aircraft shot down, Bardshar leading the way with three to "make ace." The three surviving aircraft jettisoned their torpedoes and quickly fled.

That same day (October 14), TF 38's carriers launched a second raid on northern Luzon, and followed it up 24 hours later with a sweep over the Manila area. Hellcat pilots were credited with 139 victories on the 15th, with an additional 366 aircraft being destroyed on the ground.

Despite the superb efforts of the Hellcat squadrons over Formosa and Manila, the tenacious Japanese still managed to inflict damage on TF 38 when *Canberra*'s replacement, the Cleveland-class light cruiser USS *Houston* (CL-81), was torpedoed at dusk on October 14. Halsey formed a "cripple division" with the two damaged cruisers that were both under tow. They started to slowly egress out of range of IJNAF aircraft, but not before *Houston* was torpedoed for a second time on October 16. Further attempts by enemy torpedo-bombers to sink the two cruisers were successfully repelled by Hellcats, and both vessels eventually completed the 1,300-mile trip to Ulithi.

The Japanese pilots that did survive the aerial battles over Formosa and the attacks on TF 38 reported a series of dramatic successes, and their outrageous accounts were believed at the highest levels. On the evening of October 16, the IJNAF announced that it had sunk 11 aircraft carriers, two battleships, three cruisers and one light cruiser or destroyer. Additionally, pilots claimed to have shot down 112 American aircraft. Convinced that they had inflicted serious damage on the Pacific Fleet, Toyoda ordered that an additional 600 IJNAF aircraft be transferred from Japan to Formosa, including those allocated to the remaining IJN carriers.

Operations were now complete in Formosa, and it was time for TF 38 to turn its attention to the isolation of the Leyte beachhead. On October 15, as TG 38.1 stayed behind to cover the withdrawal of the two damaged cruisers, *Princeton* and TG 38.3 steamed to a position about 300 miles to the east for refueling. Once that was completed, the carrier operated as part of what Capt Buracker termed the "firing line" to support the landings in the Philippines. TG 38.4 began five days of strikes against Luzon, and it was joined by TGs 38.1 and 38.2 three days later.

REPLENISHMENT

Referred to by some in the US Navy as its "open secret weapon," Service Squadron (ServRon) 10 moved its headquarters from Eniwetok to Ulithi in October 1944 so that a floating tank farm of obsolete oilers could provide a ready reserve of 400,000 barrels of fuel oil and aviation gasoline.

When refueling was required at Ulithi, each replenishment group of 12 oilers would sortie for a rendezvous with the fast carriers. Aircraft from the small escort carriers, nicknamed "jeep carriers," would provide air cover for the replenishment group as replacement aircraft and pilots were also ferried to the fast carriers. The ServRons gave the Third Fleet a strategic mobility unprecedented in naval warfare, and this would be needed as the demands on TF 38 reached peak proportions. In the upcoming weeks, its vessels would face another fleet battle, many weeks of CAS for ground operations, heavy weather and a deadly storm of another kind – the kamikaze.

The vanguard of MacArthur's invasion forces had been spotted by the Japanese off Suluan Island on October 17, bound for their landing beaches at Leyte, while the US Army's 6th Ranger Battalion landed on Dinagat and Suluan, at the entrance to Leyte Gulf, to destroy Japanese installations capable of providing early warning of a US attack. The IJA garrison on Suluan transmitted an alert that prompted Adm Toyoda to order the defense of the Philippines with Operation *Sho-Go 1*. That same day, Vice Adm Ozawa, Commander-in-Chief, 3rd Fleet, who was now left with carriers that lacked any aircraft, recommended to Toyoda that his vessels be used as a sacrificial decoy to allow Vice Adm Kurita's 2nd Fleet, comprised of battleships and cruisers based at Singapore, to attack and destroy the landing force off Leyte.

As a deceptive move, Ozawa's decoy Northern Force would have enough aircraft (just under 120) embarked to launch a shuttle strike to Luzon and convince Halsey, with orders to finish off the carriers of the IJN fleet, that the force was headed for Leyte, when in fact it had no intention of doing so.

The real blow would come from Kurita's Center Force, passing through the central Philippines via the Sibuyan Sea and the San Bernardino Strait to descend upon MacArthur's forces at Leyte Gulf from the north and east of Samar Island. It would include the two super battleships *Yamato* and *Musashi*, behemoths with 18.1in. main guns, two older battleships, six heavy cruisers, a light cruiser and several destroyers. The Southern Force, conducting a pincer movement and consisting of two old battleships, one heavy cruiser and destroyers commanded by Vice Adm Shoji Nishimura, would transit the Sulu and Mindanao Seas and approach the landing area from the south after sailing through the Surigao Strait. It would receive support from Vice Adm Kiyohide Shima and his three cruisers from Japan.

As was frequently the case with Japanese military campaigns during the latter stages of the war in the Pacific, the plan to defend the Philippines was overcomplicated. It was also suicidal from the start. The IJN was sacrificing its once proud and powerful fleet in the hope of protecting the Philippine lifeline, which was now a part of the interior defense of Japan itself. As these plans moved forward, Vice Adm Takijiro Onishi, commander of the land-based 1st Air Fleet in the Philippines, took desperate, sinister measures of his own. On October 19, 1944, after initially resisting such a move, he approved the official activation of Special Attack Units, better known as the kamikaze ("divine wind").

The next day MacArthur's Sixth Army landed at Leyte Island in the middle section of the archipelago under air cover provided by 18 escort carriers of TG 77.4 commanded by Rear Adm Clifton A. F. Sprague. These vessels, a handy addition to any beach assault, embarked Hellcats, Wildcats and Avengers and were organized into three task units (TUs 77.4.1, .2 and .3) known collectively as "Taffys 1," "2" and "3." This entire naval force in support of MacArthur's landing was assigned to Seventh Fleet, led by Vice Adm Thomas C. Kinkaid, who had been in command of "MacArthur's Navy" since November 1943.

The IJN's depleted 3rd Fleet (Northern Force), with Ozawa still in charge, was tasked with drawing Halsey's Fast Carrier Task Force away from the east coast of the Philippines so that Kurita's Center Force could catch "MacArthur's Navy" relatively unprotected and destroy it.

IJN 3rd Carrier Division, October 24, 1944
Commander-in-Chief, Vice Adm Jisaburo Ozawa

"UNCLE SAM'S CYCLONE"

1st Carrier Division – Vice Adm Jisaburo Ozawa
  Amagi, *Unryu*, *Zuikaku* and *Katsuragi*
3rd Carrier Division – Rear Adm Sueo Obayashi
  Chitose and *Chiyoda*
4th Carrier Division – Rear Adm Chiaki Matsuda
  Hyuga (hybrid battleship/carrier), *Junyo* and *Ryuho*

From August 1944, Halsey's forces would leave a trail of enemy ruin and destruction in the Palaus, Okinawa, Formosa, the South China Sea and the Philippines. They would inflict greater losses upon the IJN than had ever been suffered by any navy in history. Halsey's recognition of the true status of Japanese forces in the Philippines on September 13 had prompted MacArthur's return date to Leyte to be adjusted to October 20, 1944, when his Sixth Army force landed under the cover of the Third and Seventh Fleets.

During the period spanning from August 24, 1944 to January 26, 1945, when Third Fleet was engaged in supporting operations to retake the western Carolines and the Philippines, 4,370 enemy aircraft would be destroyed and 82 enemy warships and 372 auxiliaries and miscellaneous vessels sunk.

In the days following MacArthur's forces storming ashore at Leyte, the fast carriers of Mitscher's TF 38 would find themselves the target of three different IJN fleets, along with combined IJNAF and IJAAF aircraft putting them directly in their sights. What was now unfolding was the Battle of Leyte Gulf, which brought warfare on sea, on land and in the air to a level of intensity never seen before in human history.

8

Task Group 38.3 East of Luzon

The global conflict had moved into its sixth year by October 24, 1944. In Berlin, the Führer, Adolf Hitler, had informed his generals of his intention to launch a surprise counteroffensive against the weakly held Ardennes area of the Allied line. Simultaneously, the Soviet Red Army was massing along an 87-mile front, poised to invade the Third Reich. The war in the Pacific was now nearing the end of its third year, and the Japanese were reeling under the constant pressure of Allied military might. While they had suffered tremendous blows to their surface forces over the last two years and had lost an appalling number of aircraft and pilots, they were still in the fight after the IJAAF and the IJNAF had agreed to cooperate in the desperate defense of the Philippines.

TF 38 Organization in support of Gen Douglas MacArthur's landings in the Philippines, October 1944
Commander-in-Chief, United States Fleet and Chief of Naval Operations – Adm E. J. King
Commander-in-Chief, Pacific Fleet – Adm C. W. Nimitz
Commander, Third Fleet – Adm W. F. Halsey
Commander, TF 38 – Vice Adm M. A. Mitscher
Commander, TG 38.1 – Vice Adm J. S. McCain
    Wasp – Capt O. A. Weller (CVG-14 embarked)
    Hancock – Capt F. C. Dickey (CVG-7 embarked)

 Hornet – Capt A. K. Doyle (CVG-11 embarked)
 Monterey – Capt S. H. Ingersoll (CVLG-28 embarked)
 Cowpens – Capt H. W. Taylor (CVLG-22 embarked)
Commander, TG 38.2 – Rear Adm G. F. Bogan
 Intrepid – Capt J. F. Bolger (CVG-18 embarked)
 Bunker Hill – Capt M. R. Greer (CVG-8 embarked)
 Cabot – Capt S. J. Michael (CVLG-31 embarked)
 Independence – Capt E. C. Ewen (CVLG(N)-41 embarked)
Commander, TG 38.3 – Rear Adm F. C. Sherman
 Essex – Capt C. W. Wieber (CVG-15 embarked)
 Lexington – Capt E. W. Litch (CVG-19 embarked)
 Princeton – Capt W. H. Buracker (CVLG-27 embarked)
 Langley – Capt J. F. Wegforth (CVLG-44 embarked)
Commander, TG 38.4 – Rear Adm R. E. Davison
 Franklin – Capt J. M. Shoemaker (CVG-13 embarked)
 Enterprise – Capt C. D. Glover (CVG-20 embarked)
 Belleau Wood – Capt J. A. Perry (CVLG-21 embarked)
 San Jacinto – Capt M. H. Kernodle (CVLG-51 embarked)
Commander, TF 34 (battle line) – Vice Adm W. A. Lee
Commander, Southwest Pacific Theater – Gen D. MacArthur
Commander, Seventh Fleet – Vice Adm T. C. Kinkaid
Commander, Escort Carrier Group – Rear Adm T. L. Sprague
Commander, Support Aircraft – Capt R. L. Whitehead

On October 24, 1944, three of TF 38's four task groups were steaming in the vicinity of Leyte Gulf. TG 38.1, which was the strongest of the task force's fast carrier groups, had departed for Ulithi for replenishment, rest and recreation following a period of increased operational tempo, while the other task groups – 11 carriers in total – prepared to launch aircraft for searches and CAPs. Roughly 100 miles east of Luzon was the northernmost task group, Sherman's TG 38.3, consisting of *Essex, Lexington, Princeton* and *Langley*. It would handle nearly all the major aerial combat when the Battle of Leyte Gulf commenced in earnest.

 Lexington's CVG-19 shouldered most of the task group's search responsibility, with 37 of its aircraft being tasked with scouting the western quadrant to a distance of 300 miles. The search would head out over the Sibuyan Sea and the waters off Mindoro, where it was believed some units of the IJN were on the move. *Lexington*'s search aircraft launched at 0607 hrs, along with a group from *Essex*'s CVG-15, but they lost each other in heavy clouds lingering between the task group and Luzon. In other pre-dawn launchings, *Langley*'s CVLG-44 sent up anti-submarine and anti-"snooper" patrols, *Essex* dispatched a 20-aircraft fighter sweep to cover the airfields around Manila, and *Princeton* provided an eight-fighter CAP at roughly 0600 hrs to provide air protection for the task group.

Rear Adm Sherman, commanding TG 38.3 from his flagship *Essex*, was concerned about the large number of aircraft Halsey was launching on reconnaissance missions. He felt that there would be insufficient machines available to launch powerful strikes once the enemy fleet was located. Sherman was also worried that the fighter units embarked would be spread too thinly to provide adequate protection for the task force.

Furthermore, the enemy knew exactly where TG 38.3 was, as it had been shadowed throughout the night by IJNAF flying boats that seemed to be tracking its movement. VF(N)-41 had launched several radar-equipped F6F-5N nightfighters from *Independence*, and at 0227 hrs a snooping "Emily" had been downed, followed by a Kawanishi H6K "Mavis" flying boat a little over an hour later. However, there were five more still lingering in the vicinity, keeping track of Sherman's movements.

Radar screens on board vessels of TG 38.3 came to life early on October 24, revealing a number of aircraft taking off from the airfields near Manila. Sherman quickly reacted by launching 20 Hellcats to attack them. This activity involving so many enemy aircraft indicated to the commander of TG 38.3 that the approaching IJN fleet might not be the only threat facing his task group.

At 0520 hrs *Princeton* had gone to general quarters and set material condition "Able." Aircraft had been fueled and armed throughout the night in preparation for a scheduled attack group launch at 0900 hrs. Meanwhile, the IJNAF was massing for a legitimate counterattack, having flown approximately 450 aircraft from Formosa into the Philippines overnight. These would be launched in the direction of TF 38 that morning, as would large groups of aircraft from Clark and Nichols Fields, near Manila.

TG 38.3's air plotters had been aware of the surveillance on the task group, having picked up "bogeys" before Halsey had dispatched his scouts in search of the IJN fleet. Early morning flight operations were punctuated by broken clouds and intermittent rain squalls, but the hardworking crews on board the carriers got their aircraft airborne nonetheless. As the sun was rising, *Princeton* and *Langley* pilots were vectored toward groups of "snoopers." Hellcat pilots from *Langley*'s VF-44 subsequently downed a "Jake" and a "Kate," while Lt "Red" Shirley and Ens Les Blyth, manning one of two four-aircraft CAP sections put up by VF-27, each claimed a "Judy" destroyed 30 miles east of Polillo Island. Shortly thereafter, Lt Carl Brown's CAP section intercepted two Avengers with their IFF transponders turned off.

Fifteen minutes after the last of the "snoopers" had been shot down, the situation in the air intensified when a large group of enemy aircraft, estimated to be 40–50 in number, was detected on radar 75 miles west of the task group. A second group of 30, stacked at various altitudes up to 25,000ft, was also detected. The eight VF-27 fighters on CAP – including Shirley, Blyth and Brown – were vectored by "Hatchet Base" (*Princeton*'s call-sign for this operation) to intercept the approaching enemy force. Simultaneously, all of the carriers in the task group were ordered by Sherman to launch additional fighters to join the attack. *Princeton* quickly launched three more divisions (12 aircraft in total) of Hellcats into the fray to join the eight pilots already committed.

"Fighting 27's" CAP intercepted enemy aircraft approximately 50 miles from TG 38.3 before the fighters frantically launched by the task group had reached the "tally-ho" point. VF-27's two four-aircraft CAP sections that were already airborne were led by Lt Carl Brown, a truly gifted Naval Aviator with 5.5 victories already to his name, and by fellow ace Lt "Red" Shirley. The latter provided the following account of his aerial engagements on October 24:

> That day had begun about 3 am for the pre-dawn CAP. I led Division Four off the ship about 4 am and during join-up was given a vector toward two low targets. After a few steers, I sighted the bogeys and we closed to splash two "Judys." More single targets were given to us, and in the next 45 minutes we sighted and downed three more bogeys at low and mid altitudes near the perimeter of our operating area.

Shirley was then instructed by radio to climb to maximum altitude at full throttle toward a large group of enemy aircraft 60–70 miles to the west. "Just after daylight we began to make out an unusually large formation of planes of every Japanese make stacked in altitudes from 6,000 to 25,000ft headed toward our fleet."

Shirley reported the sighting by radio, telling his FDO that he would commence an attack and continue with it until he ran out of ammunition or fuel:

> We started in head-on at our altitude of about 23,000ft and worked our way down as we had to. First, we reversed course with an overhead run, and each of us took out one or more planes on the first pass. Our speed advantage was about 50 knots, so we repeatedly made runs in and through their formation, bringing down planes each time.

With all of their ammunition quickly expended, Shirley and his companions returned to *Princeton*. "On final debriefing, as best we could account, Division Four splashed four Jap planes before the large contact, and 15 of the large group, for a total of 19 planes during that one flight."

For Lt Brown, his flight on October 24 had not started according to how he had briefed it before launch:

> One of the most exciting days of my life. We had been briefed that we could expect some snoopers. At that time, I had a replacement pilot assigned to me for training. Because snoopers were likely, I put the new man in the number four spot in our division, figuring he'd learn more by following the example of the three pilots ahead of him.
>
> In the blackness of that pre-dawn launch, my regular wingman [Ens Paul E. Drury] wound up on the other division leader's wing and I had the new man on mine. My division was assigned high patrol at 20,000ft and the other division was given low patrol at 10,000ft. We usually swapped altitudes halfway through the patrol. I figured when we did, we'd reorganize, and I could get my wingman back. As it worked out, I never flew combat with my regular wingman on that flight.

After Shirley and Brown received two vectors to investigate "bogeys," and Shirley's section downed two "Judys" and Brown intercepted two Avengers, both were given the same message from "Hatchet Base": "'Hatchet Three-One' [Brown's division] and 'Hatchet Six-One'

[Shirley's division], vector 240. Gate!" VF-27's pilots were being told by the FDO to head in the indicated compass direction using all possible speed. If the FDO wanted his aircraft to get somewhere in a hurry, the code word was "buster." "Gate" was only used for urgent emergencies. Shirley's section was at 20,000ft while Brown's was 10,000ft below. Shirley's flight duly pulled ahead as it maintained that altitude, while Brown's group dropped back as they clawed for height. "When both of us got to the same vector," Brown later said, "I knew it had to be trouble." It was trouble.

As Brown's division went to "gate" speed, and at the same time began gaining altitude, the pilots shifted into a wide combat formation. On the radio, they heard Shirley call "'Tally-ho, three bogeys'." Then, moments later, three plumes of smoke trailed down in the sky, followed by another radio transmission. "This is 'Hatchet Six-One'. Grand slam. Three bogeys." Shirley downed his fifth victim of the flight with the last of his ammunition, bringing his final aerial tally to 12.5 victories in only four combats. Ens Thomas J. Conroy was top scorer for VF-27 that day with six victories, while Lt(jg) Eugene P. Townsend got five. Lt Ralph S. Taylor was shot in the leg and had to return to *Princeton* and Ens Oliver L. Scott was killed.

While Shirley's division was scything through the enemy formation, Brown and his pilots were still climbing at "gate" speed. Brown repeatedly asked how many bandits were up ahead, but the FDO was busy and likely rather stressed. Having ignored the question several times, he then blurted out, "many, many, many, many." "I was cussing a little to myself," Brown said, "as I thought the three bogeys [initially reported by Shirley] were all there were. All of a sudden, there they were. I let Hatchet Base and the other divisions know the enemy force was high at 240 [24,000ft], and added, 'the sky's black with them'."

The lower division had reached 18,000ft when Shirley "tally-hoed" two more "bogeys" in succession and downed both of them. Brown had by then closed the distance to Shirley's division, at which point he saw the huge enemy formation straight ahead, stacked from 20,000–23,000ft. Notifying *Princeton*, Brown said, "Hatchet Base, estimate 80." He got a "Roger" and "Good luck" from the FDO as he prepared to engage. At about the same time Shirley called out, "Hundreds of bogeys, high, low and in the middle. Am attacking 'til ammo runs out."

Two "Fighting 27" divisions from *Princeton*, numbering eight aircraft in total, engaged approximately 80 IJNAF aircraft without hesitation.

Figuring his best course of action was to gain as much speed as possible and pull right up into the formation, Brown tried to estimate his enemy's strength. His quick count totaled 65 fighters and 15 bombers. Over the next few minutes, aircraft fell from the sky at an unbelievable rate. Brown's recollection of the air battle while strapped into the cockpit of F6F-5 *PAPER DOLL* are vivid:

> Shortly we were into them. I pulled up, carefully keeping my speed above 160 knots indicated, for the Zero liked to get us when we were slow. We were at about 12,000ft, maybe a little higher. Some Zeros came at me from two o'clock. I turned hard into them and fired. As they flashed by, I reversed my turn. I made some violent reversals, firing at a minimum of six aircraft, while the new man, Hatchet Three-Two, was on my wing. The next thing I remember is weaving a couple of times with my wingman and shooting planes coming in on his tail. I remember, too, that as we came at each other in the weave, Three-Two's guns were going, so I knew he was firing at the enemy coming at me.
>
> Then I couldn't find Three-Two and couldn't see any of our planes. In fact, all I saw was aircraft with meatballs on them, and they were everywhere. The thought came to me, as I saw no other friendlies, that I was the only American left in the fight. I didn't believe I could get away with all those enemy planes around. From that point my memory of what happened is quite clear.

As Brown whipped out of a turn, a "Zeke" appeared dead ahead of him. He let the distance close before opening fire with his 0.50-cal. guns. He saw pieces fly off the enemy aircraft, which then came out of its gradual turn and flew straight:

> Although I knew better than to fly a straight line in combat – that's deadly – I got stubborn and followed a Zero. Just as he burst into flames, all hell broke loose in my cockpit. Bullets were flying into it and, fortunately, I reacted fast, jamming my stick all the way forward as hard as I could, with the throttle two-blocked and pitch full low. I was thrown against my safety belt as dirt, pencils and whatever else

was on the floor of my fighter came flying up and collected at the top of my canopy. When I was pointing straight down at the sea the hail of bullets stopped. No one can follow that maneuver and track for accurate shooting. I always kept it for last ditch use.

Taking a moment to assess the situation, Brown looked back. There were four "Zekes" coming down on him for another attack, "arguing about who would kill me." Still in a vertical dive, he pushed the stick hard to the right in order to enter a spiralling turn because the "Zeke" could not easily follow him at high speed. Brown then dived into large cumulus clouds, and upon re-emerging he found himself alone. He called "Hatchet Base" and requested a vector to any enemy aircraft in the area. As Brown began to follow the directions provided, he assessed the damage that had been inflicted on both him and his Hellcat:

> They had hit me pretty well. Two 20mm shells had entered the cockpit, exploding on the instrument panel. I didn't have many instruments in working condition. A piece of shrapnel flew across the cockpit just above the throttle, grazing my thumb. Another cut a fuel line leading to the transfer valve. Fuel was all over the cockpit, and I had two to four inches of it in the bottom of the bird. Even though I wanted a cigarette, I didn't dare light one. My port elevator hardly existed and my tailhook was jammed – I couldn't get it out even with my emergency extension release.

The 20mm shells that had hit the Hellcat ripped through the port wing and entered the port wheel well. Brown could see torn rubber, and so he knew that the tire was flat. Then he realized the inside of his left thigh was numb. He was bleeding. "I cut my overalls with my hunting knife and saw two small pieces of shrapnel in my leg, about an eighth-of-an-inch in diameter and three-quarters of an inch long. I pulled them out and bled like a stuck hog, so I got a compress bandage from my first aid kit to stop the bleeding."

Meanwhile, Brown was following the vector given to him toward the enemy aircraft still in the area, hoping to rejoin the fight. Eventually, another VF-27 Hellcat joined Brown, and together they headed for their carrier – a vessel they were shocked to find on fire. Brown was told *Princeton* could not take him aboard, and the presence of aviation fuel in his cockpit, coupled with other damage to his fighter, posed a landing hazard to other carriers about to receive their own aircraft. Brown radioed he would make a water landing near the lead destroyer of the formation:

> As I was preparing to let down, *Essex* came on the air and said, "Hatchet 31. If you'll land immediately, we'll take you." You can imagine my relief. Here she was volunteering to take me aboard when it was almost certain that I'd foul her deck. To say I was grateful was to put it mildly. The captain had to have great confidence in the ability of his deck crew to clear wreckage quickly.

As Brown approached the carrier, *Essex*'s LSO gave him a "Roger" for landing, although he knew he was coming in high and fast:

> I lowered my gear with my emergency bottle – I had no hydraulics, so I couldn't have flaps for landing, nor an airspeed indicator, or cowl flaps or a tailhook. The *Essex* captain had compassion and guts. I made a "British" approach from 500ft. There he stood, the LSO letting me make my own approach. I liked that. He knew my aircraft was shot up [164 holes were subsequently found], and he was letting me fly the way I thought best, at the same time ready to signal me if I got dangerous.
>   The LSO held a "Roger" on me 'til I was at the ramp, when he gave me "fast", "high dip" and "cut" signals. I had tested my controls and couldn't get the stick all the way back. I took the "cut" and snapped the stick as far back as it would go. My tail hit the ramp hard, knocked the hook out and caught the first wire.

SIBUYAN SEA STRIKE

CVLG-27 had originally been tasked (along with other TF 38-assigned carrier air groups) with a planned attack against IJN vessels in the Sibuyan Sea on October 24, with nine torpedo-armed TBM-3 Avengers from VT-27 being escorted by Hellcats from VF-27 – the *Princeton* aircraft were being led by CAG, Lt Cdr Bardshar. The nine torpedo-bombers were sitting armed and ready in the hangar bay when the incoming enemy formations were detected.

Bardshar had been anxiously watching events unfold while still on board the carrier:

> When the enemy sent out a number of planes to attack our ships, we countered in self-defense and put up increasingly more fighters. They'd call for a division from this carrier and then a division from that one and so forth. I was sitting in *Princeton*'s ready room, preparing to go on the big attack against Japanese ships, when it became clear to me that the strike wasn't going to occur. There wasn't any point in me waiting in the ready room with most of our fighters already in the air, so my division went off with the last four fighters launched from *Princeton* that morning.

Flying at 10,000ft, Bardshar requested permission from the FDO to join the "Japanese circus going on out there about 10,000ft above us," but at that point he was 'just too busy'" to handle CAG's request. This left Bardshar's division in a vulnerable position below 10,000ft about 75 miles from the task force, the four Hellcats flying just above the overcast. "Japanese fighters made a pass at us and then disappeared in the overcast," CAG recalled. Minutes later roughly 30 Nakajima Ki-43 "Oscar" IJAAF fighters dove on his division from 15,000ft, although they did not stick around. "We smoked two or three of them, but it was difficult to tell whether we scored any kills. Some of our planes had been hit, but nobody was hurt."

Bardshar's fighter had been struck in the engine, smearing his canopy with a film of oil. Nevertheless, "The old R-2800 [engine] continued to run well."

On the way back to *Princeton*, CAG's wingman, Ens Arthur H. Munson, shot down a stray "Val," which proved to be the only confirmed victory for the division that day. Shortly thereafter, Bardshar was informed that *Princeton* had a "fouled deck" and could not take his division back aboard. It was not until he approached the task group that he realized from the rising smoke and the disarray of the ship formation that his carrier had been hit. CAG was instructed to land on *Essex*.

Ens Frank P. "Smokey Joe" Kleffner was another of VF-27's pilots who returned to the carrier to find its flightdeck inoperable after taking part in a wild melee 20,000ft above TG 38.3. Following a series of dogfights in which he "shot down a couple" (Kleffner was officially credited with a single "Zeke" destroyed), he headed for home low on ammunition and fuel. As he approached *Princeton,* Kleffner was given a wave-off by the carrier's LSO:

> That upset me more than a little bit, because by then I was a fairly accomplished aviator and didn't like to get wave-offs. As I pulled up to go around, I noticed smoke was coming out where it wasn't supposed to. The LSO responded "We've taken a bomb. Land on Buick Base [*Essex*]." I did that, and compared to *Princeton*, it was like landing on a runway at Alameda Naval Air Station.

VF-27's Ens Paul E. Drury and Lt Ralph S. Taylor did manage to land before the bomb hit. Drury was a member of Shirley's division of four fighters involved in the early interception of Japanese aircraft:

> After we took off in the dark, radar vectored us out to a couple of Japanese observation planes. That was easy because they were just singles and there were four of us. Then radar said there was a huge bunch of bogeys out there and they sent us after them. We had the advantage by getting up into the sun and coming down on the Japanese. Things happened so fast, but I do recall thinking this is exactly like they said we ought to do it.

After breaking up the initial IJNAF attack formation, and a second one intercepted by *Lexington*'s VF-19, Drury returned to *Princeton*. He was in the ready room being debriefed when the carrier was struck. Drury would feel the highs and lows of combat on that fateful day, making ace by downing two "Zekes" and a "Tojo" while trying to repel the huge morning onslaught against the task force, and then having to "jump ship" when *Princeton* was mortally damaged:

> My greatest and most dramatic exposure to the Battle of Leyte Gulf was all wrapped up in one day – October 24, 1944, the longest day of my life. Actually, I guess it started the night before on the evening of the 23rd, as the Japanese had all kinds of observation planes out trying to locate our task force. In fact, I think they already had us located, and they were just keeping track of us until the next morning, when they were going to attack.

Eight of us from VF-27 were told that evening that we would have CAP duty the next morning, and that we could expect a lot of activity. So, we were awakened on the 24th at about 0400 hrs, and it was still dark when we took off. Due to a combination of the excitement on the flightdeck, the blacked-out carrier, and the fact that we were in a hurry to get off because there were already bogies on the radar screen, I didn't get to fly in my regular plane, the *PAOLI LOCAL*, nor did I get to fly in my regular division, led by Lt Carl Brown.

I found myself as wingman to Lt Jim "Red" Shirley, who was the leading ace in our squadron. But this was no big deal because I thought as soon as the sun came out I'd slide over to where I belonged and, still maintaining radio silence, I would signal for that pilot to get back where he belonged. That scenario, however, never came to pass, because as soon as we had rendezvoused after takeoff the four of us were vectored out on a bogey, which we quickly took care of. As soon as we got back to station, Carl Brown's division of four was vectored out onto a contact, so the routine continued – I never did get back into my regular division.

Following these snooper intercepts, all eight of us were given a vector to Gate at full speed to tackle a larger formation of aircraft, and as Carl Brown's section had tackled the last snooper, we had a height advantage over his division going into the dogfight. We duly spotted the enemy first, and as the sun had now fully risen, I could clearly see how large this attack was.

"Red" Shirley quickly radioed back to *Princeton*, "'Tally-ho' – 80 Jap planes," and then thoughtfully added, "Better send help." The carrier responded "Affirmative," and stated that they could send another 12 fighters out, plus contact *Essex* to launch a few more.

The four of us dived into this Japanese formation. I think that we each downed one plane on that first pass, then after that all hell broke loose and it was just one huge mass of airplanes trying to see who could shoot who down. I think the four of us shot down 15 Jap planes that morning [the division score was officially recorded as 14 – six for Conroy, five for Shirley and three for Drury – with the fourth member, Ens Oliver Scott, being killed in action]. Then we were out of ammunition and short on fuel, so we were ordered back to the task group.

I believe I was one of the last pilots to land on *Princeton* before it was bombed, as I had just gotten out of my plane and returned to

An IJNAF D4Y2 "Judy" dive-bomber of 653rd Kokutai in October 1944. It is highly likely that it was aircraft from this unit that attacked *Princeton* on October 24, 1944, leading to its demise. (Tony Holmes Collection)

Battle-damaged F6F-5 *PAPER DOLL* of VF-27, with wounded Lt Carl Brown at the controls, is taxied forward after landing on *Essex* following the squadron's epic engagement on the morning of October 24, 1944. *Princeton* can be seen burning in the background. (Tony Holmes Collection)

Princeton's stern was quickly filled with acrid smoke as a result of the fuel fires caused by the single 550lb bomb that hit it amidships and detonated several decks into the ship. (Naval History and Heritage Command)

This photograph of *Princeton*, burning but still underway, was taken from the battleship USS *South Dakota* (BB-57) about 20 minutes after the light carrier was hit. When the dive-bombers attacked, all the CVLG-27 aircraft on the flightdeck had been moved forward of the island to allow Hellcats from the morning combat air patrol to recover back on board the carrier. (Naval History and Heritage Command)

Princeton is hosed down by firefighting teams on board the Atlanta-class light cruiser USS *Reno* (CL-96). The forward elevator has been blown out of its well and the rear flightdeck is badly damaged following a series of blasts in the hangar bay from 1002 hrs, although the Avengers and Hellcats on the bow appear to be unscathed.
(Naval History and Heritage Command)

Opposite Sat off *Princeton*'s port quarter, *Reno* focuses its hoses on the carrier's stern following the hangar bay explosions fueled by the detonation of torpedo warheads. (Naval History and Heritage Command)

Above The Cleveland-class light cruiser USS *Birmingham* (CL-62) approaches *Princeton* for the first time shortly after 1100 hrs, having replaced the Fletcher-class destroyer USS *Irwin* (DD-794) minutes earlier when it became clear that a vessel with greater firefighting capacity was needed. (Naval History and Heritage Command)

Above *Birmingham* closes on *Princeton*, stationary in the water. Both of the carrier's elevators have been blown out of their mounts as a result of torpedo-fueled blasts that wrecked the hangar deck at 1005 hrs. The fires from these explosions are still smoldering, with smoke seeping through gaps in the buckled flightdeck. (Naval History and Heritage Command)

Princeton's port forward area, as seen from the bow of *Birmingham*. Note the vessel's forward gun turrets turned to port to allow the ships to meet, and the damage inflicted on the carrier's gun sponsons when the cruiser came close alongside.
(Naval History and Heritage Command)

Princeton's crowded bow (both Avengers and Hellcats can be seen in this photograph) looms over *Birmingham* and its six-inch Mk 16 turrets during the early stages of the light cruiser's doomed efforts to save the carrier. Many of the sailors seen here were subsequently killed or seriously wounded when ordnance exploded in *Princeton*'s hangar bay. (Naval History and Heritage Command)

A damage control party standing alongside the smoldering remains of an Avenger take stock of the devastation inflicted upon *Princeton*'s hangar bay when torpedo warheads "cooked off" shortly after 1000 hrs. This photograph was taken from *Birmingham*.
(Naval History and Heritage Command)

This view of *Princeton*'s port side was taken from the foredeck on *Birmingham* as the light cruiser stood alongside the carrier to help fight its fires. Note the fire hoses on the vessel's deck in the foreground, the water cascading down the side of *Princeton* and the carrier's unused whale boat and 25-man balsa life raft.
(Naval History and Heritage Command)

Princeton's forward elevator, weighing several tons, was blown from its mount and lodged sideways in its well by a blast at 1005 hrs. The firefighter walking towards the camera is wearing breathing apparatus, having just emerged from smoke-filled spaces below the flightdeck. (Naval History and Heritage Command)

Visible through the smoke, damage control parties receive instructions on *Princeton*'s forward port flightdeck. Note the 40mm twin gun mount at left whose shield has been torn off by *Birmingham*'s No. 2 six-inch Mk 16 turret as the two ships rolled and pitched while in close contact. (Naval History and Heritage Command)

Above *Princeton* survivors crowd a whaleboat launched by the Fletcher-class destroyer USS *Cassin Young* (DD-793). A line has just been thrown down to them from the vessel. With sharks taking survivors in the water, whaleboats like this one from destroyers and cruisers proved critically important in the rescue of *Princeton*'s crew. (Naval History and Heritage Command)

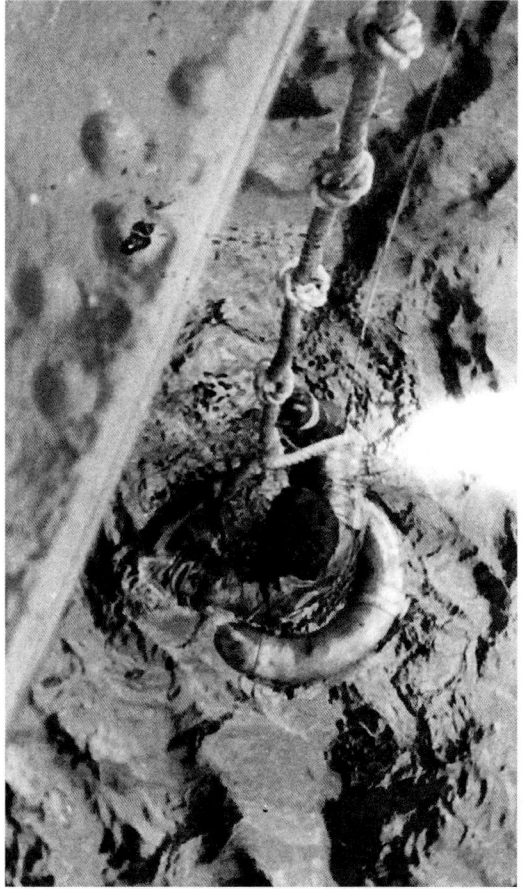

Left Coated in machine oil leaking from *Princeton*'s ruptured hull, a sailor from the carrier prepares to vacate his lifebuoy and climb up a knotted rope thrown over the side of *Cassin Young*. (Naval History and Heritage Command)

Left *Birmingham*'s skipper, Capt Thomas B. Inglis, was badly wounded when *Princeton* was rocked by a catastrophic explosion at 1523 hrs while the light cruiser was close alongside. (Naval History and Heritage Command)

Below A huge plume of smoke rises from *Princeton* following the detonation of munitions stored in the hangar bay. As this photograph graphically shows, *Birmingham* was close alongside the mortally damaged carrier at the time. The light cruiser's proximity to the explosion exacted a heavy toll on its crew. (Naval History and Heritage Command)

Cdr (here, Ens) Bruce Harwood, a highly decorated Avenger pilot and *Princeton*'s air officer, lost his life along with 25 members of his firefighting party when munitions stored in the hangar bay "cooked off" at 1523 hrs, causing a catastrophic explosion. (Naval History and Heritage Command)

This view of *Princeton*'s port midships area shows its collapsed forward elevator, buckled flightdeck and gutted hangar bay. (Naval History and Heritage Command)

Opposite *Birmingham* (left), slightly smoking following the explosion at 1523 hrs, and an unnamed destroyer tend to the now "sternless" *Princeton*. (Naval History and Heritage Command)

Left Capt (here Rear Adm) John M. Hoskins, *Princeton*'s future skipper, was in line to take the helm from Capt Buracker when the carrier was bombed and subsequently scuttled. Hoskins lost a foot to shrapnel when the vessel was rocked by the explosion that blew off its stern.
(Naval History and Heritage Command)

Below *Princeton* blows up after being torpedoed by *Reno* in what could possibly be the largest explosion of World War II in the Pacific, bar the two atomic bombs.
(Naval History and Heritage Command)

Birmingham sails slowly through San Francisco Bay on November 24, 1944, bound for the Mare Island Naval Shipyard. Here, the light cruiser would be both repaired and modified into a flagship. All work was completed by January 17, 1945. (Naval History and Heritage Command)

A close-up shot of the damage sustained to *Birmingham*'s after smokestack and superstructure following *Princeton*'s catastrophic explosion. Of the vessel's 1,285 crew, 241 were killed and 412 wounded, 212 of them seriously.
(Naval History and Heritage Command)

Under Secretary of the Navy Ralph A. Bard presents Capt William H. Buracker with the Legion of Merit on January 12, 1945, the decoration being bestowed upon him for his actions in attempting to save *Princeton* on October 24, 1944. (Tony Holmes Collection)

The Essex-class carrier *Princeton*, with CVG-13 embarked, sits at anchor off the Chinese port of Tsingtao (then headquarters for the US Navy's Western Pacific Fleet) in November 1948. The vessel was commissioned in November 1945, with Capt John M. Hoskins in command. (Tony Holmes Collection)

the ready room for a debrief when a tremendous volume of black smoke came billowing into the compartment through the ventilator system. An announcement was soon made that yes indeed we had been bombed, and that all aviators were ordered up to the flightdeck to stand beside their planes – I think the captain had at first thought that we might be able to launch.

One of the torpedoes in the hangar bay exploded and blew up the aft elevator right near where I was standing beside my Hellcat on the flightdeck, while another took out the forward elevator. The captain then ordered all crew other than select damage control to abandon ship. I went over the side down a rope and swam over to the destroyer *Irwin*, where I collapsed from exhaustion.

It had been a fighter pilot's day. Two enemy formations of more than 100 aircraft had attempted to strike TF 38, and they had been turned back with heavy losses. Twelve of Lt Cdr Bardshar's highly capable pilots had downed 36 Japanese aircraft in a matter of minutes in the defense of *Princeton* and the other ships in the task group. Seven of TF 38's pilots had destroyed five or more enemy aircraft on October 24, achieving "ace-in-a-day" status. Four of them were from VF-27. The unit's division leaders (and ranking aces), Lts Shirley and Brown, who were the first to engage enemy aircraft, were both awarded the Navy Cross for their outstanding performance that day.

ABOARD SHIP

Capt Buracker had expected some of CVLG-27's Hellcats to return shot up from the morning action on October 24, and he was correct. The very first aircraft that *Princeton* recovered that day was riddled with bullet holes, and its pilot, Lt Ralph Taylor, had been wounded in the leg.

With the exception of those who had headed to their bunks to try to get some much-needed sleep after their midnight to 0400 hrs watch, the day had gotten off to an early start. Capt Buracker was on the bridge along with Capt Hoskins, who would be taking charge of the ship after his on-the-job training period. Lt Vic Moitoret, the ship's navigation officer, was also at his general quarters station on the bridge. Lt Cdr James Large was in "air plot" along with members of his staff who were continuing their radar surveillance of the skies and waters around *Princeton*.

In the forward and aft ready rooms, just under the port side of the carrier's flightdeck, CVLG-27's air combat intelligence officers, Lts Bill Kerr and Thomas Bradshaw, were sorting through the required information (route, weather, weapons, expected enemy resistance etc.) that they would need to brief the Avenger and Hellcat pilots scheduled to attack warships in the Sibuyan Sea later that day.

On the flightdeck and in the hangar bay, fire hoses had been strung out as the ship went to general quarters at 0520 hrs. In the bake shop, three levels below the flightdeck, bakers were turning out hundreds of bread loaves and pies under the critical gaze of Chief Commissary Steward Frederick Plath – he had reported to *Princeton* after surviving the sinking of *Hornet* at the Battle of the Santa Cruz Islands in October 1942. The ship was preparing for long stretches at general quarters with the imminent threat of air attack, and the cooks and bakers had planned to bring food to gun battery crews, personnel up on the bridge and aircraft handlers at their stations throughout the carrier.

Flightdeck crews were busy in their usual routines prior to launching aircraft, carrying out arming, fueling and the delicate process of staging fighters prior to launch. Eight Hellcats had been sent aloft a little after 0600 hrs, and more would follow them as the colossal air battle intensified. Two large air engagements were duly fought between 0750 hrs and 0845 hrs, after which the carriers were ordered to recall enough fighters to provide an escort for the planned torpedo-bomber attack on IJN vessels in the Sibuyan Sea. VF-27 had been tasked with providing eight Hellcats to escort the nine Avengers from VT-27 assigned to this mission.

To make room for the returning F6Fs on *Princeton*'s flightdeck, six fully armed and fueled Avengers had to be moved below to the hangar bay. Ten Hellcats were soon recovered and two more were inbound, with CVLG-27 being optimistic that eight of those 12 would be airworthy and capable of escorting the torpedo-bombers on the strike mission. At 0910 hrs the gasoline detail commenced refueling the Hellcats that had just landed, while the six Avengers were spotted on the hanger deck in a fore and aft line on the port side of the ship, each armed with one Mk 13 torpex-loaded torpedo. All of the TBMs were topped off with fuel, and they were also carrying full auxiliary wing tanks.

The pilots of VT-27 never got the chance to carry out their scheduled attack against the enemy fleet – the wait had not been easy for them. One of those raring to go was Lt(jg) Tom Mooney:

> It was a pretty exciting prospect. Our squadron had never dropped live torpedoes against the enemy. There just weren't too many experienced torpedo pilots because of the danger involved. You get one chance. Because of the nature of the attack, you come in very low – the TBM did only about 180 knots – and you had to have the airplane well-stabilized in a proper position above the water to make a successful drop. You had to do a lot of things that made it all the easier to shoot you down.

At 0912 hrs *Essex* reported a possible "bogey," along with what was thought to be a friendly aircraft, about six miles northwest of the task group. No other identified contacts were reported within 25 miles of this pair. Less than thirty minute later, while the gasoline detail was refueling Hellcats on the flightdeck, two enemy dive-bombers, identified as "Judys," slipped through the savage aerial engagement raging above the fleet and hid in a low cloud formation off *Princeton*'s bow. At 0938 hrs both aircraft plunged out of the cloud – it appears that only one of the dive-bombers was sighted by *Princeton*'s lookouts. Capt Buracker reacted quickly, calling out hard left rudder as *Princeton* heeled over 20 degrees to port. It was too late, however. The carrier's forward gun batteries opened up at about the same time the dive-bombers each released a single 550lb bomb from 1,200ft.

Although one of the "Judys" missed its target, the other aircraft executed a perfect dive-bombing attack. The bomb struck *Princeton* in a direct hit about 15ft to port of the centerline at frame 98 on the flightdeck, nearly dead center between the two elevators. The enemy pilot could have tried that dive-bombing run over and over and never placed his weapon in a better position.

The impact caused jarring on the bridge, and a dull thud was heard in the center of the ship. Black smoke started seeping up through the small hole in the flightdeck, the forward elevator, and every access trunk to the hangar bay aft of the island. RM Ed Butler spotted one of the now-fleeing dive-bombers headed away from *Princeton*. "I saw him high-tailing it away from our stern, trailing smoke." The "Judy" leveled off at 1,000ft and flew past TG 38.3. The Atlanta-class light cruiser USS *Reno* (CL-96) fired at one of the dive-bombers, and spotters believed that they scored some hits. A Hellcat from VF-19 later claimed a "Judy" in the general area, but it will never be known if was indeed one of *Princeton*'s assailants.

Aviation Ordnanceman Pete Callan, one of the crew who had refueled and armed the torpedo-bombers, said he heard machine guns firing at a more rapid rate than any of the weapons used to defend *Princeton* were capable of. He also stated that he heard bullets striking the wooden planking of the flightdeck. Interviewed 50 years later, Callan recalled, "The Japanese pilot utilized the striking bullets to guide his aim by stitching the deck and the surrounding water, then making the appropriate corrections to his bombing run."

The bomb had penetrated the flightdeck about 75ft forward of the aft elevator. According to Capt Buracker:

> From where I stood on the bridge, the hole in the flightdeck appeared so small it seemed hardly possible major damage had been done. I visualized slapping on a patch in a hurry and resuming operations, but the bomb put out of commission the after firefighting system. It also passed right through the gas tank of a torpedo plane, spreading the fire instantly to others.

After the bomb hit, *Princeton*'s rudder was reversed and the ship rejoined the task group formation, maintaining a 20-knot speed. A radio report was made to the task group commander – "I have taken a bomb. Will keep you informed."

The weapon, more likely an armor-piercing version of a No. 25 (551lb) Ordinary Bomb, passed through the flightdeck, leaving a small hole no more than 15–18in. in diameter, and continued on a downward path, severing the main gasoline line used to fuel aircraft. It then smashed through one of the auxiliary fuel tanks suspended under the wing of Lt(jg) Tom Mooney's Avenger parked in the hangar bay. Continuing its downward path, the bomb punched through the steel plates in the hangar bay and main decks and detonated in compartment B-204-L on the second deck, or between the main and second decks. The detonation took place very near to the crew's galley on the second deck, killing most of the cooks and bakers and blowing a hole through the second deck into the third, right above the after-engine room.

The structural damage to *Princeton* was relatively minor, but a raging gasoline fire flared up in the wreckage of Lt(jg) Mooney's torpedo-bomber and spread rapidly to the other TBMs parked in the hangar bay. The severed gasoline main then started dumping large quantities of very volatile aviation fuel into the hangar bay, quickly making its way toward six Avengers topped off with 2,500 gallons of fuel and a single torpedo in their bomb-bays.

When punching through the steel hangar bay deck, the bomb had created a five-foot indentation around the small 15in. hole, which then started acting as a funnel for the gasoline spilling into the hangar bay, allowing it to find its way into the lower decks, where the fire began to rage.

Capt Buracker noted:

> The bomb exploded below the hangar bay. Flames shot through the engineering spaces aft and back into the hangar. Smoke was intense from the start, and soon was billowing up from the sides of the ship, flowing aft and making the stern untenable for personnel there. Because of the heat and smoke, men were forced to jump overboard. Circling destroyers picked them up.

Lt Frank Bell, the ship's assistant navigator, had been a prep schoolteacher and coach prior to enlisting. He had volunteered under a special naval reserve program for men with a coaching background, which meant that he also served as *Princeton*'s athletic officer. Bell was stationed at a 20mm battery near the forward corner of the flightdeck when the ship went to general quarters:

> I just happened to be looking up from my vantage point, and I spotted an enemy plane diving on the carrier. It was too late to take evasive action, for the clouds were too low. Following the plane with my eyes, I could plainly see the bomb under the fuselage. I saw the bomb released and the plane pull out of its dive. You wouldn't think one bomb could do so much damage to an aircraft carrier.

Aviation Ordnanceman Americo Mazziotti was on the wing of a Hellcat parked on the ship's bow, reloading the fighter with ammunition after it had returned from the morning engagement, when the carrier was attacked:

> I told my helper I needed boxes of right-hand feed and he had to go to the port side of the flightdeck where we had the ammunition stored. When he came back, he brought left-hand feed boxes and I had to send him back again. While he was gone, I kept an eye on the aft part of the flightdeck and the barrier – the cables which were stretched across the deck to form a sort of fence to stop planes when they had to. I had seen planes miss the arresting cables and hit the barrier, sometimes plowing right into planes forward. Anyway, while I was looking down the flightdeck, I saw splinters fly up from the flightdeck and I just knew it was a bomb. There were explosions in the hangar bay while I was still loading ammunition in the fighter. Then after a while the word came to abandon ship.

When the bomb hit, Lt Cdr Louis Levy, CVLG-27's flight surgeon, was at his battle station on the flightdeck at the base of the island structure:

> Thinking the PA system might have been damaged, I began wandering around the flightdeck to make myself fully visible in the event medical aid was needed. Shortly afterwards, I heard explosions below and machine gun firing. I felt the deck, and it was quite hot. Then I decided I had better return to my battle station. I am happy I did because the elevator I had been standing on a few seconds earlier blew up.
>
> The order to abandon ship was given. As always at general quarters, I had my flight gloves tucked under my belt and my knife, in its scabbard, hooked onto my belt. Wearing this equipment had frequently been the source of ribbing by the aviators. This time they came in very handy. I was able to cut loose two life rafts on the port side with the knife, and I went down a line using my gloves to prevent rope burns. I landed on the deck of the destroyer *Irwin* alongside *Princeton* and went to the sick bay, where there were a number of casualties needing help.

Aviation Ordnanceman Pete Callan had gone on duty at 0200 hrs when he and other members of the ordnance crew were awakened and sent to the hangar bay to rig the TBMs with torpedoes – a tough job:

> The bomb-bays had to be rigged to carry each type of ordnance. We worked for hours rigging the planes, and then started to load the torpedoes. They were stored in a peculiar manner. The warheads were kept in the magazines and the bodies were stored in racks in the hangar bay. This meant the warheads had to be brought up and the torpedoes assembled before we could load them on the planes.

The task was barely completed just before dawn when word came from the bridge to substitute 2,000lb bombs for the torpedoes. While the ordnancemen were voicing their unhappiness over the last-minute change, a second order came from topside – leave the torpedoes in the aircraft. "In view of what happened later in the day, this was fortunate for the ordnancecrewmen. A torpedo has great impact when it explodes under water. Out of water, it's about as powerful as a 500lb bomb. If we had loaded those planes with 2,000lb bombs, I don't think any of us would have survived that day."

A native Californian and the son of Greek immigrants, Pharmacist's Mate George Pantages had joined *Princeton* with a deep-rooted desire to go to sea and eventually pursue a career in pharmacy. Pantages graduated from college, took the state pharmacy examination and joined the US Navy all in July 1942. He subsequently became one of the carrier's "plank owners" – a member of the crew from the ship's commissioning. Pantages had spent his first weeks on board ship getting the pharmacy ready for the shakedown cruise and eventual departure for the war in the Pacific. "We were issued life belts when we first came aboard *Princeton* and, all the time we were at sea, I never once tested my life belt to make sure it worked properly. As we encountered more and more enemy action, I felt it was about time to check it out."

Pantages quickly found that it was impossible to manually activate the preserver, and that the only way to do it was with a pair of pliers to turn the valve:

> I thank God to this day I took a few moments then to check it out, since the preserver did play a significant part in my eventual rescue. When the bomb hit, I was sitting along the starboard catwalk, with

my feet propped up on a rail, daydreaming. I remember eating a sandwich, which suddenly disappeared from my hand. A column of smoke began to rise from amidships, and I knew we had been hit. I headed for my battle station, the farthest compartment aft on the ship. Three or four casualties were treated quickly, and then the intense black smoke from the flightdeck made our position untenable.

Pantages tried using a gas mask, but that only made matters worse. Because he was alone at the time, he made the decision to head to the hangar bay to help treat casualties:

That was a mistake. As I opened the hatch to enter the hangar bay, it appeared the place was a solid inferno. I headed back to the flightdeck and my battle station again. The smoke was so thick that I crawled along the catwalk to the port side of the carrier for some fresh air. Then the abandon ship order was given.

Quite possibly the first two sailors to leave *Princeton* did it unintentionally. Aviation mechanics Edward Montani and Leo Kieri were both stationed in the hangar bay when they were blown off the ship through a steel rolldown curtain that was kept open during daylight hours for ventilation and light. At night and during storms, the curtain was lowered, much like a garage door.

"I landed in the water without a life jacket," Kieri said. "The mechanics didn't usually wear their life preservers while working because they were bulky and subject to getting snagged." Kieri quickly realized he was alone, and the task group appeared to be steaming away from him. He began to panic, then nausea set in and soon he vomited up the sea water he had swallowed after his plunge, easing the nausea. "I took off my shoes. I thought about taking off my pants and making water wings out of them as we had been taught in survival school. Then it occurred to me sharks might be attracted to my white legs and even whiter bottom. I kept my pants on."

Like Kieri, Montani was certain he was the first sailor off the carrier: "When I heard our 40mm open up, I reached down to pick up my helmet, but I was immediately blown out the hangar bay opening, hitting my head on the safety chain. I spread-eagled myself so as to not go under when I hit the water, because I was aware of the starboard screw directly below me."

He escaped the propeller, but the ship's wake dragged him under. After surfacing, all he could see was *Princeton* disappearing, with smoke bellowing from the starboard side:

> I was minus my life jacket and got rid of my heavy work shoes to make treading water easier. I knew I was about 40 miles from the nearest land. As I prayed silently for help, I thought I was all alone. Little did I realize that Leo was so close. The waves seemed mountainous, and there was no chance of seeing one another.

Kieri could not see Montani, but he "heard someone hollering and thought they picked him up and passed me by." However, the Fletcher-class destroyer USS *Cassin Young* (DD-793) was able to gather both of them up. They had no opportunity to compare departure times from *Princeton* in those first hectic hours, but later, when the two were able to talk things over, Montani said, "We'll have to settle for a tie."

9

A New Battle

Princeton's hull, more than 600ft long, was divided into literally a mouse-maze of compartments on five different decks. These included crew berthing, galleys, mess areas, engine rooms, fire rooms, gasoline storage and munitions magazines. All of the spaces were located below the hangar bay, a huge garage-like room located directly under the flightdeck that spanned half the length of the ship from bow to stern.

The pilots' ready rooms – spaces where they prepared for their flights and conducted post-mission debriefs – were compartments suspended beneath the flightdeck on the port side of the ship.

The island, essentially the command center, was located on the starboard side and was the control tower for the carrier's small "runway." All necessary operating orders were issued from this location, and it was also where the captain and his staff spent most of their time, "on the bridge." Additionally, the island housed "talkers" manning communication lines to the various parts of the ship, along with log keepers – men who made constant routine entries into the many logs that were maintained on board ship.

The ship's executive officer, Cdr Joseph N. Murphy, was at his battle station in the CIC when the bomb struck, after which he immediately made his way to the initial location of the fire to inspect the damage and direct the battle to contain it. At much the same time, hangar bay officer Lt(jg) Henry Auclair ran to the damage control station on the port side and turned on pressure for two hoses at approximately 0945 hrs (seven minutes after the bomb had hit the ship), before activating the hangar sprinkler systems amidships. Auclair discovered the hangar bay sprinkler control switches at frame 74 smoking from an electrical short-circuit, and that several telephone talkers in that vicinity had collapsed from smoke inhalation. Soon, the flames and smoke became too much for Auclair, and he departed to report to Cdr Murphy just before the conflagration engulfed the damage control station.

When the bomb struck *Princeton*, the TBM pilots were in their ready room receiving their briefing for the upcoming mission. They collectively heard a thump or a bump similar to the sound made if a heavy object had been dropped somewhere in the ship. The ready room door led into a companionway which was normally closed, but at this time for some reason it was open. Lt(jg) Mooney looked toward the door and saw something he will never forget: "It was a fireball, a true ball made of molten flame, maybe the size of a basketball, that sailed forward through the companionway past the open ready room door."

Mooney and his fellow pilots wasted no time leaving immediately through an emergency hatch opening onto the portside catwalk, from where they climbed up to the flightdeck. Once there, Mooney witnessed controlled chaos. "Everyone had something to do, and was doing it with great vigor and proficiency."

When communications issues temporarily prevented Cdr Murphy from being in contact with Capt Buracker and the bridge, the XO hurried into his cabin nearby and used the ship's service telephone to direct the damage control officer manning the central station to activate the sprinklers from the manual controls on the third deck.

The intense heat was now boiling the water that was running down watertight hatch 01-66 and flooding the forward fireroom from the port trunk. Additionally, black smoke billowed from every access point to the hangar bay aft of the island, the bomb hole in the flightdeck and around the forward elevator. It was now also beginning to penetrate spaces at the stern of the ship.

Buracker and the bridge watch standers received numerous garbled reports that compromised their efforts to effectively direct firefighters. The captain was not adequately informed of the situation below decks and did not initially know the extent of the blaze as minutes ticked by. He then conferred with the chief engineer, and they discussed slowing or stopping *Princeton*. Buracker stated that his immediate priority was to evacuate survivors from the compartments below that were quickly filling with smoke. Buracker stood in the ship control station on the port side of the island, from where he had a clear view of the fire raging in the hangar as the elevator, flush with the flightdeck, kept the smoke from rising up over the bridge.

He tried to improve smoke conditions on board at 0950 hrs by turning the ship so that the wind was about 45 degrees on the port bow. A few minutes later, TG 38.3 commander, Rear Adm Sherman, designated the light cruiser *Reno* and the three Fletcher-class destroyers *Cassin Young*, USS *Gatling* (DD-671) and USS *Irwin* (DD-794) to stand by *Princeton* and assist the damaged carrier, while the remainder of the task group carried on with operations. During the next few minutes, the four ships began protectively circling *Princeton* as the vessels in the vicinity cleared the immediate area.

The fire spread rapidly, and the hangar bay was completely engulfed by 0953 hrs despite the best efforts of the firefighters. They reported that only one of the four hangar sprinkler bays and one of the three water curtains was turned on. Furthermore, no one had visual confirmation that any of the sprinklers were in operation – *Princeton* was being gutted.

Sailors cleared the engine room of smoke shortly before 1000 hrs, but heated water from the hose teams working above filled the bilges, raising the temperature in the small space to the point where men began to pass out. Although personnel in the engine room donned gas masks in order to breathe, the smoke and heat forced them out. Minutes later, the fire main aft lost pressure, although at that time there was no damage to machinery in the engineering spaces.

A flash, more than likely the result of a bomb detonation, penetrated the aft engine room, and it is assumed the mechanical supply ventilation systems began to draw smoke from the explosion that filled all of the engine rooms and fire rooms. Smoke also then spread to the sick bay, driving the medical team from that space. At 0956 hrs steering from the pilothouse failed, and it was transferred to aft control. Four minutes later, Sherman ordered the Cleveland-class light cruiser USS *Birmingham* (CL-62), commanded by Capt Thomas B. Inglis, to take control of the efforts to save *Princeton*.

At 1002 hrs the heat or igniting gasoline vapor in the hangar bay detonated some of the torpedo warheads, causing the first of several violent explosions. The blast, which cut men down where they stood, was so powerful it lifted the aft elevator up and completely flipped it over. Men stationed at the guns on the port side near the elevator were blown overboard. Ammunition in the aircrafts' magazines also began to "cook off" at this point, adding to the confusion and danger.

To preserve water for fire hoses forward, sailors closed the valves to hangar curtains' one and two and hangar bay one. Smoke was continuing to drive down into the forward fire and engine rooms through the ventilation ducts, and these spaces quickly became untenable. The intense heat aft, combined with the flames and twisted wreckage following the first hangar bay explosion, prevented the men in those stations from moving forward to escape. Many of them were channeled toward the stern, where they descended into the water on ropes or simply jumped. It was at this time that pilots from VF-27, after their heroic morning engagement, returned to the task group, only to be diverted to *Essex* or *Lexington*.

A second major explosion erupted in *Princeton*'s hangar bay at 1003 hrs, followed two minutes later by a much larger one, more than likely caused by torpedoes. Having emerged from their ready room, VT-27's pilots helped push aircraft over the side before tackling the raging blaze engulfing their ship. Lt(jg) Mooney grabbed a fire hose and joined a group directing streams of water down into the forward elevator shaft, which was not fully raised, sitting partially below the flightdeck. Several other crewmen were similarly engaged when an incredible eruption blasted the forward elevator out of its shaft. Mooney was an eyewitness to this:

> There was an enormous sound. It wasn't like an explosion. It was an incredible rush of air, and the elevator, which was down below flightdeck level, rose in front of me and kept on going straight up as high as the ship's radar mast. I can't remember any shock at seeing this. I don't recall being knocked out or anything either. I just thought, "Jesus, the number one elevator just flew out," and I decided there wasn't any more point in pouring water at that spot.
>
> Word then passed for all non-essential personnel to abandon ship. I caught the term "non-essential", and I was offended by it because I considered myself pretty damned essential. However, when you saw all the ship's officers and men who had duty stations being so

collected, you realized us air group types were really quite useless under the circumstances.

Mooney had on him a .45 Colt automatic pistol that his father had come by while serving in the US Army in World War I. "That forty-five was my prized possession, and I knew the old man wasn't going to like what I was about to do. But I knew I was going into the water and had no idea how long I would be swimming."

He laid the gun and holster on the deck and, with fellow torpedo-bomber pilot Lt "Doc" Manget, started down a fuel hose:

> They threw gas hoses down the side because they were handy, and they didn't have a lot of things to use. The hoses were thick, and it was tough going hand-over-hand down 50ft from the flightdeck to the water. I went first, and Manget was right behind me. He was in as big a hurry to reach the water, as was I, and on the way down he stepped on my hands several times. I remember remonstrating with him, which is a nice way of saying I wish you hadn't done that.
>
> I didn't fear the water because I was an experienced swimmer. I'll tell you, though, 15 knots of wind in the middle of the ocean is a lot of wind. You go down in a trough and can't see anything. Then you come up top on a crest and there is the ship and some people. Again, you go down and the world goes away. I had figured it would be like swimming off Hawaii, but it was not like that at all.

He and Manget were taken aboard *Irwin*. Mooney subsequently learned that the bomb had passed through the hangar bay and struck his own Avenger, which he had named *Sweet Sue* after his wife. As previously noted, all the TBMs below deck were still carrying torpedoes and full auxiliary wing fuel tanks. There simply had not been enough time for personnel to remove them when the torpedo-bombers were sent down from the flightdeck to make room for the Hellcats to recover back on board.

"My plane captain was standing on the plane's wing when the bomb came down," Mooney explained. "It torched the fuel and covered him with flames. He was just like a marshmallow – seared. Later, when we had been picked up, I saw him bandaged up like a mummy, and I thought 'He's going to die,' but he lived."

The extremely heavy blasts from the detonating torpedoes exerted incredible force against the flightdeck and the sides of the carrier. The steel and timber flightdeck surface between the forward and aft elevators buckled upwards.

Gun crews manning the 20mm and 40mm mounts along the port side were hit hard. There were many casualties with burns and shrapnel wounds. Men were blown from the carrier's catwalk to the water 50ft below. Gunnery officer Lt Jim Kelleher lost contact with three gun crews on the fantail, but those men had received word, along with other sailors crowding the stern, to abandon ship. Conditions had become too hazardous to remain on board the ship, and there was no apparent path forward to escape the thickening cloud of smoke. The gunners joined their fellow crewmen in scrambling down hoses or lines to the water. Most of these men were picked up by the destroyers circling *Princeton*.

Ens Frederick "Fritz" Hautop was among the fighter pilots who had taken part in the morning's CAP, and he was in the forward ready room being debriefed for another flight when the bomb hit:

> The initial explosion knocked us right out of our seats. I got up and headed for the wardroom, which is the officers' dining area, but at that point was being used as an aid station. One of my friends, "Swish" Taylor, had landed aboard with a bullet hole in the leg. A couple of us helped him and saw that they got him off the ship.
>
> By then the lights were dimming. People were panicking, coming up from down below badly hurt – scalded, screaming. We heard the captain had ordered "abandon ship", and I went to the forecastle where there were many people, with the *Irwin* rammed up against our bow to take aboard survivors. The ships didn't meet too well, so you couldn't jump from one to the other. Some tried it and were crushed in the attempt. Hoses and lines were put down *Princeton*'s side, and I used one to go into the water.

Although he was an excellent swimmer, Hautop realized that the carrier and destroyer being so close together meant the surge of water between them would probably keep him under for a good amount of time:

> There were bodies all over the place, plus some sharks that were kicking around. Someone on the *Irwin* dropped a line right next

to me. I got it, wrapped it around my hand, and they started to pull me up. There was a man hanging on each of my feet. By the time I got ten feet out of the water I thought the rope would cut my hands off with all that weight, so I dropped back into the sea. Another line with a loop was dropped from the *Irwin* and I grabbed it. I still had people hanging on my feet, and with my last bit of strength I had to kick them off. They finally got me on deck.

One of the ship's officers, Lt Richard Jackson, was on the crowded forecastle deck following the impact of the bomb, and he observed with shock the sight of men who jumped or went down lines and attempted to swim the gap between *Princeton* and *Irwin*:

> The eccentric wave action between the ships made this a nightmare for many, as they closed the gap only to be thrown back just as their fingers were clutching at the cargo nets, which had been dropped over the destroyer's sides. Some of the swimmers drifted aft of both ships, and with the help of machine gun fire from the *Irwin*'s fantail, eluded sharks and were picked up by small boats.

With so many sailors overboard, destroyer crewmen launched whaleboats and started throwing empty ammunition cans in the water so that the people adrift could grab onto them and stay afloat until they were picked up.

Gunner Larry Addison, who was stationed on a 40mm quad mount, was among those who later reported there were probably sharks in the water, although it did not concern him at the time. When the abandon ship order was passed, he went over the rail on the starboard side, jumping to avoid the destroyer that was then alongside *Princeton*:

> I was in the water about two hours, alone most of the time. I saw others occasionally, and we would try to get together, but the waves kept us apart. I lost all of the ships and couldn't see anything, then suddenly there was a whaleboat alongside. I heard some rifle shots, and wasn't aware of what they were doing until I got aboard. Then I found out they had been shooting at sharks. I don't know what I would have done if I had been attacked by sharks, particularly because I had no shoes on.

Aviation Boatswain's Mate Don Scheer, a plane handler assigned to flightdeck duty, helped man a hose line, then followed an officer's instructions to assist in pushing aircraft over the side near the forward elevator:

> We backed up the planes we had just landed and spotted. We pushed them onto the elevator, then turned them outboard and ran them off the edge of the flightdeck. They plunged down and sank in the sea. We were on the elevator, which kept bouncing up and down a little bit every time we went over it, and I thought, "Hey, we better get off this thing." Well, after we pushed one final, or maybe next-to-last, plane off the side the elevator exploded.

Somehow, Scheer escaped injury. He looked at the elevator cocked up on a corner in its well. "If I had been on that thing, I'd be down the hole." He crawled to the port side and went down a line to the water, along with another sailor:

> We started swimming. My life jacket was one of those air jobs. When we hit the water, the thing just went whoosh and all the air went out of it. I started swimming and the other guy was behind me. He called my name, "Don", and I turned around, but he was gone. I don't know whether a shark got him or what, but from then on, until some ship picked me up, I was alone in the water.

Fellow "airdale" (aviation rating) Percy Sherman had the assigned task of manning a foamite station in the event of a flightdeck fire. A foamite station was a small compartment with a single entrance off the carrier's catwalk. It contained a fire hose and a large hopper in the center. Stacks of pails filled with powder were lined up on the bulkheads. The powder was dumped into the hopper, which had a hose line feeding water into its bottom. The mixture of powder and water became foam, which was shot out of the hose to extinguish fires. The compartment was not tall enough inside to stand up in, but it served as a great place for five or six men to take a seat for a poker game.

After the bomb struck, Sherman began pulling out a fire hose and opening the powder pails so he could pour the contents into the hopper, which fed foam to the water line. He stayed at that station until the water pressure failed:

> When I climbed out onto the flightdeck, I was amazed to see *Princeton* all by itself when there had been so many other ships with us before the bomb hit. I then received word to abandon ship, so I went over the side with a friend. We were swimming toward one of the destroyers, and it seemed like we would never get there. My friend had a long cut on his forearm that was wrapped up but bleeding badly. We had been in the water only a short time when I saw a shark fin coming toward us on the surface. Then the fin turned under. My friend came high out of the water and shouted to me. Then he disappeared for the last time.

Cassin Young had been dispatched to *Princeton*'s aid shortly after the carrier was hit, the destroyer's crew helping with firefighting and any other duties that might be required. Thankfully, the vessel also had sailors who could handle an M1 Garand rifle. *Cassin Young* quickly launched a whaleboat to pick up sailors and Marines that had gone overboard, and its crew was kept busy plucking survivors from the water. One unnamed *Princeton* sailor recalled that once he got aboard the destroyer, he became aware of small-arms fire on the starboard side of the ship and walked over to investigate:

> I saw maybe a dozen sailors standing along the rails, and what they were shooting at from the *Cassin Young* were sharks. Suddenly I realized the wounded man I had helped off the *Princeton* and later saw floating dead near me didn't just go under when he disappeared. He had probably been eaten by sharks. Why they didn't go after me I'll never know. The thought of those sharks made me a little faint, and I had to sit down for a while.

The blast in the hangar bay that tossed the forward elevator up in the air and turned it over created an opening that released an inferno from within the hangar spaces, allowing black smoke to pour out over the bridge. This forced Capt Buracker to order all personnel out of that area. The heat and smoke prevented them from simply exiting through the hatchways, however. Buracker exited the bridge onto the ship's crane and then climbed down onto the flightdeck forward. Here, the situation was dire. The flightdeck burned furiously aft of the island back to the stern and the thick smoke grew until it became so dense that it obscured the stricken carrier from the other ships.

The scene surrounding Buracker was absolute carnage. The blast had thrown a 14ft section of flightdeck girder over the open bridge and onto the crane arm, where it remained, hanging. By now, the ship and crew had endured several major explosions, killing scores of sailors and wounding many more. Dozens of seamen had already gone overboard. Fragments from the explosions had sliced into the bridge and cut down a number of men. The most seriously wounded was one of the lookouts, who had been struck by a 4in. by 4in. piece of timber. He was lowered onto the flightdeck and then the forecastle of *Irwin*, where he died of his wounds the next day. Repeated explosions had buckled most of the flightdeck upward between the elevators, and both gyrocompasses had been knocked out.

Buracker's leadership was being tested, but he stayed focused and ordered "all hands topside" just before all communications bar the ship's service telephone failed. He then personally directed the chief engineer to get his men out of the engineering spaces. Vibration had triggered the general alarm, and some crew interpreted this as an emergency signal to abandon ship, resulting in the unfortunate evacuation of many important damage control personnel.

Princeton had lost all of its main pressure for the firefighting hoses by 1010 hrs, after which the vessel's steering failed and it assumed a position across-wind, drifting to leeward. Buracker met with Murphy on the flightdeck and they agreed to order Salvage Control Phase I as a result of the catastrophic damage. This order directed 490 men to remain behind to battle the fires and man the antiaircraft guns in case the enemy attacked again, while crew members vacated the spaces below and gathered on the flightdeck in preparation to abandon ship. *Princeton* was practically dead in the water, but its position drew the fire and smoke to the rear on the starboard side, freeing up the catwalks on the port side and allowing the crew to move toward the bow.

Following the first hellish minutes of the fire and subsequent multiple blasts, the officers concurred that the stellar efforts of the crew, along with the assistance of the ships that had come to the carrier's aid, seemed to be succeeding in getting the fires under control. At this same officers' call, it was then recommended that the ship be taken in tow. *Princeton* hailed nearby *Irwin*, and it slid alongside the carrier on the port side and hit the fire hard in the forward end of the hangar with several hoses aimed through the forward elevator roller curtain opening.

While *Irwin* was preparing to take *Princeton* in tow, men started lowering the wounded onto the destroyer's forecastle. Others jumped or slid down lines, while some threw life rafts into the water as *Irwin* continued to pull men from the sea.

As if current events were not enough to occupy *Princeton* and the vessels trying to save it, incoming reports of enemy aircraft forced *Reno* to take up station focusing on antiaircraft defense of the carrier and the other ships tending to "Sweet P" and its crew. The light cruiser headed in the direction of one of the reported raids and opened fire at a range of 3,000 yards when low-flying enemy aircraft were spotted approaching from the starboard side. Its gunners claimed a "Betty" and a "Judy" destroyed, while Hellcats from the CAP intercepted more aircraft shortly before 1030 hrs.

While *Reno* was downing incoming aircraft, 20mm and 40mm ammunition stored in *Princeton*'s ready lockers began to "cook off," prompting Capt Buracker to order Salvage Control Phase II. This meant that all gunners had to vacate their posts and abandon ship. This should have left Buracker with just under 250 men on board, consisting of mostly repair party and engineering sailors. However, the majority of the engineering personnel had been forced overboard at the stern due to their spaces being filled with acrid smoke. Furthermore, broken communications, or none at all in the forward compartments, saw crewmen in these spaces receive a mistaken order to abandon ship, sending more men overboard than was intended for these two phases. All hands were then ordered to remain on *Princeton*, regardless of their ratings, after Buracker and his officers realized they were shorthanded of these essential personnel.

Cdr Bruce Harwood, *Princeton*'s air officer, courageously remained at his station on the port side of the bridge to direct firefighting, despite the recent explosions and the threat of future ones. To determine the extent of the damage below, on his own initiative he entered the hangar bay in the face of flames that were making their way toward the torpedo and bomb stowage area. In a continuing act of bravery and persistence,

Harwood entered a number of blazing compartments, often at the lead, and when the heat or exhaustion got the better of his men, he personally pulled them from harm's way.

Meanwhile, the remaining sailors on board continued in the attempt to save "Sweet P." Crewmen pushed more aircraft overboard, and a damage control team rigged a gasoline Handy Billy to pump water to the flightdeck. Here, firefighters sent a stream of water down the forward elevator opening into the inferno.

ASSISTANCE FROM *BIRMINGHAM*

When it was quickly realized that a larger ship could add significantly more to the firefighting effort, *Irwin* was relieved at its station and cast off at 1100 hrs while the light cruiser *Birmingham* carefully made its way through the sailors bobbing in the water on *Princeton*'s port side. The vessel's commanding officer, Capt Inglis, later reported, "I found it was necessary to run a line to *Princeton* in order to keep the two ships together since the *Princeton*, with her high sides, made faster leeway than the *Birmingham*. My plan was to start fighting the fires from the forward end of *Princeton*, and as they were extinguished to work aft."

Fighting the fires from the starboard side proved difficult because of the wind and the intensity of the smoke – *Reno* attempted to slide up alongside *Princeton* but was driven away by the heat and smoke. Enemy aircraft also continued to target them, with one of *Reno*'s lookouts sighting a Zero-sen emerge from a cloud directly over the cruiser at an altitude of about 4,000ft. The vessel's light antiaircraft guns opened up, but the enemy fighter escaped without inflicting any more damage upon the US Navy ships.

In an attempt to tackle the fires more effectively, *Birmingham* moved aft of *Princeton*. Within a short space of time, it had sent 14 water hoses and 38 men from its damage control teams over to the carrier. This assistance was significant, for it helped extinguish one of two major fires in the hangar spaces. The firefighters made steady progress in the forward end of the hangar bay and had extinguished the flames in this area by 1130 hrs. A small fire remained in the forward elevator pit, however, fueled by hydraulic fluid. *Reno* also continued to maneuver alongside Princeton, and after several failed attempts to take up station close on its starboard side, resulting in damage to a 40mm gun mount, it cleared the carrier at 1202 hrs.

Princeton's chief engineer and a handful of officers who specialized in hull work had abandoned ship earlier in the morning and were now on board the Fletcher-class destroyer USS *Morrison* (DD-560). Twelve minutes into the afternoon watch, *Morrison* tried to return these men to *Princeton* by maneuvering up to the carrier's starboard side. This attempt had to be abandoned when radar operators on board one of the nearby destroyers reported a "bogey" just five miles out. *Reno* prepared to protect *Princeton* once again.

When the threat had passed, *Morrison* was finally able to move into position, and at 1245 hrs it took advantage of a lull in the smoke and eased in alongside the carrier, starboard amidships. As the crew of the destroyer pushed two hoses into the after-elevator pit through the after-roller curtain opening, the two ships ground together and *Morrison* became wedged between *Princeton*'s Nos. 2 and 3 stacks. The sponsons of the destroyer's starboard antiaircraft guns suffered severe topside damage, while the collision caused a jeep and a tractor used to tow aircraft to fall from the carrier's flightdeck onto *Morrison*'s bridge, knocking the foremast and forward gun directors overboard and badly damaging its stacks, the searchlight platform and the port side of the bridge.

Although the noon attack by enemy aircraft failed to materialize, they continued to probe the outer defenses, and at 1300 hrs radar detected another large group bearing 210 degrees at 60 miles. Rear Adm Sherman then directed *Reno* to take charge of the destroyers not battling the fire or rescuing survivors and provide a protective screen around *Princeton*.

Like a wounded beast, the carrier was attracting the enemy's attention, as word was then received by *Birmingham* that several Japanese aircraft had broken through the CAP. Minutes later, a lookout on *Cassin Young* reported spotting a submarine just 2,000 yards away. *Birmingham* reeled in nearly all of its fire hoses and broke away at 1332 hrs to gain sea room for maneuvering as the threats from above and below appeared to be increasing.

Princeton's chief engineer was able to get back aboard his damaged ship, and while the aerial threat played out, he entered the forward engine room and discovered all of the steam and fire main gages indicated zero pressure. On a more positive note, he reported that the forward diesel generator was still running. Additionally, the emergency system had operated as designed for the most part and turned on the battle lights in this space. Smoke had filled the forward engine room, and he estimated that the temperature in that compartment to be an unbearable 165 degrees.

When the submarine contact proved to be a false alarm, *Cassin Young* rejoined the rescue effort in place of *Irwin*. Debris and flotsam had clogged one of the latter vessel's condensers, putting an engine out of use and preventing it from helping in the rescue and firefighting operation. At the same time, *Morrison*'s crew were able to clear away the jeep, tractor and other debris, and it backed away at 1354 hrs to rejoin the protective screen.

Birmingham being forced to pull away to deal with a perceived enemy threat and *Irwin*'s engine problem could not have come at a worse time for *Princeton*. Its firefighters, assisted by personnel from other vessels, had battled a series of explosions and a severe blaze and were now very close to saving the carrier, having essentially got the conflagration under control. The only known remaining fire burned around the torpedo workshop and in the aft elevator pit. Capt Buracker optimistically envisaged his men ventilating the spaces below, allowing the engineering sailors to return to their stations and *Princeton* again getting up steam to come about for emergency repairs.

"The ship was not very pretty at that time," Buracker reflected, "but at least we would bring her back." When the cruisers and destroyers were forced to pull away, the fire took on a life of its own once again, blazing with renewed vigor as the afternoon winds picked up. A squall then moved in and pummeled the sailors with heavy rain, reducing visibility to barely 100 yards while 20-knot winds added to the misery. Some sailors were encouraged by the rain, thinking that it would both assist in putting out the fires and provide cover from enemy air attacks.

Yet despite the inclement weather, the aerial intruders would not go away. Another lone "Zeke" appeared overhead at 1402 hrs, only to be driven away by *Reno*'s antiaircraft batteries. Meanwhile, Capt Inglis optimistically reported to Sherman that the flames were all but out, giving him a rundown of the damage that had been sustained by *Princeton* and the other vessels.

Inglis was apparently unaware that the fire was increasing in the forward magazine, and the sprinklers failed again just as he instructed *Reno* to take *Princeton* in tow at 1445 hrs. This proved to be no easy task, for the light cruiser's stern had been hit by a crashing enemy torpedo-bomber during the raids on Formosa, effectively destroying its towing equipment. As the crew attempted to pull together something with which to tow the carrier, *Morrison* slid alongside *Princeton*'s port quarter at 1453 hrs to battle the resurgent fire in the aft end of the hangar. It had little luck tackling the renewed, persistent blaze.

10

Princeton Eternally Defiant

There are conflicting reports and recollections as to the extent and intensity of the fires that were burning in *Princeton*'s aft hangar bay as *Birmingham* approached the carrier on the afternoon of October 24. Some have stated that they had started back up with renewed vigor, while others recalled that they were subdued and hardly visible. Regardless, both Capts Buracker and Inglis felt that *Princeton* was ready to be taken in tow.

More than five hours had passed since the bomb had struck the carrier. During that time, the largest naval battle in history was unfolding. Thousands of combatants from both sides were engaged in a conflict that would rage at a level of intensity never seen before. As the afternoon progressed, the men focused on saving *Princeton* were beginning to hope that they would live long enough to see the sun rising the following day – their world was now that small.

Birmingham had begun using its hoses to assist in firefighting duties from 1100 hrs, and the crew of the cruiser had eventually played a major part in subduing a very dangerous, raging conflagration. Inglis had continually used the engines of the light cruiser to maneuver close to *Princeton* to help his firefighters tackling the blaze, while at the same time other members of the crew undertook FDO duties for Hellcats from *Essex* providing CAP over the small group of ships. The events of the 24th had all amounted to a day's worth of hard, dangerous work that was still far from over.

Birmingham held station alongside *Princeton* for two-and-a-half hours, with the two ships frequently making contact, inflicting some damage on the light cruiser's gun mounts. Witnesses commented that "it was sickening to watch – it seemed as though the two ships were attempting to destroy each other." In reality, just the opposite was occurring – *Birmingham* was doing everything it possibly could to save *Princeton*, as were the other ships within the small group surrounding the carrier. The rescue operation was continuing to go well, and this would ensure that more than 90 percent of *Princeton*'s complement of 1,569 officers and men would survive the ordeal.

By 1200 hrs, firefighters were concentrating water from 14 *Birmingham* hoses on *Princeton*, making noticeable progress on the forward blazes that culminated with the first fire being reported under control by 1212 hrs. Around 1230 hrs, Capt Inglis sent a volunteer firefighting detail of 38 men over to *Princeton*, and they were soon joined by the carrier's engineering personnel from *Morrison*.

As noted in the previous chapter, the afternoon air attack and false submarine report tore the ships away from *Princeton* at the very moment when the salvage effort was appearing to make headway. When the vessels returned, the sailors persisted. At 1406 hrs *Birmingham* reported to TG 38.3 that "prospects very good now," with *Princeton*'s fires being confined to the aft section of the ship.

Having broken away from the carrier after the near-simultaneous submarine and air strike reports, *Birmingham* began to ease alongside *Princeton* once again at 1430 hrs to allow the crew to train hoses on the troublesome aft section of the ship. Leading a firefighting detachment from the light cruiser, Lt Alan Reed estimated that one more hour of work would extinguish this final blaze in the stern, prompting Capt Buracker to suggest that the ship be taken in tow. Inglis asked Buracker if they should continue to fight the fire or take *Princeton* in tow, and Buracker recommended that the fires should be extinguished first, which was the logical thing to do.

By this time the wind was blowing at more than 20 knots and pushing *Princeton*, adding to the challenge of lining up two large warships as *Birmingham* once again moved alongside the carrier. The wind whipped up the fires aft as a spring line joining the two vessels abeam was finally secured to a forward point on the carrier at around 1520 hrs. *Birmingham* settled in in a position on *Princeton*'s port side, with roughly 50ft of space between the two ships. The light cruiser's foremast was about abreast of the carrier's midsection. *Birmingham*'s deck was packed with many more sailors than usual as men manned antiaircraft batteries and hoses, while others kept themselves busy aiding survivors and tending to lines and other gear.

In *Princeton*'s hangar bay, Cdr Harwood's party waited to receive *Birmingham*'s bow line and hoses. In that general vicinity, sitting on pallets a few yards aft, were 400 100lb GP bombs, 65 500lb fragmentation clusters and possibly some remaining charged torpedo air flasks (housing the various compartments for compressed air, fuel, water and chemicals that when combined form the propellant for the weapon). In total, more than 30 tons of explosives that had been literally baking in the heat from the fires throughout the day were nearing their limit.

At 1523 hrs those munitions cooked off in a colossal blast, cutting *Princeton* literally in two. The carrier's stern, separated from the rest of the ship, floated free and rotated horizontally, with the rudder, two big screws and the vessel's name across the fantail pointing skyward for a defiant 45 minutes before sinking. A number of the survivors later compared the explosion to that of an atom bomb. The incredible force of the blast shoved *Birmingham* – a 610ft, 11,700lb fully loaded warship – more than 15ft sideways through the water.

Just seconds after the blast, there was dead silence, then the airwaves crackled with urgent transmissions. *Birmingham* radioed *Reno*, "Take command," followed by, "We have had many casualties on *Birmingham*. Take command." *Reno*'s reply was simply, "Roger." As the smoke started to clear from the scene, the radio transmissions began to paint the ugly picture of the human carnage for those that were too far away on the other ships to see it.

"There was an explosion on *Princeton*," *Birmingham* reported to *Reno*. "I believe it has had its fantail blown off. See if you can get contact with Commander, Task Group 38.3." Moments later, *Reno* was asked to "take guard for us on all circuits but TBS [talk between ships]. We have been unable to determine damage."

Birmingham to *Reno*: "Try to contact *Santa Fe* and tell him we need our other doctor as soon as possible." *Reno* to *Birmingham*: "Do you wish for one of our doctors?" *Birmingham* to *Reno*: "Affirmative. Would you send over some corpsmen?" There was a brief pause, then *Birmingham* to *Reno*: "We have about 100 to 150 killed and about the same number wounded. Those casualties are very gravely wounded. Our commanding officer is a casualty."

One of *Birmingham*'s machinist mates, Frank Popham, was an eyewitness to the whole horrific event:

> I was perched on the after-ventilator "mushroom" between the Nos. 3 and 4 turrets, intently watching the activities on *Princeton*. From an estimated 50 to 75 yards, absolutely no smoke or fires were observed, only patches of fog-like vapors coming from the numerous openings in *Princeton*'s flightdeck. *Princeton* appeared to be serenely drifting with the current. It appeared as if the fires had gone out on their own or they had been extinguished. George, on my right, suddenly exclaimed, "Look at that flame!"

Frank and his fellow sailors then witnessed flames begin to shoot out from around the area of the aft elevator, followed by the horrific blast. All hell broke loose as the massive detonation blew 130ft of *Princeton*'s stern off, as well as 180ft of its flightdeck. Popham continued:

> The three of us were blown into the air. I landed on my back. My best friend, Vernon, landed on his feet and ran around the barbette of No. 3 turret and then dropped dead. Suddenly, it was deathly quiet. I mean just nothing, and then the hot shrapnel was raining down. It was burning the hell out of me, so I tried to stand up, but one leg wouldn't support me. It turned out that a piece of shrapnel had broken a bone in my leg, and I wasn't able to stand on it.

Popham then discovered that his other leg was wounded and that his back had also been hit. Hot shrapnel was burning the exposed skin on his neck. He could see only two or three conscious people around him, as the sailors manning the hoses and trying to get a bow line to *Princeton* had been completely wiped out.

Another shipmate, Mike Miksis, suddenly appeared from nowhere and said, "Pop, Pop, take it easy." Shock had set in, and Miksis told Popham that he was going to get help and disappeared below decks. With another shipmate, Dick Stern, he tore a bunk form from the bulkhead and rushed back to the deck to carry Popham to a first aid station below. Popham concluded: "John probably saved my life for getting me there so fast. While I waited for John's return, my limited view was of a deck strewn with assorted body parts and rivers of blood draining into the water."

PO Buhler "Buck" Glans was the chief quartermaster on board *Birmingham*, and it was his duty to take periodic readings of the sun to pinpoint the ship's position at sea:

> When it was time to take sightings, I went to the flying bridge with my first-class quartermaster. Using my sextant, I was bringing the sun down to the horizon between the smokestacks of *Princeton* when the carrier blew up. Looking up, I saw steel coming down, so I dove for cover toward the ladder to the lower decks. I made that descent hitting only two steps on the way down. Then I found I had been hit by shrapnel in the thigh, only a few inches from an important part of my body.

When the debris stopped falling, Glans returned to the open flying bridge, where he found his first-class quartermaster dead:

> I tried to get to those who were still alive. Wounded men lay all over the deck – not a pretty sight. The ship's captain, the navigator and officer of the deck were wounded. They all asked that the others be helped first. There were many heroic acts. Our specialist chief of physical fitness, who had lost both legs, told the corpsman to help others first. He died from loss of blood. *Birmingham*'s decks ran with blood.

Birmingham's bridge – from where Capt Inglis was guiding the light cruiser in to help *Princeton*, which was under the command of his naval academy compatriot, Capt Buracker – had taken the full impact of the explosive eruption. According to Inglis, "As we moved back toward *Princeton*, she looked as innocent as could be, with just a thin wisp of smoke visible. I thought to myself, 'We'd have the fire licked in no time and have her in tow.' Then *Princeton*'s stern blew."

Inglis was thrown against the far bulkhead. "I was struck by fragments. My left arm was broken – a clean break as it turned out. I had been hit by shrapnel in the head, face and at the base of my spine."

Initially, Inglis thought he had escaped serious injury, and that the latest blast was just another explosion in *Princeton*'s hangar bay, much like the others. "At first, I believed I was okay. I hardly knew I had been wounded. I kept command for some ten to 15 minutes, and then I began to feel dizzy and not really competent to handle the task of running my ship and looking out for the safety of all hands aboard."

Cdr Francis R. Duborg, *Birmingham*'s chief gunnery officer, was on the bridge with Capt Inglis. He had also been wounded by flying steel but was in far better shape than the skipper. Duborg assumed command of the ship when it became obvious that Inglis could not continue.

Naval reserve officer Lt James H. MacArt was the only doctor on board *Birmingham* at the time of the explosion. According to Duborg, "It wasn't until sometime later that MacArt was able to check on the captain, and that was when we found out how bad he was. He sent down a corpsman with a splint. The repair job was really painful." Inglis sent a message to *Reno* before being forced to leave the bridge: "We have had many casualties on *Birmingham*. Take over command. Report to CTG 38.3 that bomb magazine exploded. I consider it useless to salvage ship. Recommend that personnel be removed, and ship sunk. In the meantime, we are trying to inspect the damage on *Birmingham*."

Birmingham's executive officer, Cdr Winston P. Folk, was also on the bridge at the time of the blast:

> I was standing on the starboard side of the signal bridge a few feet from the captain. We were both struck by debris and knocked to the deck. As soon as I recovered from the shock of the concussion, I got up and went to the captain to see how he was. He said he had been hit, but was all right.

Inglis immediately instructed Folk to conduct a quick survey of the ship's condition. The XO described how he was "totally unprepared for the spectacle" he saw when exiting the bridge to take a look at the damage done and check on casualties:

> Still a bit dazed myself, I somehow thought the principal effects of the explosion had been in the bridge area. I found instead that the main deck, for 140 of our 150 frames – most of its length – was

strewn with dead, dying and wounded, many of them badly hurt. Already a few unwounded were beginning to render first aid to their companions. The communications platform was in the same condition. It is impossible, even remotely adequately, to describe the grisly scene of human fragmentation that presented itself. I felt as if I were having a horrible nightmare and wished I would hurry and wake up.

Despite the horror of the situation, Folk would never forget the collective unselfishness and remarkable heroism that left a lasting impression on him. There was the possibility that another massive blast could come shortly after this one, but that was put aside, as the sailors tended to their wounded shipmates. *Birmingham*'s surviving crew members threw sand on the deck to provide firm footing amidst the blood and carnage, harkening back to the age of sailing ships. "There was not the slightest tendency toward panic," Folk confirmed, "and many of those involved had never before been in close contact with violent death, or seen decks covered with the blood of companions."

The XO worked his way back to the bridge after completing his survey of the damage to both ship and personnel. He then discovered Inglis had given over his command, reluctantly, to Duborg, and placed *Reno* in charge of the rescue operation. Folk then relieved Duborg and took command of *Birmingham*, as he was rightfully the vessel's executive officer.

Lt Edward Ryan was *Birmingham*'s communication officer, and he was standing near the middle of the pilot house at the time of the explosion and luckily escaped injury. "When I heard the blast," he said, "I crouched down, and fortunately none of the fragments penetrated to where I was." After standing up again, Ryan had a broad view of the forward half of the ship. He left the bridge immediately, and despite having had only basic first aid training he tried to do what he could to help the wounded men.

Ryan, moving alongside a wounded sailor, tried to inject him with morphine. The seaman in turn pushed him away, telling Ryan, "No, don't take care of me. Take care of those other fellas. They're worse off than I am." "That," said Ryan, "was typical of the spirit you saw everywhere. I don't really have too coherent a recollection of what I did much of the time after that. Most of the injuries were so serious you really didn't know how to begin to help."

SHATTERED SHIP

For the few personnel still on board *Princeton*, the explosion was truly devastating. The bulk of the 13,000-ton ship lurched sideward and upward, trembled for an instant, then settled back in the water as the deadly shower of debris came down. The stillness in the instant after the blast was completely void of human sound. The silence was then pierced by white-hot steel and other objects slamming into whatever was in their path, the clank of metal on metal and hissing steam from ruptured pipes.

There were only roughly 50 men left on board the carrier at the time of the blast. Cdr Harwood and his firefighting party of 25 men that he had just led down into the hangar bay were completely wiped out. Harwood was already a two-time recipient of the Navy Cross, having received these decorations during the Guadalcanal campaign in the late summer and early fall of 1942. His selfless actions on October 24, 1944 earned him a third Navy Cross, albeit posthumously.

Capt Buracker subsequently said of Cdr Harwood, "Like every man on the ship, he thought of saving it first and not of personal danger."

Not one of the remaining survivors on the carrier escaped without some degree of injury. A small group of men standing amidships on the port side of *Princeton*'s flightdeck that included Capt Buracker and his replacement, Capt Hoskins, were rocked by the explosion. The latter officer had remained on board the carrier to help fight the fire, although he had no requirement to do so. In absolute disregard for his personal safety, he manned hose lines and pitched in wherever he felt his help was needed. A genial, red-haired officer with more than 16 years of service by then, he was destined to become a US Navy legend.

Capt Buracker recalled that the explosion was "terrifying, as the after part of the ship was blown high and fell into the sea astern. Flying fragments, some huge, some small, burst outwards and upwards. Big chunks swept *Birmingham*, causing many casualties in killed and wounded. Our ship also was showered with flying debris from stem to stern. Practically all left aboard were killed or injured. Cdr Harwood and his party aft in the hangar were lost."

Hoskins was standing next to Buracker at the time of the blast. "When the blast came, we all started crawling and running forward for protection," Buracker explained. "Someone noticed that Capt Hoskins couldn't move. Going back, I saw that his right foot was hanging by a shred. By then he had already swiftly applied a tourniquet to his leg to stop the flow of blood." Cdr Roland O. Sala, *Princeton*'s senior medical officer, along with Pharmacist's Mate Paul Robinson, rushed to assist Hoskins. According to Robinson:

> Dr. Sala had fallen heir to an amputation knife that was in a set when we put the ship in commission. He had a sheath made for it. When Capt Hoskins had this problem, which was on the flightdeck next to the island, I know there were people that said they were eyewitness to my amputation of the leg, but I didn't amputate it at all. Capt Hoskins' foot was blown off above the ankle. The ankle has many bones in it. Capt Hoskins was in great pain. I came upon him when Dr. Sala was already there, but he was also wounded. I gave Capt Hoskins a shot of morphine – one-half grain. One-quarter grain is a lot, and I think one-eighth grain now is the usual dosage for pain.
>
> I then proceeded to clean the wound up. I didn't know how bad it was. I put a tourniquet just above it – a stricture rather than a tourniquet because I cut off all the blood supply and cut through to the Achilles tendon. The people who saw me do this thought I was amputating the leg, and this is the reason for that story.

Cdr Sala was standing by with knife in hand as Robinson injected Hoskins with another one-half grain of morphine. "He just gritted his teeth. By then, he had a full grain of morphine in him. This is an awful lot for one to take, but when you are in pain, it has been proven the more pain, the more morphine you can take. A full grain might kill someone, but not someone in his state of pain."

Surrounded by the small group of survivors on the flightdeck of a mortally wounded aircraft carrier with its stern blown off and struggling to remain afloat, Cdr Sala removed Capt Hoskins' foot. Robinson recalled:

> There is a way that you do an amputation under sterile conditions where you cut the bone back a little and you cut a pattern somewhat

like a baseball cover, putting a flap over the end of the extremity that is being amputated. This was not the time or the place for that, and it wasn't sterile either. Nevertheless, Capt Hoskins survived that very well. He was a real man. Eventually, we lowered him into a whaleboat.

Capt Hoskins had no recollection of having been given the two morphine injections:

> We had fought the fires from nine o'clock in the morning to nearly 3.30 in the afternoon. Our sprinklers were knocked out, and I was knocked on my fanny three times. When the stern of the carrier was blasted off, all 20 or so of us on the flightdeck were blown flat. Then everyone started to run, but I couldn't get up. There was my bare right foot – minus shoe and sock – hanging by a tendon, almost completely severed. They carried me forward and the doctor, himself injured, went to work on me with a sheath knife.

Lt Cdr Albert R. Oesterle, *Princeton*'s dental officer, had been standing beside Capt Hoskins at the time of the explosion. "After I had regained some composure, I found Capt Hoskins near me using a belt as a tourniquet around his injured leg. Dr. Sala came up and removed the foot with his sheath knife. Dr. Sala had also been injured in the groin by a piece of shrapnel."

A still-conscious Hoskins was placed in a Stokes litter and lowered from the forward end of the flightdeck to the forecastle – an open portion of the deck at the carrier's bow. "Before he was lowered into a whaleboat and taken to USS *Gatling*, Hoskins asked that he be given a knife to use in cutting himself loose from the stretcher in case he wound up in the water before reaching the destroyer," explained Lt Cdr Oesterle. In a moment forever cemented in US Navy lore, Capt Hoskins saluted in the direction of Capt Buracker and said the words to the officer of the deck spoken by every officer or enlisted man when disembarking from a US Navy vessel: "Request permission to leave the ship."

As his litter was slowly lowered toward the bobbing whaleboat below, Hoskins called to Buracker, "Don't worry about me. I hope you save her. You deserve to."

As a testament to the skill, craftsmanship and engineering of the American shipbuilding industry at that time, *Princeton*, minus its stern section, rode the sea at an even keel and trim after the force of the blast had subsided. Without even the slightest list, the vessel showed no sign of giving in to the horrendous punishment it had endured over a six-hour period.

Capt Buracker took the carrier's state into consideration and had Lt Moitoret, the ship's navigator, make one more request for a tow. The request was denied for several reasons. Firstly, *Birmingham* was unable to handle the request for obvious reasons, as it had hundreds of dead and wounded that required immediate care, plus there were multiple damage assessments to the ship that required immediate attention. Secondly, *Reno* had been unable to rig makeshift towing gear to replace the equipment destroyed by a crashing enemy aircraft during the Formosa operation. Finally, the handful of destroyers in the immediate vicinity were too small for the job.

Several messages flashed back and forth through the air waves between *Reno* and the commander of TG 38.3 concerning the status of the situation. Eventually, the decision was made at fleet command level to abandon *Princeton* and scuttle it.

In the meantime, some of the walking wounded on board the carrier had been given the grim assignment of going below to the hangar bay to look for possible survivors, where they discovered a grisly scene of mangled bodies against the bizarre, grotesque backdrop of the carrier's open stern. The search party then rejoined the group topside on the flightdeck to report their findings. They soon became very disconcerted by how hot the wood and steel plating beneath their feet was becoming. The majority of them were well aware that below their feet was the forward magazine and a huge tank containing 100,000 gallons of high-octane aviation gasoline that would literally obliterate what was left of the vessel if ignited. At 1604 hrs Capt Buracker ordered all hands to abandon ship.

Two whaleboats from *Gatling* were bobbing in the swells close to *Princeton*'s bow, and they took aboard the majority of the survivors who were immediately conveyed to the destroyer lying to nearby. Seven hours after the enemy bomb had struck the ship, the executive officer, Cdr Murphy, stepped off the carrier and into a whaleboat, followed by Capt Buracker. In the age age-old tradition calling for the captain to be the last to leave his ship, Buracker joined Murphy aboard the whaleboat at 1654 hrs.

Lt Cdr Large had made it into the whaleboat the hard way:

> Murphy and I went down the Jacob's ladder, which didn't quite reach the water. The whaleboat was bobbing around, and there was a pretty good sea running. We had to let go and drop maybe the last 15ft. Murphy, who had been a US Naval Academy football player, was a huge man and a wonderful officer. When I looked up and saw him there above me on the ladder, I thought I better get out of his way. I let go and was caught by a sailor in the whaleboat.

Lt Moitoret also exited *Princeton* via the Jacob's ladder and boarded the first whaleboat. While on his way down, he paused briefly. "When my head got level with the deck, I leaned over and kissed *Princeton* goodbye."

The two boats pulled away from the mortally damaged carrier, with one heading for *Gatling* while the other, with Capt Buracker on board, toured the gutted, blasted stern of the vessel to look one last time at the damage, and to make one last visual check from sea level to make sure there were no signs of life on board. From there it sailed on to *Reno*.

11

So Long "Sweet P"

The biggest naval battle the world has ever seen was being waged across thousands of square miles of the Pacific Ocean and the Philippine archipelago. While *Princeton* was lost, the intensity of the fighting in the waters around the vessel heightened, as 64 warships of the IJN with 43,000 officers and men embarked attempted to disrupt and destroy the landings at Leyte. Opposing this counterattack was TF 38 under the command of Adm Halsey and Seventh Fleet, led by Vice Adm Kinkaid, with a combined force totaling 216 combat vessels manned by 143,000 officers and men.

Seventh Fleet turned back the Southern Force during the early hours of October 25 in the Battle of Surigao Strait, while the Central Force transited through the San Bernardino Strait unopposed and caught Rear Adm Sprague's escort carriers, protecting the landing beaches, by surprise. During the Battle off Samar that duly ensued, the undersized and under-gunned destroyers and destroyer escorts, providing protection for the flattops, turned back Kurita's battleships with help from 450 aircraft scrambled by the carriers in one of the most heroic naval stands in history. Three destroyers and the Casablanca-class escort carrier USS *Gambier Bay* (CVE-73) were nevertheless sunk. Later that same day, in one of the first organized kamikaze attacks, *Gambier Bay*'s sister ship, USS *St Lo* (CVE-63), was struck by a bomb-carrying Zero-sen. The carrier sank in just 30 minutes.

The Northern Force was able to successfully pull off its decoy mission and lure Halsey away from Leyte Gulf, but in the process it lost all four of its carriers and their cruiser and destroyer escorts. The IJN was now effectively finished as a fighting force, and it no longer posed a significant threat to the US Navy in the Pacific.

Late in the afternoon of October 24, Capt Buracker, after boarding *Reno* from *Gatling*'s whaleboat, looked back across the water at *Princeton* and wondered if there was still hope that the defiant, sturdy carrier could be saved. It was not going to happen – his superior officer, Vice Adm Sherman, had given the order. The ship could not be left adrift on the high seas with even the slightest chance that the Japanese could get hold of it. These situations had not changed over the centuries, as any warship would be considered a high value prize if captured by the enemy, along with being a gold mine of vital information. As the sun set and visibility across the waves slowly diminished, the destroyer *Irwin* was ordered to torpedo *Princeton*.

The vessel carried a normal complement of slightly more than 300 officers and men, but due to the circumstances, it was packed with survivors from *Princeton* – there were nearly 1,000 men occupying every inch of space on board the destroyer. Furthermore, *Irwin*'s torpedo director had been severely damaged while banging up against *Princeton*'s hull during the long afternoon of firefighting and rescue operations. The initial effort to sink the carrier saw *Irwin*'s captain, Lt Cdr Daniel B. Miller, position his ship 2,500 yards from *Princeton* on its port beam. He then ordered the torpedo crew to fire a salvo at the carrier, using "local control" to aim the tubes. This effectively meant that the sailors would sight down the tubes like one would draw a bead through the open sights of a rifle.

Irwin sent two "fish" down range at 1706 hrs and one missed the target completely. The other struck the extreme end of the forward bow but failed to inflict any visible damage. Making a repeat attempt, *Irwin*'s sailors peered down the tubes and fired two more torpedoes, with one shooting wide of the target. The other, in what must have been an absolutely surreal moment, ran erratically and, to the shock of those on board *Irwin*, commenced a sweeping circle that brought it back on a collision course with *Irwin* itself. Lt Cdr Miller immediately ordered, "Flank speed, everything we're capable of, and fast!"

Princeton's survivors on board the destroyer had just battled the enemy, fire, smoke, explosions, stifling heat, humidity, wind, rain, injuries, wounds and sharks. Hundreds of them were also survivors of the *Hornet* sinking almost two years earlier, and now it appeared that they were about to be sunk yet again, but this time by an American torpedo. Fortunately, it missed. *Irwin* resumed position, and for a third time fired a brace of torpedoes by local control. Once again, one missed and the second started back toward them, forcing the destroyer to take evasive action to avoid being blown out of the water.

Avenger pilot Lt(jg) Tom Mooney, whose aircraft had been struck by the bomb that hit *Princeton*, had been fished out of the sea by *Irwin*. After 30 minutes of lying on his back on the deck and crawling over to the destroyer's rail to vomit sea water, Mooney had been ordered to go below deck with the rest of the carrier's survivors:

The ship was rolling, and because there was a lot of extra weight on board in the form of sailors from the carrier, this posed a danger to the destroyer. I went below with the others, and after a bit, a Catholic chaplain came along and asked me to help him talk to the men. This guy knew it was his mission to restore some form of sanity to these guys. I don't know how long it lasted, maybe an hour or two. We just walked around in circles and told people to stay cool, glad you made it, and all that. Then for some reason – I'm not sure why – I was allowed to go up on deck.

It was at that point *Irwin* was ordered to sink *Princeton*. Being a torpedo-bomber pilot, Mooney was very familiar with the US Navy's "tin fish." "I looked at the torpedo mounts on *Irwin* and I thought, 'Jesus, they don't look right. They look like they're bent or something', and they were. They had been damaged in all the colliding with *Princeton*."

Mooney stood by as an observer as *Irwin* positioned itself to fire the torpedoes at the carrier. "There was *Princeton*, this big, beautiful ship that was my home, sitting in the water, looking like it could sail if there was someone on it, and they were going to sink it."

Irwin's torpedo tubes were hand-cranked into position as Mooney stood by, observing:

I saw this one big fish leap off and then, impossible to believe, it started turning, I thought, "It's going to miss us", but it kept turning, and pretty soon it was coming right back toward the *Irwin*. I looked up toward the bridge and thought, "Jesus Christ, full right rudder, full speed", and then the destroyer started shaking and trembling until it got up enough speed to make a slight turn. The US Navy torpedo went right past us, and I thought, "You know, that's fantastic. This can't be happening."

The ship's captain, after the first scare, brought the *Irwin* back into a firing position. This time, however, he maintained a little forward speed just in case. He needed the boat to be ready, because, once again, one of *Irwin*'s torpedoes circled back around toward it. The torpedo had not gone very far before it also turned, and I thought, "I'm going to die". Well, it too went right by. It seemed to me I could read *U.S. NAVY* on the fish, it was that close. After that, I figured if they fired another one, we were going down. There was no question – we'd be going down.

Irwin's 5in./38 guns then tried to administer the death blow, firing 27 rounds into the carrier. They reignited the hangar bay fires, with an explosion occurring – more than likely one of the aircraft stowed there. *Princeton* refused to yield. *Reno* was then ordered to move in and finish it off. The light cruiser took *Irwin*'s place on the firing line, and at 1746 hrs, with the first torpedo launched set at a 12ft depth, let it loose. One minute later, a second torpedo was fired. It took them three long minutes to reach the target, and they struck at 1749 hrs almost simultaneously in the forward magazine and forward gasoline tank.

There was a tremendous explosion, with observers believing that both torpedoes had struck the ship and detonated. Flames shot 500ft into the air and a dense, mushroom-shaped cloud of smoke rose beyond a height of 1,000ft. After the air had cleared, there was no more ship, only smoke and burning debris on the water.

The blast was monstrous. *Reno*'s torpedoes had detonated *Princeton*'s forward magazine and forward gasoline tank. The former contained 313 bombs ranging in size from 350lb to 2,000lb and with a total weight in excess of 150 tons of explosives, while the latter held 100,000 gallons of aviation gasoline. Some torpedo warheads that had failed to detonate earlier also possibly added to the force of the explosion. Fleet radar operators reported that *Princeton* disappeared immediately from their screens. There are some reports that the loss of the Atlanta-class light cruiser *USS Juneau* (CL-52) on November 13, 1942 after it was torpedoed by an IJN submarine during the Naval Battle of Guadalcanal was the biggest explosion of the war besides the two atom bombs. The blast that obliterated *Princeton* may have outdone *Juneau*.

Whatever was left of the carrier went down roughly 80 miles east of Polillo Islands in the Philippine Sea, sinking into a massive Pacific Ocean trench 2,700 fathoms (16,200ft) deep – more than three miles straight down. "Sweet P" was gone.

Princeton sailor George Green witnessed the scuttling from the deck of *Cassin Young*:

> When the *Reno* fired its two torpedoes, *Princeton* literally disintegrated. It went up in a wall of fire. Our position was one-and-a-half miles away, and my pant legs were flattened against my legs from the concussion. Some people said they could see part of the carrier sink into the sea, but all I saw were the flames, the fire and the mushroom cloud that subsequently formed. Later, when I saw films of the A-bomb explosion at Bikini Atoll, I recalled that the *Princeton*'s finish looked just like that.

Sgt Adrian Chisholm of the US Marine Corps was on board *Irwin* when these events unfolded:

> We were about a mile away from *Princeton*. I was a mess after being in the water a couple of hours. I'm standing there, looking at the carrier and thinking, "My God, I've lost everything I owned, and I don't even know where my boys are." I saw the damn thing go down. I'm alone in the middle of that little tin can. I had a couple of tears in my eyes, and I saluted her. I don't think anybody saw me do that, but she was a good ship.

A *Princeton* survivor, thinking of the carrier's codename – "Hatchet Base" – for this operation in the Philippines, was heard to say, "Well, they've buried the Hatchet."

Princeton was the first fast carrier to have been lost in more than two years of warfare in the Pacific. Prior to its demise, the last such carrier sunk in action in-theater had been *Hornet* during the Battle of the Santa Cruz Islands on October 27, 1942.

With the exception of scattered floating debris, *Princeton* was gone when *Reno* radioed the commander of TG 38.3. "This is *Reno*. Duty completed. Am rejoining." The three destroyers were assigned screen positions around *Reno* for the return to the task group. The hard-hit *Birmingham* was told to follow astern at 1,500 yards from the other ships, with one screw locked out of use due to damage sustained after it struck *Princeton*'s free-floating stern. With darkness setting in, *Reno* sent the following status report to the task group by radio at 2015 hrs:

> *Reno* group has 134 officers and 1,227 enlisted personnel from *Princeton*. Damage to *Birmingham* topside casualties two 5-inch mounts, two 40mm, four 20mm smashed. *Reno* has one 40mm smashed. *Morrison*'s mast gone, portside smashed. *Irwin*'s forward director out. *Birmingham* has about 85 killed, 300 wounded, 200 seriously. Casualties include captain. *Princeton* captain on *Reno*. *Irwin* limited to twenty-five knots.

Casualty figures would climb during the night.

Birmingham, *Morrison*, *Irwin* and *Gatling* were separated from TG 38.3 at 2242 hrs and designated TU 38.3.6, with orders to proceed to Ulithi and rendezvous with tankers en route to refuel. *Gatling* was included because it had 221 survivors on board, plus it was the only ship in the group with completely operable radar. *Reno* rejoined the task group with Capt Buracker and his executive officer, Cdr Murphy, on board. They were joined by the heroic *Cassin Young*.

At 2121 hrs, Adm Halsey radioed TG 38.3: "You and your group have done a fine job today. I am proud to ride with TG 38.3."

Later that night, *Birmingham*'s skipper radioed the task group commander: "*Birmingham* will do her utmost to return as soon as possible. Goodbye, good luck. Hit them hard for us."

After temporary duty on board *Santa Fe*, *Birmingham*'s chief medical officer was back on board, along with *Reno*'s doctor. Unfortunately, despite their incredible efforts, they could not save all of the badly wounded. Indeed, many were beyond their help from the instant *Princeton* had exploded. The medical teams faced a long night ahead, with several more to follow. *Birmingham*'s logbook told the grim story of those difficult hours: "At 0138 completed burial of four officers and 67 men. 0700, resumed collection, identification and burial of the dead. 1145, completed burial services for three officers and 154 enlisted men."

Pharmacist's Mate George Pantages was transferred, along with two of his shipmates, from *Morrison* to *Birmingham* on the morning of October 25 when a call was sent out for more medical help. "We changed ships by breeches buoy, and believe me, that's an experience. The lines between the ships kept sagging to the point where you could be dunked into the sea, and next they would be taut. The secret was to try to take off when you thought the two vessels would not be rolling too much."

Nothing could have prepared Pantages and his two shipmates for the horrific scene on *Birmingham*:

> It was beyond description. The deck of *Birmingham* was a shambles, and sand had been spread about in places so you wouldn't slip on the bloody mess. Below decks, much of the interior space had been cleared of bunks and other objects to make room for the wounded and medical supplies. The ship was divided up into sections, and each was given as many wounded as we expected to care for in the best possible manner. They had only three doctors aboard, and a few medical corpsmen, so all hands had to pitch in and do whatever was needed. My first night aboard *Birmingham* was really the most critical and exhausting.
>
> I applied splints to five men with compound leg fractures, using Thomas splints and sufficient morphine to keep the men from suffering too much during the procedure. Probably the worst incident I encountered as far as splinting fractures was concerned involved a sailor with his left leg at a right angle to his body, about ten inches above the knee. It took all the strength and courage I could muster to straighten that leg and apply the splint. God and perseverance were on my side. I finally got the job done to my own satisfaction.

That first night, medical personnel and others that were caring for the wounded were focused on saving as many of the most seriously injured as possible, and making sure the others were as comfortable as they could be under the circumstances. "Plasma was used by the hundreds of units," Pantages said. "Monitoring all the casualties was no easy matter. There were approximately 100 wounded in the compartment I was assigned to. To the best of my recollection, we lost only one man in our group."

Not enough can be said about "Doc" Pantages and the others who assisted the wounded during the post-sinking hours and days, their performance being simply remarkable:

> Most of us in the medical department labored around the clock for five days without any real sleep. At the very most I got just a wink or two. Food was brought to us while we worked for the first couple of days. The center of the deck was a mountain of bandages and medical supplies, and thank God for the fact we had plenty [of supplies] to work with. I feel certain that meant the difference between making it or not for quite a few of the more severely wounded.

Pantages subsequently recalled some of the patients he attended to with great clarity:

> One sailor had a gaping hole in his chest. Air was bubbling from his lungs, and it really looked like he was a goner. After trying desperately for some time to administer plasma, I finally found a vein suitable enough to get a needle in. The usual spots on his arms turned up only collapsed veins. A doctor closed his chest wound after the plasma had been injected. In about two hours, the patient showed pretty good signs of recovery. After several units of plasma, he really rallied and ended up on the right side of the roster. Experiences like that on *Birmingham* always will be etched on my mind.

Doctors boarded *Birmingham* immediately after it had pulled into Ulithi Atoll, and to Pantages' extreme gratification, every splint he and his comrades had applied passed their inspection without question. After the last patient had been transferred to a hospital ship, Pantages found a quiet corner on the deck and went to sleep.

Pharmacist's Mate Paul Robinson, who helped treat Capt Hoskins after he had been severely wounded in the *Princeton* blast, was taken aboard *Gatling* with his patient and the carrier's chief medical officer, Cdr Sala. Although the latter had also been wounded in the groin by shrapnel, he had continued with his duties and performed the amputation of Hoskins' foot. According to Robinson, "Cdr Sala was peeing blood. We didn't have X-rays and didn't have any way of knowing the extent of his injuries. He stayed in the wardroom, and everyone in extremely critical condition we put there with Cdr Sala."

Other wounded personnel were treated by *Gatling*'s own doctor and corpsmen that included Robinson in the destroyer's mess compartment. "We had a real good system, and we didn't have any infections. We had sulfadiazine and we had some penicillin, but not very much – penicillin wasn't any good for treating burns in any case. Our big problem was dealing with burns."

Robinson instructed other corpsmen to administer sleeping pills to those who needed them, and pain killers, including morphine, to those who required such relief:

> We had a lot of casualties on *Gatling*, including burns cases. We gave sulfadiazine to those patients. Rather than changing their bandages, if arms or legs were involved, where swelling might develop, we looked for blue fingernails or toenails. In those cases, instead of taking the bandage off, we would just cut the bandage and put a new one on the outside. The odor was bad, but the serum oozed from the burns through the cut in the bandage and a lot of sulfadiazine killed any bacteria. As far as I know, we didn't have any burn infections on the *Gatling*.

The night brought sleep and rest for those who had been severely wounded and called for sedation. For others, the night was long, troubled and difficult. The next morning was brightened, possibly, by the knowledge that they had been spared from something much worse.

"Things on *Irwin* were really crowded, and we had to sleep on deck," said *Princeton* survivor Aviation Machinist's Mate Larry Morgan. "However, out in the Pacific in October it was warm, and we weren't too uncomfortable. Some of our shipmates who had died from their wounds were awaiting burial. They had been placed on deck in canvas bags. We laid down among them, wherever there was room."

In the morning, the crews of *Birmingham* and the three destroyers, with the continued welfare of their shipmates on their minds, pulled together and prepared enough food for everyone who wanted to eat. "I know I didn't feel too much like eating," Morgan said. "We were all pretty much shook up. During the morning, we buried five of our *Princeton* shipmates."

Shortly before noon, two enemy twin-engined aircraft began shadowing the four cripples, adding anxiety to an already difficult situation. Morgan watched the Japanese machines approach the small group, and he wondered when *Irwin* and the others would open up on them:

> I started to shake, my knees were knocking together and my teeth were chattering. Anyhow, the guns opened up and the two Jap planes took tail. After the guns stopped firing, I was okay. I talked about this later to one of the officers, and he said he had experienced the same sort of thing. He was lying on his bunk a couple of nights after we had been sunk. He said he started to shake and get sick to his stomach. He went to see a doctor, and the doctor told him that was quite normal under the circumstances. I felt better about it after hearing that.

Gatlin had repeated radar contacts throughout the day, both air and surface, and all of them had to be looked upon as a potential threat until proven otherwise. To those who had been through the ordeal of losing their ship and shipmates, these enemy contacts were a nerve-wracking ordeal. Thankfully, most of the radar contacts were friendly and the task unit did not have to go on the defensive or prepare for evasive action. *Birmingham*'s CO, Capt Inglis, who had remained in command despite being injured, was conscious of lurking submarines. This prompted him to radio a reminder to the other ships – "Do not throw floatable trash over the side."

Birmingham established radio contact with the task group of oilers that had been dispatched to refuel the cruiser and its three destroyer companions. After a rendezvous location had been established and a course set, *Birmingham* radioed: "Request services two oilers to give drink [fuel] to one CL [cruiser] and three destroyers simultaneously. Please designate oilers and drinking course speed and formation. One destroyer would also like to get about 10,000 gallons of water."

Each of the damaged vessels was assigned a port or starboard position beside one of the oilers – *Irwin* received a port approach due to its starboard side being smashed. The subsequent refueling scene was one that was conducted literally hundreds of times in the Pacific in order to keep combat ships stocked with fuel and the supplies that they needed. Nevertheless, such an evolution could never be taken lightly due to the inherent danger posed by two vessels sailing in such close proximity.

The thirsty ship would take a position close beside the oiler, after which the two vessels would proceed in an identical direction at the same speed while a weighted line was fired from the oiler to the warship by a specially designed gun. The initial line was attached to a heavier line and then came the hose after that. On the bridges of both vessels, crews had to keep the two ships perfectly aligned in a potentially rolling sea, with the hose line linking them as highly combustible fuel was transferred between the oiler and the warship.

After the refueling was complete, the oilers and their escorts sent two doctors and five corpsmen over to *Birmingham*, using destroyers to complete the transfer. Along with the medical personnel came much-needed morphine syrettes, bandages, plaster of Paris for casts and a variety of other items. Finally, large quantities of mail – warmly received by the crews – were passed by line to *Gatling* and *Morrison*. The wartime delivery system in which mail moved from its origins stateside to its eventual recipient by leapfrogging from ship to ship across the vast Pacific Ocean had finally caught up with these beleaguered sailors.

Birmingham, via radio transmission to the oilers, expressed the feelings of all on board the four ships of TU 38.3.6. "We are eternally thankful to you for your assistance. We shall now proceed on our way." The commander of the oiler group responded with, "Thank you and good luck." As the sun came up the following morning (October 26), with *Birmingham* still 24 hours from Ulithi, radio monitors picked up the text of a communiqué issued by Gen Douglas MacArthur's Philippine headquarters. The men packed on board the cruiser and three destroyers were shocked to learn that the sinking of *Princeton* had been revealed. Lt(jg) Mooney recalled his reaction:

> When a Navy ship was lost at sea, there were no public reports until the next of kin were notified. The loss of *Princeton* was announced the instant battle reports came in to MacArthur. As a result, the relatives and friends of more than 1,200 men didn't know for days who had survived. It wasn't a matter of national importance, but in terms of the people involved, we were outraged.

Only Gen MacArthur's staff could answer to that horrible mistake – an episode of inexcusable behavior by senior officers. It was not until the four ships reached Ulithi that the survivors were able to get brief notes sent off to their families. These were flown back to the United States, and it would be five days or more before the letters were delivered to anxious families and friends.

Once Ulithi had been reached, the *Princeton* drama concluded for many of its former crew. The dead had been committed to the sea and the survivors were sent from there to other assignments and various hospitals. *Birmingham* proceeded on to Pearl Harbor and reached its destination on November 10, 1944 with the majority of the survivors still on board.

After reports from *Princeton*'s crew and CVLG-27 were painstakingly recorded, the men were granted leave. From there, some of the survivors embarked aboard the troopship *Matsonia*, which was owned and operated by the Matson Company for the War Shipping Administration. *Matsonia* cruised into San Francisco Bay on November 24, and once they had disembarked, *Princeton* personnel departed for destinations across the United States for much-needed leave. *Birmingham* also sailed to San Francisco Bay, dropping anchor at the Mare Island Naval Shipyard. Here, the light cruiser underwent battle damage repairs and conversion into a flagship – the work was not completed until January 17, 1945, when the vessel returned to service.

The war was not over for CVLG-27 either, with Lt Cdr Fred Bardshar remaining in command after it reformed on January 2, 1944. Sent far from the beautiful California coastline, its squadrons underwent refresher training at a location on the opposite side of the country – NAAF Sanford, Maine. CVLG-27 (still comprised of VF-27 and VT-27) was eventually sent to the Philippines, where it embarked in *Independence* on June 16, 1945 for the final push on Tokyo. Flying off *Princeton*'s sister ship, CVLG-27 saw action alongside other carrier air groups in TF 38 sailing off Japan from July 10. Both VF-27 and VT-27 targeted enemy installations ashore and ships in Tokyo Bay itself, with the Hellcat-equipped unit chalking up one last aerial victory.

On September 2, 1945 in Tokyo Bay, CVLG-27 participated in a multi-squadron flyover as representatives of the Empire of Japan signed the Instrument of Surrender on the deck of the Iowa-class battleship USS *Missouri* (BB-63). As the Hellcats and Avengers flew in tight formation over the vast Allied fleet at anchor, a pilot commented over the radio, "Too bad the *Princeton* isn't here."

Capt Hoskins, standing on one prosthetic foot after convincing the US Navy that he was fit to serve, ordered the first watch set on board the new Essex-class carrier USS *Princeton* (CV-37) – the fifth United States ship to bear the name – at Philadelphia Naval Shipyard on November 18, 1945.

Epilogue

Princeton participated in a revolutionary period in naval warfare. Although originally built as a stopgap carrier, the vessel's stellar performance in combat that saw its crew earn nine battle stars during a series of campaigns which included the largest carrier clash in history off the Marianas and culminated in the largest naval battle in history at Leyte Gulf proved that "Sweet P" was a worthy addition to the Pacific Fleet.

President Roosevelt's initial request to the US Navy to convert nine light cruisers into light aircraft carriers was initiated due to the fact that the new Essex-class vessels would not be ready until late 1944. While the Essex-class carriers did in fact arrive well before their projected date, the Independence-class carriers were proceeded with nevertheless to fill the void left in the Pacific Fleet following high attrition in 1942.

The light carriers proved themselves worthy from the start, sailing alongside their larger counterparts from day one of their introduction until war's end. The numbers associated with the Independence-class vessels speak for themselves as a testament to their contribution to operations in the Pacific Theater. The light carriers would collectively form more than a quarter of the US Navy's carrier striking power in the Pacific after joining the fleet from 1943, and they would earn 81 battle stars, three Presidential Unit Citations and one Navy Unit Citation between them.

Princeton had joined the fleet in August 1943 and was scuttled on October 24, 1944, having served with Fifth Fleet for much of that time.

The carrier's first commanding officer, Capt George R. Henderson, started his career as an enlisted man and eventually achieved the rank of vice admiral before retiring in August 1954 following 37 years of naval service that had seen him participate in three wars.

Capt William H. Buracker, a Naval Academy graduate in 1919, relieved Capt Henderson of command of *Princeton* on February 7, 1944 and served on board until its loss on October 24. Buracker's leadership was instrumental in the attempt to save *Princeton* on that fateful day, and he was awarded the Purple Heart, Legion of Merit with the Combat "V" and the Navy Cross for his actions. Buracker retired from the US Navy as a rear admiral on May 1, 1947.

Capt John M. Hoskins, a Naval Academy graduate in 1921, was to take command of *Princeton* in November 1944 but he had not been on board long enough to officially relieve Capt Buracker when the carrier was lost. Following the amputation of his foot after it had been all but blown off on *Princeton*'s flightdeck on October 24, Hoskins received an artificial foot and was able to demonstrate to a US Navy medical board his ability to climb up and down a ship's ladders with his new prosthetic. Fittingly, he was named the commanding officer of the newly commissioned *Princeton* in November 1945. John Hoskins retired in 1957 as a vice admiral, having received the Navy Cross, Navy Distinguished Service Medal, Silver Star, Legion of Merit and Purple Heart during his long, distinguished career.

Cdr Joseph N. Murphy, *Princeton*'s executive officer from December 1943, was instrumental in the attempt to save the ship. During those frightful final hours, Murphy was fully engaged in manning hose lines, and assessing damage in flame-swept and potentially explosive areas of the ship. Alongside Capt Hoskins, he suffered shrapnel wounds in the final blast, but was able to assist Hoskins off *Princeton*. Murphy was awarded the Navy Cross for his actions on board the carrier, and he was eventually recognized as being one of the US Navy's leading aeronautical engineers, achieving the rank of rear admiral.

Cdr Bruce Harwood, *Princeton*'s air officer, and 25 men that he was leading as a firefighting party lost their lives in the final blast that ultimately doomed the carrier. He had courageously remained at his station on the port side of the bridge to direct the firefighting effort, and despite the danger of imminent detonations, he also ventured

EPILOGUE

below decks on his own initiative in an attempt to fight fires that were threatening the ship.

Harwood had joined the US Navy on June 6, 1935, and after training as an aviation cadet at NAS Pensacola, he was commissioned an ensign on July 7, 1939 and started flying torpedo-bombers. Harwood received the Navy Cross for extraordinary heroism on August 24, 1942 during the Battle of the Eastern Solomons when he led Avengers of VT-8 from *Saratoga* in an unsupported aerial torpedo raid against an IJN task force, pressing home the attack through a hail of antiaircraft fire. Harwood subsequently received a Gold Star in lieu of a second Navy Cross for extraordinary heroism as VT-8's CO while flying from *Hornet* against Japanese forces in the Guadalcanal area between September 20 and October 5, 1942. Harwood posthumously received a second Gold Star in lieu of a third Navy Cross when he lost his life on October 24, 1944. The Gearing-class destroyer USS *Harwood* (DD-861), commissioned in September 1945, was named in his honor.

Lt Cdr Henry L. Miller, prior to wearing two hats as commanding officer of both CVLG-23 and VF-23, was personally involved in the training of the USAAF B-25 pilots who participated in the incredibly dangerous Doolittle mission. The all-volunteer crews from the 17th Bombardment Group (Medium) flew 24 B-25s to Eglin Field on March 1, 1942 for extensive training. There, the men received three weeks of tuition in a wide range of subjects that included carrier deck takeoffs out of nearby Auxiliary Field 1 due to its isolated location.

Then-Lt Henry Miller, stationed at nearby NAS Pensacola, supervised the takeoff training, and on March 25, 1942, 22 B-25s departed Eglin for McClellen Field, arriving two days later for final inspection and modifications. A total of 16 bombers were then flown to NAS Alameda on March 31. The following day the modified B-25s were loaded onto *Hornet* at NAS Alameda, from where the carrier would sail under the Golden Gate Bridge for a launch point east of Tokyo. Lt Miller accompanied the crews on board *Hornet* to their launch point, and for his efforts he would always be considered an honorary member of the Doolittle Raiders group.

Lt Cdr Frederic A. Bardshar had the difficult duty of taking over CVLG-27 after the loss of Lt Cdr Ernest Wood. After embarking aboard *Princeton* in late May 1944, VF-27 posted an incredible record in combat, flying F6F Hellcats with their famous ferocious faces painted on the cowlings. With the war still raging in the Pacific after the loss of *Princeton*, CVLG-27 reformed in January 1945 and was posted back into action six months later. It boarded *Independence* (part of TG 38.4) at Leyte–Samar anchorage on June 16, and during the final months of the war VF-27 and VT-27 undertook combat missions against Honshu and Hokkaido from the carrier.

Following the Japanese surrender, CVLG-27's Hellcats and Avengers undertook prisoner of war searches and peace patrols. On September 26, the carrier air group was detached from *Independence* at Saipan and arrived in Portland, Oregon, on October 19. Exactly one week later, both squadrons and CVLG-23 were disestablished. "Fighting 27" had been credited with 147 aerial victories during World War II – the most recorded by a squadron operating from a US Navy light carrier. Additionally, while operating with Fifth Fleet for five months, the unit had produced ten aces for a combined total of 78.5 victories. Three had been awarded the Navy Cross, three were double aces and five had achieved "ace-in-a-day" status.

Appendix 1

US NAVY RANKS

Officers

Rank	Abreviation	Insignia
Fleet Admiral	Fleet Adm	Five stars
Admiral	Adm	Four stars
Vice Admiral	Vice Adm	Three stars
Rear Admiral	Rear Adm	Two stars
Commodore	Commodore	One star
Captain	Capt	Silver eagle
Commander	Cdr	Silver oak leaf
Lieutenant Commander	Lt Cdr	Gold oak leaf
Lieutenant	Lt	Two silver bars
Lieutenant (junior grade)	Lt(jg)	One silver bar
Ensign	Ens	One gold bar

Enlisted Ranks

Rank	Abbreviation
Boatswain's Mate	BM
Coxswain	COX
Gunner's Mate	GM
Quartermaster	QM
Signalman	SM
Fire Controlman	F

Gun Rangefinder	GR
Machinist's Mate	MM
Water Tender	WT
Boilerman	B
Motor Machinist	MoMM
Electrician's Mate	EM
Yeoman	YM
Store Keeper	SK
Pharmacist's Mate	PhM
Radioman	RM
Radarman	Rdm
Torpedoman	TM
Carpenter	CM
Painter	Ptr
Patternmaker	PM
Shipfitter	SF
Molder	ML
Metalsmith	M
Photographer's Mate	PhoM
Chief Commissary Steward	CCS
Officer's Cook	OC
Ship's Cook	SC
Baker	Bkr
Steward	St

Appendix 2

SPECIFICATIONS

USS Princeton (CVL-23)
  Class and type: Independence-class aircraft carrier, light
  Builder: New York Shipbuilding Corporation
  Laid down: June 2, 1941
  Launched: October 18, 1942
  Commissioned: February 25, 1943
  Displacement: 11,000 tons, roughly 13,000 tons loaded
  Length: 622.5ft
  Beam: 71.5ft (waterline), 109.2ft (extreme)
  Draft: 26ft
  Speed: 32 knots
  Complement: 1,569 officers and men
  Armament: 22 x Bofors 40mm cannon and 16 x Oerlikon 20mm cannon
  Aircraft carried: 45 (30–35 in combat)
  Fate: scuttled by Atlanta-class light cruiser USS *Reno* (CL-96) after being severely damaged by Japanese air attack on October 24, 1944 in the Battle of Leyte Gulf

Grumman F6F-3 Hellcat
Crew: 1
  Wing area: 344 sq. ft.
  Wingspan: 42ft 10in.
  Length: 33ft 7in.

Height: 11ft 1in.
Empty weight; 9,023lbs
Loaded weight: 12,415lbs
Wing loading: 37.17lbs/sq. ft.
Engine: Pratt & Whitney R-2800-10 Double Wasp
Engine rating: 2,000hp
Speed at altitude: 388mph
Speed at sea level: 312mph
Initial climb rate: 3,650ft per minute
Time to altitude: 7 min 0 sec to 20,000ft
Service ceiling: 35,500ft
Maximum range, clean: 1,085 miles
Internal fuel: 250 gallons
External fuel: 150 gallons
Armament (standard): six Browning M2 0.50-cal. machine guns
Number manufactured (excluding prototypes): 4,403

Grumman F6F-5 Hellcat
Crew: 1
Wing area: 344 sq. ft.
Wingspan: 42ft 10in.
Length: 33ft 7in.
Height: 11ft 1in.
Empty weight; 9,238lbs
Loaded weight: 12,483lbs
Wing loading: 38.17lbs/sq. ft.
Engine: Pratt & Whitney R-2800-10W Double Wasp
Engine rating: 2,200hp
Speed at altitude: 400mph
Speed at sea level: 318mph
Initial climb rate: 3,200ft per minute
Time to altitude: 7 min 30 sec to 20,000ft
Service ceiling: 36,000ft
Maximum range, clean: 1,300 miles
Internal fuel: 250 gallons
External fuel: 150 gallons
Armament (standard): six M2 Browning 0.50-cal. machine guns
Number manufactured (excluding prototypes): 7,868

APPENDIX 2

Grumman TBF-1C Avenger
Crew: 3
- Wing area: 490 sq. ft.
- Wingspan: 54ft 2in.
- Length: 40ft
- Height: 16ft 5in.
- Empty weight: 10,555lbs
- Max loaded weight: 17,364lbs
- Engine: Wright R-2600-8 Twin Cyclone
- Engine rating: 1,700hp
- Maximum speed: 271mph (maximum), 145mph (cruise)
- Rate of climb: 1,075ft per minute
- Service ceiling: 22,400ft
- Range: 1,215 miles (combat), 2,335 miles (maximum ferry)
- Internal fuel: 330 gallons
- External fuel: 116 gallons in two droppable slipper tanks under outer wings, with provision for a jettisonable 275-gallon bomb-bay ferry tank
- Armament: two wing-mounted M2 Browning 0.50-cal. machine guns, one M2 Browning 0.50-cal machine gun in dorsal turret, one M1919 Browning 0.30-cal. machine gun in ventral position, one Mk13 aerial torpedo or 2,000lbs of bombs (4 x 500lbs) or 350lb depth charges
- Number manufactured (all variants): 9,839

Appendix 3

VF-27 ACES

Lt James A. Shirley – 12 victories (Navy Cross, double ace, "ace-in-a-day")
Lt Carl A. Brown – 10.5 victories (Navy Cross, double ace, "ace-in-a-day")
Lt(jg) Richard E. Stambook – 10 victories (Navy Cross, double ace, "ace-in-a-day")
Lt(jg) Gordon A. Stanley – 8 victories
Lt Cdr Frederick A. Bardshar – 8 victories
Ens Thomas J. Conroy – 7 victories ("ace-in-a-day")
Lt(jg) Robert L. Blyth – 6 victories
Lt(jg) Paul E. Drury – 6 victories
Lt Cdr William E. Lamb – 5 victories (plus MiG-15 in Korea on November 18, 1950)
Lt(jg) Eugene P. Townsend – 5 victories ("ace-in-a-day")

Appendix 4

CASUALTIES

Princeton Personnel Killed in Action (October 24, 1944)
Officers
    Bradley, Robert Graham, Lt
    Burns, J. P., ChMach
    Christie, A. A., Ens
    Harwood, Bruce Lawrence, Cdr
    Hoecker, Esper Harry, Chief Pay Clerk
    Kaser, J. M., Lt(jg)
    Steele, James C., ChElec
    Suarez, J. L., Mach
    Thurman, R. E., Lt(jg)
    Vandenburg, Edward J., Lt(jg)

Enlisted Personnel
    Adolph, Adrian Lawrence, F1c
    Arsics, Michael George, EM1c
    Bentley, John Steele, MM1c
    Bloecher, Fred William, Bkr1c
    Blomstrom, Russell Carl, S1c
    Brunelle, Joseph Alberie, S1c
    Bryant, Theodore Wayne, SF1c
    Cardoza, David Frausto, MM3c
    Cerny, Joseph Lawrence, WT3c
    Chagnon, Oscar Omer, AM2c

Corum, Paul Leroy, S1c
Daly, Walter Leo, EM3c
Doherty, James Bernard, SF3c
Fiorita, Frank Edward, SF3c
Flynn, John Francis, EM2c
Fredette, John Arthur, F1c
Garrison, Dorris Gwin, RM3c
Glen, Richard Harold, F2c
Gormley, John Francis, AOM2c
Gravell, William M., AMM2c
Harrell, Robert Reed, WT3c
Hauser, Gary, Ptr3c
Heisler, Donald Ralph, S1c
Hill, Donald Norman, AM3c
Hirleman, Richard Dean, WT3c
Holden, Paul Leo, EM3c
Jarrell, James Clarence, S1c
Jones, John Norbert, WT3c
Kotlas, Johnny, EM3c
Laird, Richard Francis, CM2c
Lamb, Lonnie Leo, EM3c
Lawrence, Austin Levie Jr, Bkr3c
Letton, James Wendell, SC3c
Lewis, John Selby, S1c
Lind, Herbert James, SM2c
Mason, Booker Thomas Jr, StM2c
Mason, Ferrell Duane, S2c
Maxson, Henry Duayne, MM2c
Meza, Vicente Onesimo, SKD3c
Milano, Ralph Frank, S1c
Mirando, Mario Gabe, AMM3c
Moon, Bernard Paul, S1c
Morrison, Lewis Henry, AMM3c
Morrissey, Fred Joseph, AMM3c
McLendon, Wallace Howard, WT2c
McMahan, Jack Taylor, S1c
Newton, Lester Frank, F1c
O'Leary, James Joseph, AMM3c

APPENDIX 4

Padula, Joseph Michael, S1c
Page, Nelson Keller, F2c
Patton, Jimmy Don, S2c
Pelletier, Lucien Ernest, AMM2c
Pino, Manuel Lupe, WT3c
Probst, Herbert Lawrence, PhM2c
Reed, Wayne Markham, S1c
Reimers, Fred Lee, Y3c
Reynolds, Earl Russel, Ptr3c
Ricketts, Henry Thomas, S1c
Rigdon, David Mitchal Jr, S1c
Ringwelski, Frank, S2c
Robbe, Robert Raymond, S1c
Rogers, Everett Keith, F1c
Ross, Bernard Melvin, F1c
Sargent, William Thomas, S2c
Sassenberger, James Anthony, S2c
Saxton, William Allen Jr, AM3c
Seabrooks, Charlie, Ck3c
Sedicavage, Stanley Frank, Bkr2c
Shannon, William Jacob, AMM3c
Smith, George Thomas, S2c
Smith, Milford Hoyt, Bkr3c
Spencer, William Joseph, WT2c
Stevens, Russell Lowell, S1c
Strauch, Adam, CEM
Strickland, Young Edward, CWT
Tanner, William Joe, S1c
Tilley, Owen Edgar, AOM3c
Toporski, Edward, S1c
Vallante, Pasquale F1c
Van Dusen, Robert Jay, WT3c
Van Winkle, James Alex, S2c
Vendrely, Donald La Von, F1c
Vickers, Lawrence Virgil, BM2c
Vincent, Ivan Ray, S1c
Vydfol, Fred Albert, MM1c
Wachunas, Charles Stanley, EM3c

Walker, Ernest, Eugene, S1c
Walsh, David Samuel, M1c
Westfall, Robert William, MM1c
White, Ralph Alexander, CSF
Zaicek, Ralph Steven, WT3c
Zlatnik, Henry Frederick, MM3c

US Marine Corps
  Brutoski, Joseph John, Pfc
  Gentry, James Everett, Sgt
  Krall, Henry, Plt Sgt
  Nolan, Ernest La Verne, Pfc
  Nulph, Harold Walker, Pfc
  Rattler, Mark Jack, Pfc

Princeton Personnel Wounded (October 24, 1944)
Officers
  Beckett, J. C., Lt
  Blanchard, W. A., Ens
  Brinton, W. L., Lt
  Cochrane, G. D., Lt(jg)
  Crawford, E. E., Radio Elec
  Davis, A. H., Cdr
  Dorr, E. L., Ens
  Hoskins, J. M., Capt
  Hughes, P., Lt
  Jacobs, R. B., Ens
  Kelleher, J. N., Lt Cdr
  Moitoret, V. A., Lt
  Nelson, W. J., Lt(jg)
  Sala, R. O., Cdr
  Searles, G. B., Ens
  Smith, C. A., Ens
  Stasney, L. H., Lt
  Stebbings, H. E. Jr, Lt Cdr
  Turlington, O. R., Gunner
  Williams, L. D., Lt MC

APPENDIX 4

Enlisted Personnel
- Adams, Elvin Leighton, Cox
- Armenta, Juan Calderon, S2c
- Bellavance, Henry Roland, S1c
- Benway, Lee Walter, S1c
- Billiet, Leopold Jr, S1c
- Brown, Merle D., MM2c
- Byrnes, Stephen J., AM1c
- Carrello, Nicholas, SC1c
- Cavanaugh, Edwin Curtis, ACMM
- Chun, Leong Jin, RT2c
- Cleven, Edward Joseph, CSp
- Conda, Leonard R., S1c
- Cook, Carl Dewayne, AEM3c
- Couch, Bert Cline, AMM1c
- Cusick, Thomas Vincent, AMM2c
- Davis, Edward C, EM1c
- Deslongchamp, Irving Edward, S1c
- Degre, Adrien Joseph, SC3c
- Ditheodore, Nicholas M., MM3c
- Dunbar, Jack Frederick, S1c
- Eagle, Jess LeRoy, AN2c
- Ehrhardt, Leo, S1c
- Elwing, James Edward, S1c
- Emmets, Jacob Otto, MM1c
- Ewing, Joseph Sherman, S2c
- Fagan, William John, S2c
- Fesh, John, S2c
- Foote, George Denton Jr, SC3c
- Frazier, George Wesley, S2c
- Franklin, Bobby Leo, WT3c
- Frederick, Franklin Clifford Jr, CM2c
- Giddle, Lyel Burdette, AMM1c
- Gilmore, Charles Leo, EM1c
- Girofalo, Joseph William, MM3c
- Girvin, Harold Hayes, AMM1c
- Goode, James Franklin, WT3c

Graber, C. A., AOM2c
Hartgrove, Harold R., S1c
Havemann, Clayton John, MM3c
Herrick, Hiram Harold,, BM2c
Heydon, Darrel Gene EM3c
Hill, William R., S1c
Hite, Bert Reilly, WT3c
Holland, Kenneth W., S2c
Howard, George Wendell, S1c
Hunnicutt, James Archie, QM1c
Jessup, Carl L., CMM
Kasko, John, F1c
Kerr, Thomas, S2c
Kindt, Varon Robert, S1c
Kingsfather, Harold Jr, S1c
Knaub, Phillip Jr, MM3c
Kubiak, Donald Joseph, S2c
Kubicka, Edward L., Y3c
Indt, Varon Robert, S1c
LaFevre, Ivan Lyle, AMM1c
Lautensschlager, Cloyd Emory, S1c
Linsenmaier, Richard Carl, AMM2c
Little, William Zack, S1c
Loftis, William Franklin, S2c
Luenemann, Victor Henry, CBM
Manchester, Edward Wilbur, MS3c
Manuels, Charles Thomas, AMM3c
Martin, Frank William, F2c
Mathews, Charles, StM1c
Mazur, Anthony Eugene, AM3c
Medeiros, John Allen, MM3c
Mentzer, Chalmers O., S1c
Miller, Donald Bacon, StM1c
Miller, John A., AMM2c
Mitchell, Eugene Victor, BM1c
Moore, Bird Anderson, S2c
Moses, Henry Lee, StM2c
Muir, George Marcel, AMM3c

APPENDIX 4

Mularcik, Edward Peter, AM3c
Mullen, Carl, PtrV1c
Nelson, Walter Elihu, EM2c
O'Connor, George Gettios, F1c
Otterson, Ralph Elbridge, SK2c
Packard, James E., S1c
Palmer, Lawton Evans Jr, S1c
Parkola, W., AMM1c
Phillips, Joseph Jeremiah, AMM2c
Peter, Robert E., EM2c
Peters, Gerald Joseph, S1c
Peterson, William George, S1c
Rader, Russel E., MM3c
Ralph, Edward Anthony, S1c
Ramos, Julian Ambrose, S1c
Reid, John Johnston, S2c
Reishus, Orin Alden, Bkr2c
Reno, Robert Jr, MM2c
Ricketson, Fred Albert, S2c
Robinson, Paul, PhM1c
Rubin, Seymour, S2c
Schrott, Kenneth Henry, MM1c
Smith, James C., MM3c
Sorger, Joseph Robert, SF3c
Souza, Joseph Gomes, S2c
Stoian, Thomas, S1c
Sumrall, Thomas B., S2c
Talaba, Paul, GM3c
Therrien, Hector Normand, S1c
Tolley, William Hubert, S2c
Trafford, Richard George, AMM2c
Trudeau, Paul L., F2c
Tutino, Anthony, MM1c
Van Horn, James Glen, S2c
Wadsworth, Glenn A., F1c
Walck, Lloyd A., PhM2c
Walker, Robert Ansel, S2c
Wendel, George Daniel Jr, S2c

Weyhmuller, Alfred Victor, ACMM
Whipple, Albert Haywood, S2c
Zaborowski, Ralph, S1c

US Marine Corps
Anderson, Arthur A., GySgt
Chisolm, Adrian C., 1st Sgt
Claypool, James C., Pfc
Conklin, Walter K., Pfc
Heumann, Carl W., FM Cpl
Hollar, Frank W., Pfc
Keilman, Maurice F., Pfc
Rutkowski, Frank S., Cpl
Walker, Frank E., Pfc

Birmingham Personnel Killed in Action (October 24, 1944)
Officers
Cooper, Roland, Lt
Ekstrom, Stanley Edson, Lt
Hoagwood, George Holl, Machinist
Kerr, Robert Charles, Ens
McCormick, Donald, Lt
Perkins, Van Ostrand, Cdr
Reed, Alan, Lt
Smith, Mirel Ralph, Rad Elect

Enlisted Personnel
Agnew, Charles Vincent, RdM3c
Austin, Carl Samuel, S2c
Babbs, Marshall Lewis, S2c
Babger, Thomas Earl, EM2c
Barron, Samuel John, S1c
Bassett, Albert Joseph Jr, S2c
Bates, Robert Harrison, QM1c
Benzie, Paul, GM3c
Bishop, Joseph Edward, CEM
Blanco, Anthony Perry, S1c
Blankenship, Cleo, S2c

APPENDIX 4

Bodnar, John Paul, SC1c
Bowers, Harry Leroy, CRT
Buckingham, Ernest Archie, MM2c
Burckhard, Mike Thomas, S1c
Burnham, Robert Lee, S1c
Burns, Rodger M., Cox
Butkiewicz, Daniel N., S1c
Butler, Collie Harding, S2c
Caputo, Vincenzo James, RdM3c
Carl, Robert Paul, S1c
Carmody, Kenneth James, GM3c
Carr, James Robert, FS3c
Carroll, John Francis, S1c
Corbin, Charles Oswald, S2c
Corini, Carlo Louis, S1c
Costigan, Joseph Frank, S2c
Cottrill, Harold Richard, S2c
Cramer, Winfred Lee, S1c
Creaven, John Anthony, Cox
Crockett, Thaddeus Hamp, SC3c
Culotta, Dominic Peter, S1c
Deakin, Billy Wayne, MM2c
Deane, Norman Goodrow, CWT
DeCenzo, Frank Joseph, F2c
Dickerson, Alfonzo Jr, S1c
Dietrich, Howard Bill, GM1c
Dobbins, Robert Henry, S2c
Doughman, Clarence Leroy, S2c
Droste, Albert Henry, SSML3c
Duke, Robert Clayton, S2c
Dymond, Charles David, S1c
Elkins, Samuel Eli, S2c
Ellison, Harold Pond Jr, S1c
Elsinger, Francis Joseph, S2c
Elson, William Junior, F1c
Englert, Harry Joseph, S1c
Ericksen, Ralph John, WT1c
Estes, George, S2c

Evankoe, Steve, F1c
Farish, James William, MM1c
Filip, James William, CSP
Flynn, Gerard Edward, GM3c
Folkman, Leon J., GM3c
Ford, Simon Patrick, Cox
Fowler, Arthur Jesse, GM3c
Frazier, Paul Dewitt, S1c
Fulton, Richard E., MM3c
Gerson, Paul William, WT3c
Gifford, Winford Bundy, Cox
Gilbert, Charles Hugo Jr, EM1c
Gluscic, Joseph John, S1c
Golitco, Edward Paul, S2c
Godin, Vincent Richard, Y2c
Graham, James Paul, S1c
Graves, Joe Earl, S1c
Griger, Arthur, Y3c
Gwinn, Charles Parker, S1c
Haas, Edward Joseph, S1c
Hahn, John Edward, GM3c
Hartle, Raymond Lewis, S2c
Hedges, Wilbert, GM3c
Hoegerl, Anthony Joseph, MM2
Hoff, Ralph William, SSML3c
Holley, Hubert Henry, S2c
Howard, Henry Franklin, S2c
Howze, James Edward, QM3c
Huckaby, Brodie David, S2c
Huey, Hubbard Pool, S1c
Huls, Joseph Francis, S2c
Hunter, Norman Elwood, S2c
Jackson, David Elwood, S1c
James, Raymond, S1c
Jaramillo, William, S2c
Jones, George Franklin, FCO3c
Johnson, John Thomas, Jr S1c
Johnston, Richard Henry, GM3c

APPENDIX 4

Kenley, Lee Charles, F1c
Kuminga, Chester Stanley, M3c
Kwitkowski, Peter Paul, BM1c
Kwolek, John Joseph, MM3c
Large, George Hathaway, SC3c
Landin, Johan Ambrose, F1c
Latorre, Joseph, S2c
LaValle, John Arthur, S2c
Lawson, William Dallas, M3c
LeBlanc, Osias Joseph, S1c
LeClaire, Ovila Joseph, S2c
Leonard, Daniel Jr, SC3c
Leta, Domenico Michael, S2c
Libengood, James Ralph, QM3c
Liebman, Marion Albert, S1c
Loeber, Edward Conrad, SRT3c
Loeffler, Ernest Edward, S2c
Longkabel, Gordon Jr, S2c
Low, Frederick John, S1c
Lowe, Wimpy, F1c
Mahin, Charles William, SK2c
Mara, George Philip, Cox
Marker, Franklin Leroy, GM3c
Marriott, Oscar Ferdinand, CEM
Marsland, Alvah Irwin, MM3c
Martin, Wendell Linzy, S1c
Mauter, Paul Thomas, F1c
Medellin, Pedro Martinez, S1c
Medina, Norberto, RT3c
Mensenkamp, Walworth Thomas, S1c
Menius, Billy Odell, MM3c
Menallo, Nunzio Danial, BM2c
Michalik, George Edward, S1c
Mierzekewski, Paul Raymond, WT2c
Miller, Joseph James, Cox
Miller, Robert William, FC3c
Minahan, John Patrick, S1c
Minks, Everett Russel, S2c

Mitchell, Wallace Harry, S2c
Molzahn, Albert Lester, WT2c
Moore, Carroll Edwin, MM2c
Moos, Robert Francis, WT2c
Mount, James Watson, S2c
Mugridge, Paul Clayton, Cox
McGee, Donald Eugene, S1c
McGinnis, Arthur James, S1c
McClain, Charles Edward, F1c
Neal, Earl Arthur, AMM3c
Nelson, Laverne Nels, S2c
Nelson, Lowell Rainard, GM3c
Nettles, Edward Marvin, S1c
Nielsen, Kenneth Reher, WT3c
Oleson, Harald Reio Arild, CT
Owens, Luther Birchel, S1c
Payton, Larus Elmer, SF2c
Peregud, Harry, S2c
Peterson, Robert Hamilton, EM2c
Piggott, Tom Edward, Bkr3c
Pires, John Paul, F1c
Popa, Emil, S1c
Postle, Lewis Wiley Jr, RM3c
Pote, Robert Lee, S2c
Purvis, John Mitchell, GM3c
Quinn, Edward Joseph Jr, S1c
Ramsey, Charles Homer, Cox
Reed, Donald Otis, S1c
Richard, Omer Adrian, S2c
Richie, Eugene Anthony, S1c
Ritchey, Edward Gilbert, MM2c
Roberts, Roberts Ewing, CCSTD
Rod, Ernest David, S1c
Rogers, Harold Floyd, S1c
Rogers, Louis Richard, S2c
Roleder, Howard Stanley, MM2c
Romo, Jesus Antelno, S2c
Russo, Anthony Thomas, MM2c

APPENDIX 4

Sabino, Peter Anthony, S1c
Samuelson, Laurence Albert, S1c
Sanders, Charles Ernest, S1c
Savage, Jack Milton, CPhM
Savey, John Henry, S1c
Schaffer, William Arthur, MM3c
Schieble, Robert Frances, S1c
Schmidt, John Mathew, S1c
Schoen, Roy Adam, BM2c
Schultz, Alvin Leo, Cox
Sears, Billy D., S2c
Shaver, Frank Jr, Bkr1c
Sheil, Joseph Patrick, S1c
Sidor, John, S1c
Simkins, Clarence Marcellus, GM2c
Smith, Harold Truman, F1c
Solano, Isidro, CST
Spillane, Charles William, Cox
Staymates, Albert Harrison, S2c
Stepp, Billie, S2c
Studden, Arthur, MM3c
Taylor, Clair Elwood, BM2
Taylor, Lloyd, S2c
Teague, Jesse Zachaus, S2c
Thompson, John Robert, RT1c
Thurman, Joseph Allen, S2c
Tice, William Lester, SC1c
Tipps, Everett Shirman, S2c
Tonka, George Joseph, S2c
Tomlinson, Frank Ellis, S1c
Treventhan, Vernon Erwin, MM3c
Truett, James Melvin, S1c
Trujillo, Daniel Carmen, S1c
Turner, Daniel Junior, S2c
Ulery, Roy Levon, MM1c
Vaughn, Clyde Everett, MM2c
Vicknair, Warren Joseph Jr, EM2c
Voelker, Delmer Oswald, S2c

Voigt, Ferdinand Max, F1c
Volk, Wendelin J., Cox
Wade, Jack Wayne, S2c
Walden, Charles Orville, S2c
Walker, Paul Allen, S2c
Walls, William Howard, S2c
Walters, James Truman, SK3c
Walterman, Lee, F1c
Waynick, Delbert Lee, S2c
Weaver, Marlin Andrew, S2c
Weaver, Bruce Edward, S1c
Webb, Edward Perry Jr, SC1c
Wedeking, James Linard, FC3c
Weigand, Ralph John, S1c
Wells, Paul Raymond, SK3c
West, Clayton Clifford, F1c
Westfall, Howard Venton, S2c
White, Fred Hoyt, S2c
Wilczynski, Tadausz Bernard, S2c
Wilson, Max, FCO3c
Wolff, Warren William, S2c
Wollerman, Fritz August, GM2c
Wong, Harry, Bkr3c
Wood, Russell Devere, F1c
Wytrykowski, Henry Thomas, F1c
Zespy, Jerome Anthony, GM3c

US Marine Corps
  Hoyt, Dale Hoel, Plt Sgt
  Mauck, Wayne Vincent, Pfc
  Maxwell, Harry Guy, Pfc
  McGuire, Raleigh Maxwell, Pfc
  Turcott, Charles Augustus, Pfc

Birmingham Personnel Wounded (October 24, 1944)
Officers
  Adey, Edward Alonzo III, Ens
  Inglis, Thomas Browning, Capt

APPENDIX 4

Marocchi, John Louis, Lt
Reid, John, Lt
Votto, Frank V., Ens
Wingfield, William Henry, Elect

Enlisted Personnel
Adams, Edward Berry, EM3c
Adams, Smith Cantrell Jr, S1c
Allen, Richard Stephen, ARM2c
Askren, Kenneth Lee, S2c
Austen, William Ephram, SSMB3c
Battistin, Celeste Louis, MoMM3c
Belcher, John Lee, S2c
Bennett, James Claiborne, RdM3c
Bierhaus, Milford Leslie, S2c
Blackstock, Clarence Edwin, S2c
Bowen, Clovis Armster, S2c
Brown, Charles Francis, MM1c
Brown, Bernard Jones, BM2c
Brown, Clyde O'Neil, S2c
Brown, Hansel, S1c
Brown, Mitchell, RdM3c
Bryant, Ellis Franklin, S1c
Bull, Kenneth Arthur, S2c
Campbell, Jesse J. Jr, Y2c
Carmean, Eugene Vernon, Cox
Carmichael, Harry Robert, F1c
Carney, Keith Lester, S2c
Chaney, John Russell, S2c
Cholewa, Mitchell Joseph, S1c
Coleman, Leon, StM2c
Costa, Antonio Thomas, Cox
Cripe, Lawrence R., S2c
Cuppett, Leslie Joseph, S1c
Dangles, Christ, S1c
Davidson, Jewel Richmond, S1c
Davis, Delbert Barney, Cox
Davis, Eddy Junior, S2c

Decker, Richard Lawrence, F2c
Deitchler, Harlan Hans, S1c
DeJarnett, Rudolph, S2c
Delph, Paul Donald, S1c
DeMillion, Vernon Edward, S2c
Denton, James Earl, S2c
DeWitt, Harrell Lee, F1c
Drzazinski, Edward Joseph, BM2c
Dull, John Carl, S2c
Dunn, Merle Palmer, S1c
Dyer, Harry, EM2c
Eleew, Nathan, F1c
Engen, Lawrence Allen, FC3c
Fischer, Robert Donald, SK3c
Fox, Levin Thomas, MM3c
Franke, Frederick L. Jr, SF3c
Futch, Leonard Forrest, Cox
Gaddy, William Albert, S2c
Gannon, Bernard Michael, S2c
Gardner, Raymond W., S1c
Gavgler, Anthony Richard, F2c
Geiger, Martin Frank, Jr, Bkr2c
Gold, John Jay, Y3c
Gould, Wayne Emery, S1c
Gower, John Oscar, GM3c
Graves, Robert Calvin, SC1c
Greene, Forrest Monroe, S2c
Hale, Lloyd Mack, ARM2c
Harris, Robert James, S1c
Hensinger, Neile L., CEM
Herring, Bert Everett, S2c
Herzberg, William C., EM1c
Hill, Bertrand Louis, S2c
Holbert, John Marvin, S1c
Holmes, Kenneth Roger, Cox
Horner, Nelson Robert, S2c
Hudson, Clyde Thomas, S1c
Janke, Grover Cleveland, S2c

APPENDIX 4

Jennings, Marvin Edgar, S1c
Jones, James Martin, S1c
Joseph, David Lee, F1c
Kalck, Wendell August Jr, EM3c
Kane, William Donato, S1c
Kimble, Volta Edison, F1c
Klonoski, Edward James, RM2c
Lanterman, Howard Melvin, BM1c
Learn, Wayne Emmett, RM2c
Ledo, Philip Tavares, F1c
Lee, Kenneth Sheldon, S2c
Lewis, Chester, F1c
Lloyd, Ashby Wheeler Jr, S2c
Lucero, Frank, AMM2c
Lyle, Lewis Evertte W., S1c
Lynn, Harry Charles, QM3c
Mancuso, Joe, RdM3c
Mann, George Edward, S1c
McCann, Gordon Louis, S2c
McCreary, Robert Leroy, EM1c
McLaughlin, James, SM3c
Meldrum, Lynn Albert, S1c
Meyer, William Joseph, MM3c
Michalak, Henry Walter, S2c
Miller, Crockford, MM1c
Miller, Harold Irvine, S1c
Mills, Marion Carlile, Cox
Mills, Virgil, Cox
Minter, Harold Lee, S2c
Mislevy, Joseph, MM2c
Monroe, Robert Walter, S2c
Murphy, Daniel James, FC3c
Nielson, Alton, S2c
Occhipinti, Saverio, AM3c
O'Keefe, Richard William, S2c
Okray, Robert Nicholas, S2c
O'Neal, William Haynes, F1c
Patrick, William Lane, S1c

Pennington, Harold Walker, S2c
Pennington, Hollis Alvin, S2c
Perkins, Leslie James, S1c
Pickens, George Swope, GM3c
Pisor, John Perry, S2c
Polito, Crist Tony, S2c
Popham, Harry Junior, MM2c
Porter, Charles Edwin, RM3c
Prince, Merle, RdM3c
Puc, Adam Mike, Cox
Purpura, Francesco, S1c
Raimondi, William Charles, S2c
Ramon, William, S1c
Rasmussen, Carl Sophus, S1c
Readnour, Robert, S2c
Reed, Ulessess Zellen, S2c
Rees, John Pursel, MM1c
Reiff, Arvin Edward, MM2c
Rittner, Keith Haynes, S1c
Roberts, Thomas Joseph Jr, RdM3c
Robinson, Emmet Ray, FCO3c
Robnolite, Charles Nelson, S1c
Runnion, Richard, S1c
Schaeffer, Albert Andrew, S2c
Schoch, Richard, S1c
Scoltoch, John Joseph, GM3c
Searfos, Melvin Raymond, S1c
Shears, James, Ck3c
Shermer, Floyd Vernon, S1c
Shuler, Irvin Alva, MM3c
Simmons, Charles, S2c
Smith, Kermit Lyle, SM2c
Sniadecki, Francis Chester, S2c
Springman, William Walter, S1c
Steele, Irvin Robert, S2c
Steele, William Buford, S2c
Stevens, Eugene Leo, S1c
Stoneking, Floyd Delbert, Cox

APPENDIX 4

Straub, Thomas Arthur, S2c
Summers, Charles Frederick, Cox
Swinney, Robert Clyde, BM1c
Tamlyn, Calvin Cleveland, F1c
Thawsh, Martin Frank, S1c
Thiessen, Russell Clark, S1c
Thompson, George Bernard, F1c
Thompson, Richard Ellsworth, S1c
Thorpe, Delbert Franklin, S1c
Toth, Sigmond William, F1c
Vaden, Billy Earl, S2c
Vagnier, Robert Lee, S1c
Vest, Jack Emerald, S1c
Vicars, James McConnell, S1c
Vitullo, Joseph Felix, S1c
Volcke, Albert Maurice, Y3c
Wallace, Onnie Cyrus, S2c
Wallo, John Joseph Jr, S1c
Walter, Ralph, S2c
Walters, Elmer George, S2c
Walton, George Raymond, S2c
Warren, Dale Olin, S1c
Webb, Floyd Eugene, F1c
Weger, Martin Glenn, EM2c
Weiss, William Arnold, MoMM2c
White, Robert Edward, S1c
Whittington, George Alvin, S2c
Wiant, Edward Arnold, S1c
Wicker, Philip William, Cox
Wieszkowiak, Alexander, GM3c
Wiilainen, Edward Ronald, S2c
William, Johnnie Lee Jr, S2c
Williams, Homer Reed, S2c
Williams, Kenneth Arthur, F1c
Williams, Lynn, WT3c
Wilson, Joseph Lloyd, S2c
Wilson, Richard Lee, Y2c
Wirkus, Jerome Albert, FC3c

Wisniewski, Joseph Thomas, S2c
Witkovski, Russell Earl, S2c
Wojtowicz, Joseph Chester, S1c
Wolford, William Percival, S2c
Wood, LeRoy James, S1c
Wrinkle, D. T., S2c
Zea, Ward Homer, S1c
Zielinski, Michael Bruno, S2c

US Marine Corps
    Cundiff, William Henry, Pvt
    Maynor, James Lewis, Cpl
    Smith, Opie Drexel, Pfc
    Spinks, William John, Pfc
    Vendemia, James Anthony, Pfc

Bibliography

OFFICIAL SOURCES

"Early Raids in the Pacific Ocean February 1 to March 10, 1942," Naval History and Heritage Command, November 18, 2020 (www.history.navy.mil/content/history/nhhc/research/library/online-reading-room/title-list-alphabetically/e/early-raids-pacific-ocean.html).

"U.S.S. Princeton (CVL23) Loss in Action Battle for Leyte Gulf 24 October 1944," Naval History and Heritage Command, January 21, 2016 (www.history.navy.mil/research/library/online-reading-room/title-list-alphabetically/w/war-damage-reports/uss-princeton-cvl23-war-damage-report-no-62.html).

BOOKS

Alexander, Joseph H., Raymond Callahan, Richard Fran, Theodore Gatchel, Bruce Gudmundsson, David Horner, Tomoyuki Ishizu and Ken Kotani, *The Pacific War – From Pearl Harbor to Hiroshima* (Oxford: Osprey Publishing, 2005).
Alexander, Joseph H., *Utmost Savagery – The Three Days of Tarawa* (Annapolis: Naval Institute Press, 1995).
Blackburn, Tom with Eric Hammel, *The Jolly Rogers – The Story of Tom Blackburn and Navy Fighting Squadron VF-17* (Minnesota: MBI Publishing Company, 1998).
Bradshaw, Thomas I. and Marsha L. Clark, *Carrier Down – The Story of the Sinking of the USS Princeton (CVL-23)* (Austin: Eakin Press, 1990).
Chambers, Mark with Tony Holmes, *Osprey Combat Aircraft 119 – Nakajima B5N 'Kate' and B6N 'Jill' Units* (Oxford: Osprey Publishing, 2017).
——*Osprey Combat Aircraft 140 – Yokosuka D4Y Units* (Oxford: Osprey Publishing, 2021).

Costello, John, *The Pacific War 1941–1945* (Rawson: Wade Publishers, 1981).
Cutler, Thomas J., *The Battle of Leyte Gulf* (Maryland: Naval Institute Press, 1994).
Faltum, Andrew, *The Essex Aircraft Carriers* (Baltimore: Nautical & Aviation Publishing Company, 1996).
——*The Independence Light Aircraft Carriers* (Charleston: The Nautical & Aviation Publishing Company, 2002).
Gailey, Harry A., *The War in the Pacific – From Pearl Harbor to Tokyo Bay* (Novato: Presidio Press, 1995).
Hammel, Eric, *Aces in Combat: The American Aces Speak: Volume V* (independently published, 2020).
Hastings, Max, *Retribution – The Battle for Japan, 1944–45* (New York: Random House, 2007).
Hornfischer, James D., *The Fleet at Flood Tide – America at Total War in the Pacific* (New York: Bantam Books, 2017).
Kurzman, Dan, *Left to Die – The Tragedy of the USS Juneau* (New York: Pocket Books, 1994).
Marston, Daniel (ed.), *The Pacific War – From Pearl Harbor to Hiroshima* (Oxford: Osprey Publishing, 2005).
McKelvey Cleaver, Thomas, *Pacific Thunder – The US Navy's Central Pacific Campaign, August 1943–October 1944* (Oxford: Osprey Publishing, 2017).
McManus, John C., *Fire and Fortitude – The U.S. Army in the Pacific War, 1941–1943* (New York: Random House, 2019).
——*Island Infernos – The U.S. Army's Pacific War Odyssey, 1944* (New York: Random House, 2021).
Miller, Donald L., *D-Days in the Pacific – Guadalcanal, Tarawa, Saipan, Iwo Jima, Okinawa* (New York: Simon & Schuster, 1945).
Olynyk, Frank J., *USN Credits for the Destruction of Enemy Aircraft in Air-to-Air Combat World War 2* (independently published, 1982).
——*Stars & Bars – A Tribute to the American Fighter Ace 1920–1973* (London: Grub Street, 1995).
Prange, Gordon W., *At Dawn We Slept – The Untold Story of Pearl Harbor* (New York: Penguin Putnam Inc., 1981).
Pratt, Fletcher, *The Compact History of the United States Navy* (New York: Hawthorne Books, Inc., 1957).
Reynolds, Clark G., *The Fast Carriers – The Forging of an Air Navy* (Annapolis: Naval Institute Press, 1968).
Russell, David Lee, *Early U.S. Navy Carrier Raids, February–April 1942 – Five Operations That Tested a New Dimension of American Air Power* (Jefferson: McFarland & Company, Inc., 2019)

BIBLIOGRAPHY

Stille, Mark E., *US Navy Aircraft Carriers 1942–45 – World War II-built Ships* (Oxford: Osprey Publishing, 2007).
——*Pacific Carrier War – Carrier Combat from Pearl Harbor to Okinawa* (Oxford: Osprey Publishing, 2021).
——*Leyte Gulf – A New History of the World's Largest Sea Battle* (Oxford: Osprey Publishing, 2023).
Sears, David, *Pacific Air – How Fearless Flyboys, Peerless Aircraft, and Fast Flattops Conquered the Skies in the War with Japan* (Cambridge, Massachusetts: Da Capo Press, 2011).
Thomas, Geoff, *US Navy Aircraft Colours – Units, Colours, Markings and Operations during World War 2* (New Malden: Air Research Publications, 1989).
Tillman, Barrett, *Hellcat – The F6F in World War II* (Annapolis: Naval Institute Press, 1979).
——*Hellcat Aces of World War 2 – Osprey Aircraft of the Aces 10* (Oxford: Osprey Publishing, 1996).
——*U.S. Navy Fighter Squadron in World War II – Chronologies, Deployments, Combat Records* (North Branch: Specialty Press, 1997).
——*Clash of the Carriers – The True Story of the Marianas Turkey Shoot of World War II* (New York: Penguin Group, 2005).
——*Enterprise – America's Fightingest Ship and the Men Who Helped Win World War II* (New York: Simon & Schuster, 2012).
Toll, Ian W., *Pacific Crucible – War at Sea in the Pacific, 1941–1942* (New York: Norton, 2012).
——*The Conquering Tide – War in the Pacific Islands, 1942–1944* (New York: Norton, 2015).
Winton, John, *War in the Pacific – Pearl Harbor to Tokyo Bay* (New York: Mayflower Books, 1970).

ARTICLES AND PAPERS

Bisno, Adam, "Securing New Guinea – The U.S. Navy in Operations Reckless and Persecution 21–22 April 1944," Naval History and Heritage Command, May 31, 2019 (www.history.navy.mil/browse-by-topic/wars-conflicts-and-operations/world-war-ii/1944/reckless-and-persecution.html).
——"Operation Forager – The Battle of Saipan 15 June–9 July 1944," Naval History and Heritage Command, June 11, 2019 (www.history.navy.mil/browse-by-topic/wars-conflicts-and-operations/world-war-ii/1944/saipan.html).

Cheser, S., Mathew and Nicholas Roland, "Galvanic – Beyond the Reef – Tarawa and the Gilberts, November 1943," Naval History and Heritage Command, July 26, 2022 (www.history.navy.mil/research/publications/publications-by-subject/galvanic.html).

Cox, Samuel J., "H-024-1: Operation Cherryblossom – The Invasion of Bougainville and Victory in the Solomon Islands," Naval History and Heritage Command, December 27, 2018 (www.history.navy.mil/content/history/nhhc/about-us/leadership/director/directors-corner/h-grams/h-gram-024/h-024-1.html).

———"H-026-1: Operation Flintlock – The Invasion of Kwajalein, 31 January 1944," Naval History and Heritage Command, May 3, 2019 (www.history.navy.mil/about-us/leadership/director/directors-corner/h-grams/h-gram-026/h-026-1.html).

———"H-026-2: Operation Catchpole – The Invasion of Eniwetok, 17 February 1944," Naval History and Heritage Command, May 3, 2019 (www.history.navy.mil/about-us/leadership/director/directors-corner/h-grams/h-gram-026/H-026-2.html).

———"H-026-3: Operation Hailstone – Carrier Raid on Truk Island, 17–18 February 1944," Naval History and Heritage Command, May 3, 2019 (www.history.navy.mil/about-us/leadership/director/directors-corner/h-grams/h-gram-026/H-026-3.html).

———"H-004-4: The Doolittle Raid – 'Shangri-La'," Naval History and Heritage Command, May 7, 2019 (www.history.navy.mil/content/history/nhhc/about-us/leadership/director/directors-corner/h-grams/h-gram-004/h-004-4.html)

———"H-032-1: Operation Forager and the Battle of the Philippine Sea," Naval History and Heritage Command, June 26, 2019 (www.history.navy.mil/about-us/leadership/director/directors-corner/h-grams/h-gram-032/h-032-1.html).

———"H-Gram 038: Battle of Leyte Gulf," Naval History and Heritage Command, November 25, 2019 (www.history.navy.mil/content/dam/nhhc/about-us/leadership/hgram_pdfs/H-Gram_038.pdf).

———"H-038-2: The Battle of Leyte Gulf in Detail," Naval History and Heritage Command, November 25, 2019 (www.history.navy.mil/about-us/leadership/director/directors-corner/h-grams/h-gram-038/h-038-2.html).

———"Operation Galvanic – Tarawa and Makin Islands, November 1943," Naval History and Heritage Command, February 23, 2022 (www.history.navy.mil/about-us/leadership/director/directors-corner/h-grams/h-gram-025/h-025-1.html).

BIBLIOGRAPHY

Evans, Mark L., "Princeton IV (CV-23) 1943–1944," Naval History and Heritage Command, August 26, 2022 (www.history.navy.mil/research/histories/ship-histories/danfs/p/princeton-iv.html).

Gamble, Bruce, "The 'Reluctant Dragon' Awakens: Saratoga's Brave Raid on Rabaul," *World War II Magazine*, November 1, 2019 (www.navytimes.com/military-honor/salute-veterans/2019/11/01/the-reluctant-dragon-awakens-saratogas-brave-raid-on-rabaul/).

HistoryNet Staff, "World War II: Raids on Rabaul in November 1943," History Net, June 12, 2006 (www.historynet.com/world-war-ii-raids-on-rabaul-in-november-1943/).

History.com Editors, "Battle of New Britain (Rabaul)," History.com, August 21, 2018
(www.history.com/topics/world-war-ii/battle-of-new-britain-rabaul).

Marks, Chris, "Ten Minutes Over Truk," Warfare History Network, June 2021 (https://warfarehistorynetwork.com/article/ten-minutes-over-truk/).

Robbins, Michael W., "The Allies' Billion-dollar Secret – The Proximity Fuze of World War II," History Net, October 19, 2020 (www.historynet.com/proximity-fuze/).

Nasuti, Guy J., "'The Great Marianas Turkey Shoot' 19–20 June 1944," Naval History and Heritage Command, May 21, 2019 (www.history.navy.mil/browse-by-topic/wars-conflicts-and-operations/world-war-ii/1944/battle-philippine-sea/turkey-shoot.html).

Naval History.net, "Campaign Summaries of World War 2: Japanese Conquests 1939–1942," accessed September 12, 2023 (https://navalhistory.net/WW2CampaignsJapConquests.htm).

Popham, Harry, "Eyewitness to Tragedy: Death of USS Princeton," History Net, Augusts 19, 1997 (www.historynet.com/eyewitness-to-tragedy-death-of-uss-princeton-may-97-world-war-ii-feature/).

Ray, Michael, "Battle of Leyte Gulf World War II," Encyclopaedia Britannica, last updated January 5, 2024 (www.britannica.com/event/Battle-of-Leyte-Gulf).

US Naval Academy Memorial Hall, "Lucky Bag, Ernest Wetherill Wood, Jr.," accessed January 12, 2024 (https://usnamemorialhall.org/index.php/ERNEST_W._WOOD,_JR.,_LCDR,_USN).

Waldman, Martin R. "'Calmness, Courage, and Efficiency' – Remembering the Battle of Leyte Gulf," Naval History and Heritage Command, October 22, 2019 (www.history.navy.mil/browse-by-topic/wars-conflicts-and-operations/world-war-ii/1944/battle-of-leyte-gulf/calmness-courage-and-efficiency.html#F).

"World War II Shipbuilding in the San Francisco Bay Area," National Park Service, accessed January 18, 2024 (www.nps.gov/articles/000/world-war-ii-shipbuilding-in-the-san-francisco-bay-area.htm).

Wilkinson, Stephan, "Goldilocks Fighter: What Made the F6F Hellcat "Just Right"?" Historynet, March 8, 2017 (www.historynet.com/goldilocks-fighter-f6f-hellcat/).

Index

Page numbers in **bold** refer to maps.

Abell, Ens Jack M.   40
Abell, Lt(jg) J. M.   117
Abemama Island   82, 89
Addison, Gunner Larry   225
Alabama, USS   118, 162
Albacore, USS   162, 171
Allied strategy   43–44
Altemus, Lt(jg) J. P.   63
antiaircraft guns   33, 45, 52–54, 90, 100
Arnold, Gen Henry H.   81
Auclair, Lt(jg) Henry   219–220
Aylwin, USS   155–156

Baker, Lt Herman J.   135–136
Baker Island, occupation of   58–62
Bardshar, Lt Cdr Frederick   131–132, 132–133, 135, 138, 139, 145, 163–164, 165–166, 181, 183, 184, 191–192, 205–206, 209, 263–264, 270
Barnett, PH1c   75–76
Bataan, USS   27, 144
Bechtel, Warren   50
Bell, Lt Frank   147, 213
Belleau Wood, USS   27, 32, 38, 41, 46, 47, 48, 58, 59, 60–61, 62, 63, 98, 105, 144, 161
Berlin, Ens Ted   78
Bethlehem Shipbuilding Corporation   50
Betio Island   82, 87, 89

Birmingham, USS   62, 221, 230–233, 235–241, 245, 252–254, 256–258, 278–290
Blackburn, Lt Cdr Tommy   74
Blanchard, Cdr James   162
Blyth, Ens Les   163, 200
Blyth, Lt(jg) Robert L.   270
Bogan, Rear Adm Gerald F   180
Bonis, attack on   68–70
Bougainville Island, invasion of   67–73
Bradshaw, Lt Thomas   131, 210
Brakeley, George A.   34
Bransfield, Lt(jg) Charles   64
Brotherton, Lt Hank   165
Brown, Lt Carl A.   133, 187, 200–205, 209, 270
Brown, Lt George   83–84
Brown, Larry   128
Brown, Rear Adm Wilson   29
Buckalew, Lt(jg) William G.   40, 105–106
Buie, Lt Cdr Paul   87–88
Bunker Hill, USS   78, 87, 89–90, 97, 105, 116, 118
Buracker, Capt William H.   108–109, 123, 146, 188, 192, 209, 212, 213, 220–221, 227–228, 229, 232, 235, 239, 242, 245–246, 248, 262
Bureau of Ships (BuShips)   23–25
Burke, Capt Arleigh   157

Butler, RM Ed 211
Butler, Lt R. P. 138–139

Cabot, USS 27, 34, 105, 161, 191
Caldwell, Cdr Henry H. 72–73, 74–77, 75–77
Callan, Aviation Ordnanceman Pete 212, 214–215
Canberra, USS 104, 191
Cantrell, Ens Oscar 40
Carolines and Philippines campaign 180–181
Carter, Lt(jg) Van 165
Cassin Young, USS 217, 227, 231, 232, 251
Cavalla, USS 153, 156, 157, 169–171
Central Pacific 43–44
Central Pacific Force 44–45, 82–91, 95, 107, 120
Chafee, Lt Cdr George M. 34
Chisholm, Sgt Adrian 251
Clark, Rear Adm Joseph J. 99, 180
Cleveland-class light cruisers, conversions 23–28
Clifford, Lt Cdr Edward L. 35, 127, 139
Clifton, Cdr "Jumpin" Joe 73, 74
Coleman, Lt(jg) Thaddeus T. 60–61
Combat Direction Center (CDC) 47, 51
Combat Information Centers (CICs) 168–169
Connaway, Lt Cdr Fred 83
Conolly, Rear Adm Richard L. 104
Conroy, Ens Thomas J. 202, 270
Coral Sea, Battle of the 29–30, 46
Corvina, USS 82–83
Cowpens, USS 27, 85, 105, 144, 191
Crews, Lt H. W. 60–61, 63
Crockett, Lt(jg) Stanley 75–77
Cromwell, Capt John P. 83–84
Curtis, Lt W. L. 35
Curtiss SB2C Helldiver 54–55
CVG-12: 66, 68–69, 72–73, 74–77, 80–81
CVG-19: 198–199
CVLG-27: 129, 131, 135, 139, 145, 156, 174, 181, 188, 258–259, 263–264

Dashiell, USS 42
Davison, Rear Adm Ralph E. 180
Doolittle, Col James 30
Douglas SBD-5 Dauntless 36, 54, 57
Drury, Lt(jg) Paul E. 207–208, 270
Duborg, Cdr Francis R. 240, 241
Duncan, Ens Robert W. 66

Edwards, USS 66–67
Empress Augusta Bay, Battle of 70, 71
Eniwetok 109–113, 175–178
Enterprise, USS 28, 30, 31, 89, 98, 104–105, 122, 134, 146, 159, 169, 173, 182
Erickson, Ens Lief 165
Espiritu Santo Naval Advance Base 67–68, 79, 114
Essex, USS 48, 60, 78, 81, 87, 98, 105, 144, 165, 199, 205, 211, 222, 235
Essex-class fleet carriers 25–26, 31–32, 42, 45, 51, 52–54, 54, 55, 261
Eubank, Ens Elwyn P. 103

Fast Carrier Task Force 44, 45, 51, 100, 102, 120, 179–180
Fifth Amphibious Force 45, 84
Fifth Fleet 44, 120, 142, 261
fightback, 1942 28–31
fighter direction officers (FDOs) 52
Finback, USS 158, 159
Fletcher, Rear Adm Frank J. 29
Flying Fish, USS 152–153
Folk, Cdr Winston P. 240–241
Formosa 191–192
Fukudome, Vice Adm Shigeru 149–150
Funk, Lt Harold 61, 62

Gatling, USS 244, 245–246, 252, 254–255, 257
Giddle, Lyle 176, 176–177
Gilbert Islands 62, 82–91, 93–94
Ginder, Rear Adm Samuel P. 103, 112, 119–120
Glans, PO Buhler 239
Gordon, Ens P. H. 63
Green, George 251

INDEX

Gregg, Lt(jg) Howie 163–164
Grove, Lt(jg) Robert B. 133
Grumman F4F-3 Wildcat 29, 34, 36, 40, 41, 46, 55
Grumman F6F-3 Hellcat 36, 45, 46, 54, 55–56, 57–58, 60, 65, 66, 75–77, 87–88, 132, 267–268
Grumman F6F-5 Hellcat 41, 166–168, 268
Grumman TBF-1 Avenger 36, 54, 58, 75–77, 132, 269
Grumman TBF-3 Avenger 136
Guadalcanal 31, 44, 54, 66, 95, 131
Guadalcanal, Naval Battle of 157, 180
Guam 141, 142, 156, 161, 169

Hadley, Lt S. M. 132
Halsey, Vice Adm William F. "Bull" 28, 29, 30, 44, 67, 70, 72, 73, 78–79, 80, 81, 91, 110, 120, 179, 179–180, 181–182, 182–183, 191–192, 247–248, 252
Hanks, Ens Ralph 88
Harris, Lt(jg) Cecil E. 131
Harwood, Cdr Bruce 229–230, 237, 242, 262–263
Hatcher, Lt Cdr Martin T. 36
Hautop, Ens Frederick D. 185–187, 224–225
Hawk, Chief Boatswain R. C. 33
Haynes, Lt(jg) L. W. 63
Henderson, Capt George R. 31, 33–34, 38, 58, 66, 108–109, 262
Hill, Ens J. R. 117
Hoover, Vice Adm John H. 86, 102
Hornet, USS 30, 31, 34, 47, 103, 116, 144, 161, 187
Hoskins, Capt John M. 188, 209, 243–244, 259, 262
Houston, USS 191–192

Imperial General Headquarters 29, 30
Imperial Japanese Army 18, 19, 20, 21, 29
Imperial Japanese Army Air Force (IJAAF) 54

Imperial Japanese Naval Air Force (IJNAF)
  aircraft 54
  attack on Darwin 20
  attack on Pearl Harbor 16
  Battle of Leyte Gulf 199–205, 205–209
  Battle of Midway 30
  Battle of the Philippine Sea 159–169
  casualties and losses 29, 87–88, 95, 98, 117, 145–146, 161, 172, 191–192, 200, 202, 206, 209
  fighting over Rabaul 73–78, 80–81
  Marianas campaign 145–148, 149, 151, 152, 156, 157–158
  Operation *Galvanic* 87–89
  Operations *Sho-Go* 190–192
  snoopers 115–116, 121, 122–123, 144
Imperial Japanese Navy 18, 70
  2nd Carrier Division 110
  3rd Carrier Division 194–195
  aircraft carriers 19
  Battle of Leyte Gulf 205–209, 247–248
  Battle of the Philippine Sea 159–175
  casualties and losses 30, 118, 170–171, 174, 175, 195
  Combined Fleet 94, 95, 111, 148, 148–149
  Marianas campaign 148–159, 159–175
  Operations *Sho-Go* 190–192
  Philippines defense plan 193–195
  strength 49
Independence, USS 26, 27, 31, 48, 57, 58, 60, 78–79, 87, 199, 258, 264
Independence-class carriers 26, 45, 51, 261
  aircraft 28, 54
  antiaircraft guns 52–54
  armor 26
  aviation handling facilities 27
  ballast 25
  complement 28
  conversions 23–28
  cruising radius 25
  defense 28
  design 24–25

displacement 26, 27
fitting out 27
flightdeck 25, 27
hangar bay 25, 27
hydraulic catapult 27
island superstructure 25, 26–27
launched 31–42
powerplant 26
specifications 25–28
Indianapolis, USS 84, 104, 115
Intrepid, USS 105, 131
Irwin, USS 223, 224–225, 228, 230, 232, 248–250, 251, 255–256
Iwo Jima 153, 182

Jackson, Lt Richard 225
Japan 23, 96, 102, 110, 264
  occupation of Southeast Asia 17–22
  surrender 258–259
Jaskilka, 2Lt Sam 176
Joint Chiefs of Staff 43, 44, 102, 141, 142
Joint Strategic Survey Committee 43–44
Juneau, USS 250–251

Kaiser, Henry 50
Kakuta, Vice Adm Kakuji 150–151, 158, 161
Keener, Ens Leonard 70
Kelleher, Lt Jim 224
Kerr, Lt Bill 131, 210
Kerr, Lt(jg) L. H. 117, 121
Kerr, Lt(jg) Leslie 61
Kieri, Leo 216–217
King, Adm Ernest J. 27, 43, 44, 48, 94, 141–142, 144
Kinkaid, Vice Adm Thomas C. 44, 247–248
Kleffner, Ens Frank P. 154–156, 206–207
Koehler, Lt Cdr John 108
Koga, Adm Mineichi 71, 91, 93–94, 149
Kurita, Vice Adm Takeo 71, 150

Lamb, Lt William 131, 163, 164–165, 184–185, 270
Landing Operations Doctrine Fleet Training Publication No. 167: 94–95

Langley, USS 27, 49, 103, 104, 105, 111, 124, 144, 200
Large, Lt Cdr James 115, 116, 139, 146, 189, 209
Layton, Cdr Edwin T 148, 150
Lee, Vice Adm Willis A. 58, 157, 160
Levy, Lt Cdr Louis 214
Lexington, USS 29, 29–30, 46, 47, 48, 62, 63, 64, 85, 87–88, 98, 99, 115, 116, 143, 159–160, 160, 165, 166, 182, 198–199, 207, 222
Leyte 183, 192, 193–195
Leyte Gulf, Battle of 195, 196–217, 235, 247–248
  casualties and losses 200, 202, 206, 209
  opening actions 198–205
  Princeton bomb strike 209–217
  Sibuyan Sea strike 205–209
Light Carrier Air Group (CVLG) 23: 34, 35, 36, 37–38, 41, 45–46, 47, 57, 59, 63, 64, 65, 66, 73, 74, 77, 80–81, 90, 105–106, 112–113, 121–122, 125, 127–129
light carriers 31–42, 261
Lockwood, Rear Adm Charles A. 61–62
Loesch, Lt(jg) Robert 59, 59–60
Loveland, Lt(jg), Hugh 165

MacArt, Lt James H. 240
MacArthur, Gen Douglas 20, 21, 43–44, 81, 96, 119, 141, 183
McCain, Vice Adm John S. 179–180
McCampbell, Cdr David 131
McMahon,, Lt(jg) John L. 133
McWilliams, Ens Lawrence F. 117, 124
Madison, Lt(jg) J. D. 63
Majuro 114, 118–119
Makin Island 82, 86–87, 89
Marcus Island 29, 58, 60
Marianas campaign 120, 125
  Battle of the Philippine Sea 159–169
  casualties and losses 145–146, 161, 164, 170, 172, 174–175
  first strikes 144–147
  forces 142–144

INDEX

"Great Marianas Turkey Shoot"
    172–173
Guam 142
IJN 148–159
planning 141–142
pursuit of the Combined Fleet
    173–175
Saipan 142, 143, 144–148, 152, 156, 175
submarine strike 169–171
Tinian 142, 144, 153
Marshall Islands
    casualties and losses 98, 105–106, 107
    Eniwetok 106, 109–113
    invasion planning and
        preparations 93–97, 101–104
    Kwajalein campaign 97–99, 100, 101–102, 104–109
    Lexington damaged 99–100
    Operation *Catchpole* 109–113
    raid on Truk 113–114
Marshalls–Gilberts raids 28
Matsonia, USS 257–258
Mazziotti, Aviation Ordnanceman
    Americo 213–214
Merrill, Rear Adm Aaron S. 69, 70
Midway, Battle of 30, 46
Miksis, Mike 238–239
Miller, Lt Cdr Daniel B. 248
Miller, Lt Cdr Henry L. 34, 36, 47, 61, 66, 69, 73, 74, 77, 105, 106, 108, 112, 114, 115, 116–117, 118–119, 120, 121–122, 123, 124, 159, 179, 263
Miller, PO Doris 88
Mindanao 181–183
Mitnich, Lou 32
Mitscher, Rear Adm Marc 30, 102–103, 112, 115, 119, 123, 125, 143, 152, 160, 161, 162, 174, 190
Mitsubishi A6M Zero-sen 55, 66, 76, 166–168
Moitoret, Lt Vic 108–109, 209, 246
Montani, Edward 216–217
Monterey, USS 27, 89–90, 97, 105, 127, 159–160, 182

Montgomery, Rear Adm Alfred E. 78–79, 80, 86, 98, 120
Mooney, Lt(jg) Tom 177–178, 211, 220, 222–223, 249–250, 257
Moore, Joseph 50
Morrison, Rear Adm Samuel Eliot
    113–114
Morrison, USS 231, 232, 252, 257
Muhlfeld, Lt(jg) F. B. 117
Mullinix, Rear Adm Henry M. 88
Munson, Ens Arthur H. 165, 206
Murphy, Cdr Joseph N. 219–220, 228, 245–246, 262

Nauru Island 85, 86
New Guinea 21, 29–30, 44, 96, 116, 119–124
New York Shipbuilding Corporation 31, 32–33
Nimitz, Adm Chester W. 22, 28, 43–44, 48, 56, 95–96, 101–102, 110, 113, 120, 123, 142, 183
North American B-25 Mitchell 30
North American SNJ Texan 34
Nyquist, Ens Albert W. 59–60

Oahu, Hawaii, Japanese attack 16–17
Oesterle, Lt Cdr Albert R. 244
O'Hare, Lt Edward "Butch" 29, 58, 89, 134
Operation *Cartwheel* 44, 68
Operation *Catchpole* 109–113
Operation *Cherryblossom* 68
Operation *Flintlock see* Marshall Islands
Operation *Forager see* Marianas campaign
Operation *Galvanic* 82–91
    aerial clashes 87–90
    casualties and losses 83, 87, 88, 89, 94
    forces 84, 85–86
    landings 86–87
    lessons-learned statement 93–94
    submarine operations 82–84
Operation *Hailstone* 113–114
Operation *Overlord* 144
Operation *Persecution* 119, 120, 121, 122
Operation *Reckless* 119, 120, 121

301

Operation *Torch* 129–130
operational control dispute 43–44
Operations *Sho-Go* 190–192
Outlaw, Lt Cdr E. C. 124
Ozawa, Vice Adm Jisaburo 150, 151, 156, 158, 159, 160, 168, 171, 193

Pacific Fleet **10–11**, 19, 49
Palau 114–118
Pantages, Pharmacist's Mate George 147–148, 215–216, 253–254
Pearl Harbor 16–17, 19, 28, 48, 136–139
Peleliu 181–182, 182
Phaler, Lt Cdr Walt 33
Philadelphia 35–36, 42
Philippine Sea, Battle of the 159–175
Philippines, the 20, 21, 43, 192–195, 197–198
Phillipe, Ens Edward 61
Phillips, Lt Cdr John 89
Plath, Chief Commissary Steward 210
Popham, Frank 238–239
Pownall, Rear Adm Charles A. 58, 60, 61–62, 62, 63–64, 64, 85, 86, 97–98, 99, 100
Pride, Capt A. M. 38, 62
Princeton, USS
  air group training 34
  aircraft 54
  antiaircraft guns 33, 90
  assault on New Guinea 120–124
  Battle of the Philippine Sea 160, 163–168, 169
  beer supply 127–128
  career 261
  Carolines and Philippines campaign 181–189
  commissioned 26, 33–34
  crosses equator 64–65
  CVLG-23 rotated home 125, 127–129
  CVLG-27 embarked 139
  fighter strength 57–58
  fighting over Rabaul 71–78, 79–81
  first anniversary 114
  first commanding officer 31
  first deployment 57
  island superstructure 219
  joins fleet 45–48
  joins TF 58: 103–104
  Kwajalein campaign 104–106, 108–109
  launch 31
  Leyte Gulf opening actions 199–205
  Leyte Gulf Sibuyan Sea strike 205–209
  Marianas campaign 144, 145–148, 153–156, 160, 163–168, 169, 171–172, 175
  occupation of Baker Island 58–62
  Operation *Catchpole* 111–113
  Operation *Galvanic* 85, 86, 89
  outfitting detail 31–33
  Philippines landings support 192
  radar 52
  receives CVLG-27: 129
  rest and recreation, Eniwetok 175–178
  rolling 90
  shaft repair 90
  shakedown cruise 35–42
  Sibuyan Sea strike 205–209
  specifications 42, 267
  strikes against Palau 114–118
  Tarawa mission 62–64
  Truk raid 124–125
  typhoon 188–189
  voyage to Solomon Islands 66
Princeton, USS (CV-37) 259
Princeton, USS, loss of
  abandon ship order 214, 216
  attempt to save 219–237
  Birmingham aids 221, 230–233, 235–241
  bomb strike 207, 209–217, 219–220
  casualties and losses 224–225, 228, 237–238, 240–242, 242–244, 252, 253–255, 271–290
  demise 248–251
  evacuation 223–228, 245–246
  explosion 237–242, 242–243
  final evacuation 245–246

INDEX

fire 213, 216, 220–221, 228, 230, 232–233, 235–236
  first sailors to leave 216–217
  flooding 220
  hangar bay explosions 221–224
  munitions cook off 229, 237
  rescue operations 217
  Salvage Control Phase I order 228
  Salvage Control Phase II order 229
  scuttle decision 245
  smoke 221, 222, 230, 232
  stern blown off 237–242
  structural damage 213
  survivors 236, 257–258
  treatment of wounded 253–255
  unselfishness and heroism 241

Rabaul 29, 44, 66, 68, 70–71, 71–78, 79–81, 91, 94, 110
Raby, Lt Cdr John 130
radar 51–52
Radford, Rear Adm Arthur W. 58, 86
Reed, Lt Alan 236
Reeves, Rear Adm John W. 120, 123, 160
Relief Carrier Group 68
Reno, USS 228, 230–231, 232–233, 237–238, 245, 248–252
Ringgold, USS 37, 41, 62
Roberts, Ens Carlton 75–76
Robinson, Pharmacist's Mate Paul 243–244, 254–255
Rocky Mount, USS 104, 143
Rodgers, Lt John R. 184
Roosevelt, Franklin D. 22, 23
Roudebush, Lt Cdr J. 131
Royal Navy 20, 48
Royal New Zealand Air Force 68–69
Ryan, Lt Edward 241–242

Saipan 141, 142, 143, 144, 144–148, 148, 152, 156, 175
Sala, Cdr Roland O. 243–244, 254–255
Samar, Battle off 247
San Diego, USS 68, 73, 86
San Jacinto, USS 27, 145–146

San Juan, USS 68, 73, 86, 115
Sangamon-class escort carrier 24–25, 27
Santa Cruz Islands, Battle of the 47, 148, 180
Saratoga, USS 31, 46, 66–67, 70, 71–78, 79–81, 85, 86, 89, 104, 105, 106, 111, 134, 179
Scheer, Aviation Boatswain's Mate Don 226
Schmidt, Lt C. C. 117
Scott, Ens Oliver 184, 185, 202
Sculpin, USS 83–84
Service Squadron (ServRon) 10: 193
Seventh Fleet 44, 247–248
Sherman, Percy 226–227
Sherman, Rear Adm Frederick C. 68, 69, 71, 77–78, 80, 85, 89–90, 101, 179, 180, 199, 221, 231
shipbuilding program 48, 48–51, 144
Shirley, Lt(jg) James A. 133, 163–164, 200–203, 209, 270
Sims, Lt(jg) Charles A. 152
Skon, Ens W. A. 89
Smith, Maj Gen Holland M. 45, 84, 97, 102, 104, 110
Solomon Islands 66–69
South Dakota, USS 157, 169
Southeast Asia, Japanese occupation of 17–22,
Spear, Lt(jg) G. W. 111–112
Spruance, Vice Adm Raymond A. 44–45, 56, 84, 89–90, 95, 97, 101, 104, 110, 115, 120, 142, 153, 156, 158, 159, 171, 172–173, 179
Stambook, Lt(jg) Richard E. 133, 133–135, 145, 154, 163, 166–168, 172, 183–184, 270
Stanley, Lt(jg) Gordon A. 270
Stark, Adm Harold R. 24
Steelhead, USS 63, 64
Stern, Dick 238–239
Stump, Capt Felix B. 62, 87
Submarine Lifeguard League 62
Surigao Strait, Battle of 247
Syme, Lt(jg) J. W. 63, 69, 117, 118

Tallahassee, USS 23, 27
Task Force (TF) 11: 29, 58–62
Task Force (TF) 15: 58, 60, 62–64, 65
Task Force (TF) 38: **13**, 67–78, 71–78, 94, 179–195, 247–248
  TG 38.1: 180, 192
  TG 38.3: 180, 192, 196–217, 252
  TG 38.4: 180, 182, 192
Task Force (TF) 39: 69, 71
Task Force (TF) 50: 85, 98–99
Task Force (TF) 51: 104, 142–143, 156–157
Task Force (TF) 58: **12**, 103–119, 124–125, 179
  Battle of the Philippine Sea 159–175
  Marianas campaign 142, 144–147, 153–159, 159–175
Taylor, Lt Ralph S. 202, 207, 209
Third Fleet 44, 56, 78–79, 120, 179, 193, 195
Tillar, Ens Thomas C. 182–183
Tinian 141, 142, 144, 153
Tokyo, Doolittle raid 30, 34
Townsend, Lt(jg) Eugene P. 202, 270
Toyoda, Adm Soemu 148, 149, 151–152, 191, 193
Trathen, USS 58, 60
Trinidad 37, 41
Truk 81, 84, 89, 110, 113–114, 124–125, 141
Turner, Rear Adm Richmond K. 45, 84, 87, 93, 97, 101–102, 109, 110, 142–143
Two-Ocean Navy Act 48
Tyner, Lt(jg) Robert S. 40, 122–123

US Army 58, 84, 111, 112, 142, 193
US Army Air Force (USAAF) 30, 68–69, 70–71, 113, 142
US Marine Corps 45, 68–69, 94, 152
  1st Marine Division 31, 95, 182
  2nd Marine Division 82, 84, 142
  4th Marine Division 104, 142
  22nd Marine Regiment 111, 112

US Navy 28–31, 48–49
US Navy–US Marine Corps amphibious assault force 44

VC-23: 36, 41, 63–64, 66
VC-38: 68–69
Vernon, John 238–239
VF-6: 57–58, 58, 59–60, 63, 65, 89
VF-12: 73, 74, 75
VF-16: 87–88, 159–160
VF-17: 68–69, 74, 81
VF-18: 131, 191
VF-23: 36, 41, 48, 61, 63, 65, 66, 69, 70, 75, 77, 86, 105, 111, 112, 116–118, 120, 121–122, 124, 128
VF-26: 62, 131
VF-27: 129–139, 145, 154–156, 163–168, 171–172, 174, 175, 181, 182, 183–187, 191–192, 200–205, 205–209, 210, 222, 258, 263–264, 270
VF-28: 131, 159–160
VF-33: 80–81
VF-51: 145–146
VGF-27: 129–130
Vought F4U Corsairs 55
VT-23: 103, 111–112, 124, 128–129
VT-27: 131, 132, 132–133, 136, 153, 174, 181, 182, 205–209, 210–211, 222, 258, 264

Wake Island 20, 29, 66, 182
war expenditure 48–49
Warakomski, AMM2c J. S. 77
Wasp, USS 46–47
Wavell, Gen Archibald 20
Webb, Lt(jg) J. M. 69, 122–123
Wilkinson, Rear Adm Theodore 78
Wood, Lt Ernest W. 130, 135, 136, 137, 139, 163–164, 263–264

Yamamoto, Adm Isoroku 17, 29, 149
Yorktown, USS 28, 29–30, 30, 46, 48, 60, 85, 98, 99, 103, 115, 127, 144, 161